Signs of the Times

SOURCES IN MODERN HISTORY

British Political History, 1900-51

DAVID ADELMAN

Hodder & Stoughton
LONDON SYDNEY AUCKLAND TORONTO

To Val, with thanks.

British Library Cataloguing in Publication Data
Adelman, David
  Signs of the times : British political history, 1900–1951.
  – (Sources in modern history).
  1. Great Britain, 1901–
  I. Title II. Series
  941.082

  ISBN 0–340–50828–0

First published 1991

Typeset by Wearside Tradespools, Fulwell, Sunderland
Printed in Great Britain for the educational publishing division of Hodder
and Stoughton Ltd, Mill Road, Dunton Green, Sevenoaks, Kent by
Thomson Litho, East Kilbride.

CONTENTS

Introduction: how this book might be used   4

1   Social and Political Reform 1900–14   7
      Special Topic: The House of Lords Crisis 1906–11   21

2   British Foreign Policy and the Coming of War 1900–14   26
      Special Topic: The Decision for War, 1914   39

3   Lloyd George and the Decline of the Liberal Party 1914–35   46
      Special Topic: Lloyd George and the Coalition Government of 1918–22   59

4   Baldwin and the Conservatives 1922–37   63
      Special Topic: Baldwin and the General Strike 1925–26   74

5   The Rise and Fall of the Labour Pary 1900–31   82
      Special Topic: The Second Labour Government and the Crisis of 1931   93

6   British Foreign Policy and Appeasement 1919–40   104
      Special Topic: Neville Chamberlain and the 'Munich' Crisis, 1938   116

7   Consensus and Collectivism: Labour in Power 1940–51   124
      Special Topic: The Labour Victory in the 1945 General Election   125

Acknowledgements   143

INTRODUCTION: HOW THIS BOOK MIGHT BE USED

Unless students studying A-level History are excited, challenged, and intellectually involved in the way they learn about the past, few will develop a genuine interest and expertise in the subject. This is particularly hard to achieve in the teaching of British political history in the first half of this century, which has none of the superficial (and dubious) glamour and excitement which the study of revolutions, fascism and communism in European history in the same period involves. Yet in many respects it seems doubly important to find ways of kindling the enthusiasm of students in the study of their own country's history and indeed in stimulating them to decide for themselves which versions of modern British history are the 'right' ones. If lessons can be learned from the past then it is the recent past of this country which is likely to provide us with the most valuable insights about how the society we live in now has been shaped, and how it might be changed in the future. The aim of this book, then, is to provide a wide range of activities and exercises designed to involve, interest and motivate students in their study of A-level Modern British History. In this way the quality of a student's learning might be improved and his or her performance in examinations enhanced.

GENERAL APPROACH

Each theme is organised into sections with the following common headings: 'Introduction', 'Outlining the Events', 'Contemporary Views and Opinions', 'Historians' Views and Opinions', 'Special Topic', 'Simulation' and 'Back to the Present'. The order in which these sections appear differs from theme to theme and not all of these sections appear in every theme. The activities in the themes are usually related to a multiple set of primary or secondary extracts. They have been devised to enable students to develop a knowledge of the main events of the theme; to analyse the reasons, motives and factors involved; to appreciate different historians' interpretations and to come to their own conclusions; and to gain an awareness of the continuing relevance of many of the political and moral debates at the heart of the historical changes being studied. The assumption is that studying History at A-level must involve both the learning of historical facts – mastering the content – and the practice and development of the full range of intellectual skills. Furthermore, it is assumed that this can be best achieved through students working individually and in groups, deciphering, analysing, evaluating, researching and discussing a variety of historical evidence for themselves. At the same time it should be said that this approach is not designed to replace but to complement the textbook, the specialist work, and the teacher's own knowledge and know-how. Indeed the activities here are intended to develop for the students a basic framework of understanding from which they can study British History in greater depth and with greater comprehension and enjoyment than they might otherwise have been able to.

CONTENT

Each of the seven themes in the book is roughly equivalent to an A-level topic in most standard Modern British History courses. It should be possible for the teacher to use the themes in the book, which cover the period 1900–51, as the basis for teaching a large part of any Modern British History syllabus. However, for reasons of space it has not proved possible to provide a treatment of certain topics or parts of topics within the given time period. These include the Irish Problem 1900–23, the Liberal Government and Social and Political Unrest 1910–14, and some of the social and economic topics which sometimes appear in General British History syllabi. More to the point, as a perusal of the themes and their activities will reveal, this book is intended to be used in conjunction with in-depth works of history and the teacher's own materials. It has not been the intention for the sources and information here to provide a comprehensive coverage of the subject-matter on their own.

THE FLEXIBLE USE OF THIS BOOK

There are a variety of ways in which the teacher can use this book. Firstly, each theme consists of a complete scheme of work for the teaching and learning of the particular topic of British History. The sections in each theme have been sequenced to take the student through the historical events and ideas in a logical order, allowing the student to build up a cumulative understanding and interpretation of a topic. Secondly, many teachers will want to use their own schemes of work – in which case individual sections within a theme can be used as discrete pieces of work at appropriate points within the teacher's scheme. Thirdly, the teacher can choose to use the source material in a particular section with their own activities rather then the ones here. In addition, the activities themselves are very adaptable and can be re-worked to suit the teacher. Many provide the option of being carried out either individually or in groups, and either as discussion or as written exercises. Finally, most of the activities here can be used for homework as well as for work in the classroom. Teachers using a theme as a complete scheme of work will find it necessary to use some of the sections and their activities as homework exercises if they are to cover the topic in a reasonable period of time.

THE INDIVIDUAL SECTIONS

Here is a brief description of the aims and format of each of the individual sections within each theme with some further advice for the teacher:

Introduction

This consists of a paragraph which sets the scene for the theme followed by four or five Key Questions. The Key Questions provide the focus for the investigation of the particular piece of history and also serve as a checklist of questions which students should be able to answer fully by the time they have finished studying the theme.

Outlining the Events

This section consists of a range of secondary source materials – short summaries, descriptive passages, extracts from historical dictionaries, statistics and maps. These have been selected to provide a factual coverage of the main events and developments within the particular period of history. The accompanying activities usually require students to sort out for themselves a narrative of events through analysing, comparing and contrasting, and synthesising the various pieces of evidence in the section.

Contemporary Views and Opinions

The source extracts in this section have been selected to permit the student to encounter the views, ideas and explanations of the politicians and people who were involved in the historical events. Invariably several contrasting passages have been selected to allow students to perceive for themselves differences in individual reasoning, motivation and political outlook. The contemporary sources used include official documents, letters, diaries, speeches, memoirs, autobiographies, polemical works and statistics. The questions in the activities tend not to be of the historical comprehension kind, but are concerned with helping students recognise and explain the range and the complexity of the views of contemporaries in the given historical situation.

Historians' Views and Opinions

Included in this section is a selection of the different interpretations which historians have reached about the individuals and events in the theme. The intention is to introduce the students to the debates and differences of opinion between historians in their evaluations. It is hoped that in this way students will appreciate the controversial nature of history and the way in which different historians construct different general versions of history from the same raw materials. It is further hoped that students will be encouraged to read more fully the works of history from which the extracts have been selected. Also, the aim is to persuade students to reach their own judgements and opinions about what happened and why.

Special Topic

The Special Topic is designed as a concentrated piece of study of a particular aspect of the theme. This should allow students to develop in greater depth the knowledge of the personalities and issues they have gained from work they have done previously. These Special Topics can themselves sometimes be the basis for questions in examinations. The sources used as a basis for the activities can be either primary or secondary.

Simulation

Five of the themes include simulations which involve students playing the parts of politicians, leaders, and civil servants in some of the critical and determinate historical situations of Britain in the period. The aim of the simulations is to encourage students to understand history from the inside and to appreciate the different arguments and courses of action available to decision-makers at key moments. By permitting students to make their own decisions from the point of view of the contemporary situation and therefore giving them the opportunity of 'rewriting history', it is hoped they will begin to understand that the history of Britain could have developed in different directions and along different paths from the ones it actually followed. Above all, simulations are enjoyable experiences and help develop the interest of the student.

Back to the Present

This section links the political and moral issues and arguments involved in the different themes of British History studied by students with similar issues and arguments today. It attempts to make the history of our country in the first part of this century relevant to the present. It attempts to help the student appeciate that the conflicts, controversies and difficulties in Britain's recent past and the events in which these were reflected are not somehow over and done with — that our present society is the product of our past and that our future will be determined by the way in which our present conflicts, controversies and difficulties are resolved. Thus this section enables students to express their views and opinions about their own society whilst at the same time recognising that the ensuing debates and discussions have their roots in and reflect similar debates and discussions in the past.

1 SOCIAL AND POLITICAL REFORM

1900–14

I NTRODUCTION

Britain in the 1890s was the richest country in the world. One hundred years later it is no longer a great economic power, yet it is an immeasurably wealthier country. However, in spite of this economic progress the problem of poverty still has not been overcome, though the creation of what is loosely called a Welfare State has done something to mitigate its worst effects.

In Victorian Britain the state through the New Poor Law of 1834 provided support only to the most destitute and helpless who were deemed to have failed as individuals – the 'undeserving poor'. The governing classes, guided by the ideas of *laissez-faire*, did not believe the state had a responsibility to relieve poverty in general: the working class poor, it was felt, ought to help themselves. The state had a role only to assist those on the verge of starvation, and this assistance was available only on the harshest of conditions – the principle of deterrence. Clearly, the way in which our society considers and provides for 'the poor' has changed considerably since this basic system was in operation.

Change began to take place towards the end of the nineteenth century when poverty came to be perceived as a problem once again in need of urgent remedies. Of course for 'the poor' poverty had always been a problem. The Poor Law system and the ideas of *laissez-faire*, or individualism, upon which it was based started to be questioned by those in power. Different political interpretations and approaches in relation to the problem of poverty began to be voiced, and governments between 1900 and 1914 translated some of these ideas into social reforming policies. Some historians view this legislation, especially that of the Liberal administrations 1906–14, as the beginnings of the 'Welfare State'. In this first topic you will have the opportunity of studying the social reforms and accompanying political arguments of the period. In addition, in the Special Topic, you will be looking at the related issue of 'The House of Lords Crisis 1906–11', and the political warfare between the Liberal government and the Conservative opposition over the powers of the Second Chamber.

K EY QUESTIONS

1 What was the nineteenth-century approach to poverty in society?

2 How did thinking about the question of poverty change around the turn of the century and why?

3 How did governments deal with poverty in the period 1900–14 and what were their motives?

4 How significant an achievement were the Liberal social reforms in the period 1900–14?

5 What was 'The House of Lords Crisis 1906–11' and how well did the Liberals deal with the problem?

CONTEMPORARY VIEWS & OPINIONS

THE PROBLEM OF POVERTY BEFORE 1914

The following activities are based on a range of primary extracts and statistics selected to give a cross-section of contemporary views on the problem of poverty in society in the decades up to 1914. The activities are devised to help you understand the complex nature of the problem of poverty and to gain an insight into different political perspectives on the issue.

Activity I

The first four extracts provide a glimpse into the nineteenth-century middle class approach to poverty – rooted in the ideas of liberalism and *laissez-faire*. Working individually, you should study the extracts and work out answers to the following questions:

a What do the authors in extracts 1, 2 and 3 suggest are the ways in which a working class person should cope with poverty?
b Use the same extracts to work out what were the aims of the Poor Law and the workhouse in relation to poverty.
c What do extracts 3 and 4 indicate about the extent of poverty towards the end of the nineteenth century?
d According to the views expressed here, whose fault is poverty?

Activity II

a Working individually or in pairs, use the remaining sources to construct a list of reasons and arguments which explain why the nineteenth-century approach to poverty was being seriously questioned in the 20 years up to 1914. Check your list with those of other people in the class to make sure there is nothing you have missed out or misunderstood. Bear in mind that every piece of source material here is of relevance.
b Try to work out the specific approaches to poverty associated with the ideas of 'old liberalism' (extracts 1, 2 and 3), 'new liberalism' (extracts 8, 11, 13, 16 and 17) and 'socialism' (extract 15). Discuss these important concepts as a class, and then write into your notes short definitions of each of them.

Discussion

In groups or as a class hold a brief discussion around the question: 'Why was poverty becoming such a major social and political issue by the early 1900s?'

Further Reading and Research

Find out a little more about the following: the work of Booth and Rowntree; the social implications of the Boer War; the state of the British economy in the 1900s; the early careers of Lloyd George and Churchill.

Now, compile a set of notes summarising what you've found out so far on the whole question of the problem of poverty. Use textbooks, other works of reference and information from your teacher to help you with this.

1 *Report of the Charity Organisation Society, 1876*
The principle is, that it is good for the poor that they should meet all the ordinary contingencies of life, relying not upon public or private charity, but upon their own industry and thrift, and upon the powers of self-help that are to be developed by individual and collective effort. Ample room will still be left for the exercise of an abundant charity in dealing with exceptional misfortune, and also in connection with large schemes for the benefit of the working classes which may require, in the first instance of all events, the fostering of wealth and leisure. But it is a hurtful misuse of money to spend it on assisting the labouring classes to meet emergencies which they should themselves have anticipated and provided for. The working man does not require to be told that temporary sickness is likely now and then to visit his household; that times of slackness will occasionally come; that if he marries early and has a large family, his resources will be taxed to the uttermost; that if he lives long enough, old age will render him more or less incapable of toil – all these are the ordinary con-

tingencies of labourer's life, and if he is taught that as they arise they will be met by State relief or private charity, he will assuredly make no effort to meet them himself. A spirit of dependence, fatal to all progress, will be engendered in him.

2 *Evidence of J.S. Davy to the Royal Commission on the Poor Laws, 1906*
Q.2229 (T. Hancock Nunn): I think you said that the fundamental principle of the Poor Law was to relieve destitution, and that it aimed at doing so humanely to the individual pauper, while it safeguarded the community by making the lot of the pauper less eligible than that of the independent labourer ... that is the principle of the poor law understood by the Local Government Board?—Yes.

Q.2230 ... Does ineligibility consist of these three elements: firstly, of the loss of personal reputation (what is understood by the stigma of pauperism); secondly, the loss of personal freedom which is secured by detention in a workhouse; and thirdly, the loss of political freedom by suffering disenfranchisement. Are those the main elements in ineligibility, or have I left any out?—I think those would be the main elements.

3 *Robert Giffen, an economist, writing in 1887*
The general conclusion from all the facts is, that what has happened to the working classes in the last fifty years is not so much what may properly be called an improvement, as a revolution of the most remarkable description. The new possibilities implied in changes which in fifty years have substituted for millions of people in the United Kingdom who were constantly on the brink of starvation, and who suffered untold privations, new millions of artisans and fairly well-paid labourers, ought indeed to excite the hopes of philanthropists and public men. From being a dependent class without future and hope, the masses of working men have in fact got into a position from which they may effectively advance to almost any degree of civilisation. Every agency, political and other, should be made use of by themselves and others to promote and extend the improvement. But the working men have the game in their own hands. Education and thrift, which they can achieve for themselves, will, if necessary, do all that remains to be done.

4 *Paupers Relieved in England and Wales 1895–1914*

Year ending Lady Day	Indoor paupers Mean number	% of population	Outdoor paupers Mean number	% of population	Total Mean number	% of population
1850	123,004	0·77	885,696	5·0	1,008,700	5·7
1895	208,746	0·69	588,167	2·0	796,913	2·7
1900	215,377	0·68	577,122	1·8	792,499	2·5
1910	275,075	0·78	539,642	1·5	916,377	2·6
1914	254,644	0·69	387,208	1·0	748,019	2·0

Adapted from M.E. Rose The Relief of Poverty 1834–1914 (1972)

5 *J.F. Oakeshott in a Fabian essay 1894*
... many men and women every year deliberately prefer death by starvation outside the workhouse to accepting relief from the rates with its deprivation of the privileges of citzenship and its dishonorable stigma of pauperism on aged and young, infirm and able-bodied, deserving and undeserving alike ...

6 *Jack London:* People of the Abyss (1903)
Nowhere in the streets of London may one escape the sight of abject poverty, while five minutes walk from almost any point will bring one to a slum: but the region my hansom was now penetrating was one unending slum. The streets were filled with a new and different race of people, short of stature, and of wretched or beer-sodden appearance. We rolled along through miles of bricks and squalor, and from each cross street and alley flashed lost vistas of bricks and misery. Here and there lurched a drunken man or woman, and the air was obscene with sounds of jangling and squabbling. At a market, tottery old men and women were searching in the garbage thrown in the mud for rotten potatoes, beans, and vegetables, while little children clustered like flies around a festering mass of fruit, thrusting their arms to the shoulders into the squalid corruption, and drawing forth morsels but partially decayed, which they devoured on the spot.

7 *Seebohm Rowntree*: Poverty: A Study of Town Life (1901)
From the commencement of my inquiry I have had opportunities of consulting with Mr. Booth, and comparing the methods of investigation and the

The upper classes at leisure at the Eton vs Harrow cricket match, Lords 1895

Salvation Army queue in the 1890s

standards of poverty adopted. As a result I feel no hesitation in regarding my estimate of the total poverty in York as comparable with Mr. Booth's estimate of the total poverty in London, and in this Mr. Booth agrees.

The proportions arrived at for the total population living in poverty in London and York respectively were as under:—

    London . . . . 30.7 per cent
    York . . . . 27.84 per cent

We have been accustomed to look upon the poverty in London as exceptional, but when the result of careful investigation shows that the proportion of poverty in London is practically equalled in what may be regarded as a typical provincial town, we are faced by the startling probability that from 25 to 30 per cent of the town populations of the United Kingdom are living in poverty.

8 *Motion passed by the Birmingham Chamber of Commerce, 1907*

Mr J. S. Taylor (Birmingham) moved:
'That this association is of opinion that the time has arrived when His Majesty's Government should take into serious consideration the subject of national insurance for the working classes against accident, sickness, invalidity, and old age on the lines, so far as is practicable, of the comprehensive system which has operated so successfully in Germany; and that a memorial be presented to the prime minister and the home secretary praying that they will be pleased to receive a deputation from

this association to urge upon them the desirability of a royal commission being appointed to inquire into and report upon the subject.'

In doing so, he said the resolution related to a question of serious moment to taxpayers – a question upon the proper solution of which the future industrial efficiency of this country largely depended.

9 *Percentage distribution of world manufacturing production*

Year	United Kingdom	United States	Germany
1870	31.8	23.3	13.2
1913	14.0	35.8	15.7

From A.E. Musson: The Growth of British Industry *(1978)*

10 *The social background of Cabinets 1895–1914*

Date	Party	P.M.	Cabinet Size	Aristo-crats	Middle Class	Working Class
Aug 1895	Con.	Salisbury	19	8	11	–
Jul 1902	Con.	Balfour	19	9	10	–
Dec 1905	Lib.	Campbell-Bannerman	19	7	11	1
Jul 1914	Lib.	Asquith	19	6	12	1

Adapted from W.L. Guttsman: The Political Elite *(1963)*

11 *Herbert Samuel:* Liberalism *(1902)*

It was realized that the conditions of society were in many respects so bad that to tolerate them longer was impossible, and that the *laissez faire* policy was not likely to bring the cure. And it was realized that extensions of law need not imply diminutions of freedom, but on the contrary would often enlarge freedom.

Such are the facts and arguments which brought about this change. In them we find the answer to those who use the doctrine of the old Liberalism to attack the policy of the new. The State is not incompetent for the work of social reform. Self-reliance is a powerful force, but not powerful enough to cure unaided the diseases that afflict society. Liberty is of supreme importance, but State assistance, rightly directed, may extend the bounds of liberty.

12 *Edwardian ownership and income distribution*

Class	Total number	Percentage of the population	Percentage of national weath	Income per year (£)
(i)	300,000	1	55	1,000–1,500 (or more)
(ii)	600,000	2	25	400–1,000
(iii)	2,500,000	8	11	160–400
(iv)	16,500,000	56	8	60–160
(v)	11,000,000	33	1	Under 60

(i) rich; (ii) upper middle class; (iii) lower middle class; (iv) skilled working class; (v) casual and agricultural labour

Adapted from Leo Chiozza Money: Riches and Poverty *(1905)*

13 *Arnold White:* Efficiency and Empire *(1901)*
In the Manchester district 11,000 men offered themselves for war service between the outbreak of hostilities in October 1899 and July 1900. Of this number 8000 were found to be physically unfit to carry a rifle and stand the fatigues of discipline. Of the 3000 who were accepted only 1200 attained the moderate standard of muscular power and chest measurement required by the military authorities. In other words, two out of every three men willing to bear arms in the Manchester district are virtually invalids.

14 *General elections 1892–1910*

	Conservative		Liberal		Labour		Irish Nationalist	
	% vote	No. of seats won	% vote	No. of seats won	% vote	No. of seats won	% vote	No. of seats won
1892	47.0	314	45.1	272	0.3	3	7.0	81
1895	49.1	411	45.7	177	1.0	0	4.0	82
1900	51.5	402	44.6	184	1.8	2	2.5	82
1906	43.6	157	49.0	401	5.9	29	0.6	83
1910 (Jan.)	46.9	273	43.2	275	7.7	40	1.0	82
1910 (Dec.)	46.3	272	43.8	272	7.2	42	2.5	84

M. Pugh: The Making of Modern British Politics 1867–1939 *(1982)*

15 *Labour House of Commons Resolution, 1901*
'That considering the increasing burden which the private ownership of land and capital is imposing upon the industrious and useful classes of the community, the poverty and destitution and general moral and physical deterioration resulting from a competitive system of wealth production which aims primarily at profit-making, the alarming

FORCED FELLOWSHIP.

Suspicious-looking Party. "ANY OBJECTION TO MY COMPANY, GUV'NOR? I'M AGOIN' YOUR WAY"—*(aside)* "AND FURTHER."

Punch *1909*

growth of trusts and syndicates able by reason of their great wealth to influence Governments and plunge peaceful Nations into War to serve their interests, this House is of the opinion that such a condition of affairs constitutes a menace to the well-being of the Realm, and calls for legislation designed to remedy the same by inaugurating a Socialist Commonwealth founded upon the common ownership of land and capital, production for use and not for profit, and equality of opportunity for every citizen.'

16 *Speech by Lloyd George, a leading Liberal MP, in 1906*
There are ten millions in this country enduring year after year the torture of living while lacking a sufficiency of the bare necessaries of life; and all this exists amid a splendid plenty, which pours into a land so wealthy that it can afford to lend, out of its spare riches, thousands of millions to less well endowed lands in other parts of the world . . .

Christians think that their main duty towards their unfortunate fellow-beings is discharged for the current half-year when they pay their poor-rate, and they certainly think that the charity which they dispense from time to time to the occasional suppliants appearing before them to entreat their assistance deals exhaustively with the few odd cases that escape the meshes of the Poor Law. They now know that there are millions of their fellow-workmen living in a condition of chronic destitution and suffering privations which are not tempered in the least either by the organised action of the law or by the sporadic influence of personal charity . . .

The careful investigation of men like Mr. Charles Booth and Mr. Rowntree, conducted with scientific minuteness and precision, has revealed a state of things, especially in the towns, which it would be difficult even for the orators of discontent to exaggerate . . .

What are some of the direct causes of poverty! There is the fact that a man's earnings are not adequate to maintain himself and his family; there is the inability to obtain employment for economic reasons; and there is the inability of men to pursue their avocation owing to sickness, old age, or inherent lack of physical stamina or vitality. Then there is the most fertile cause of all – a man's own improvident habits, such as drinking and gambling.

17 *Winston Churchill, a leading Liberal MP, in* Liberalism and the Social Problem *(1909)*
Liberalism has its own history and its own tradition. Socialism has its own formulas and aims. Socialism seeks to pull down wealth; Liberalism seeks to raise up poverty. Socialism would destroy private interests; Liberalism would preserve private interests in the only way in which they can be safely and justly preserved, namely, by reconciling them with public right. Socialism would kill enterprise; Liberalism would would rescue enterprise from the trammels of privilege and preference. Socialism assails the pre-eminence of the individual; Liberalism seeks, and shall seek more in the future, to build up a minimum standard for the mass. Socialism exalts the rule; Liberalism exalts the man. Socialism attacks capital; Liberalism attacks monopoly.

▌SIMULATION

THE POLITICS OF POVERTY IN 1906

Introduction

The aim of the simulation is to help you think about the whole question of poverty in society from the point of view of the governing classes in Edwardian England immediately after the overwhelming Liberal victory in the 1906 General Election. This should enable you to appreciate the different mentalities and assumptions of politicians at the time, and the various political possibilities available to them.

The Situation

You are a House of Commons Select Committee on Social Reform meeting just after the General Election of 1906. Your brief is to agree on a set of policy proposals to deal with the problem of poverty in society. The information and guidelines on which to base your discussion are in 'The Problem of Poverty' section which you may have already studied, and in the sections under 'Background Information' given below. Your committee will very roughly reflect the balance of power in the new House of Commons. However, in the simulation you should not be too bound by what you understand as the party positions of 1906. It is equally important to bring your own opinions and responses into the discussion.

Background Information

General Issues
- Whose fault is poverty?
- How great should the role of the state be in helping the poor?
- Is it better for a poor person who cannot help himself or herself to receive help from charity or the state?
- Should the rich be made to pay for welfare provision? Or should the working classes themselves pay towards the alleviation of poverty?
- Rather than relieving the poor, shouldn't we be trying to remove poverty from society altogether through the creation of some sort of socialist system?

Options
- What categories of people are to be helped in your proposals?
- In what ways are these people to be helped?
- Are there to be any limitations or conditions as regards who receives help from the state?
- What are the details of some of the ideas for welfare provision which you are thinking about (eg levels of benefits and for how long)?
- How are the welfare policies you are considering going to be paid for?
- Are you going to advocate no changes and thus support the existing system of poor relief (self-help, private insurance, charity, and in the last resort the Poor Law)?

Additional Factual Information
- Two and a half million men in work earn less than £1.25 week – the average wage to

maintain a family of five in mere 'physical efficiency'. Seven shillings (£0.30) is the 'physical efficiency' figure for a single adult person.

— There are over two million people aged 65 and over who can no longer work.

— Average real wages are in decline because pay increases are not keeping in line with inflation.

— The number of strikes on average per year is on the increase.

— Average unemployment a year is four–five per cent or about 700,000 people.

— Current public expenditure at about £170 million is about nine per cent of National Income. Of that expenditure the largest single item is defence spending at 35 per cent of the total. Three per cent is for welfare.

— Taxation is one shilling in the pound on incomes over £160 per annum: that is, five per cent of a person's income.

Procedure

1 Rather than the whole class forming a Select Committee, it would be better if there were two or three smaller committees.

2 MPs in each Select Committee should be divided in the following ratio: three Liberal MPs, two Conservative MPs, one Labour MP.

3 Each Committee should select someone to chair proceedings and someone to take notes of decisions. Deadlock within the Committee should be resolved by taking a vote.

4 There is no set method of proceeding, but one idea is to go through each of the 'General Issues' outlined in the 'Background Information' section in an attempt to reach a general agreement on principles. Then you could use the 'Options' questions to assist you in discussing and agreeing on specific decisions.

5 How you use the various kinds of factual information with which you have been provided and to what level of detail is up to you.

6 The exercise should finish with a general class discussion when each Select Committee presents its proposals to the rest of the class, maybe under the headings 'Ideas', 'Policies' and 'Details'. The class should then see what agreement they can reach on a programme of welfare reforms appropriate to the times.

7 The whole simulation could take anything between one and two hours, but your teacher will set appropriate deadlines.

8 Finally, it might be worth considering (when you have completed the simulation) the historical problems involved when people living in the present (such as yourselves) try to simulate the thinking of people who were experienced politicians living over 80 years ago.

O UTLINING THE EVENTS

SOCIAL REFORMS 1900–14

In this section there are seven short accounts, by historians, describing in different ways and with different emphases the social reforms of the period. These provide the basis for the following activities designed to help you establish a factual grasp of, in the main, Liberal government policies and actions in the period.

Activity I

Read through all the secondary accounts. Working on your own or in pairs, use the different extracts here to construct a chronology of social reform developments. In your chronology write down a sentence or two of essential detail explaining each development. The narrative of events you should finish up with will serve as a basic set of notes for the theme.

Activity II

Here are a set of questions and tasks to help ensure that you have understood the information and ideas in the secondary source extracts. They can be used for class consideration or for an individual piece of written work.

a What different kinds of poverty and disadvantage were dealt with by which measures?
b What was the difference between the financing of the Old Age Pensions Act and the National Insurance Acts?
c What was the significance of the following, in relation to Liberal social reforms: a labour exchange, a trade board, an approved society.
d What had the 'People's Budget' got to do with social reform?
e What seems to have been the outcome of the deliberations of the Royal Commission on the Poor Laws?
f What was the Conservative (Unionist) attitude to social reform, as far as you can tell, and what did they achieve?

Further Reading and Research

Using textbooks, reference books and information from your teacher, find out more about what governments were doing to reduce poverty in the period. In particular, check up on aspects of the topic you are not sure about from the work so far and any references in the seven historians' extracts which you don't understand. Make additional notes where appropriate.

Discussion

By this stage you should be forming some opinions of your own about how much was achieved in the way of helping 'the poor' between 1900 and 1914. As a class hold a discussion based on the following questions:

- How effectively were the Liberals tackling the problems of poverty by 1914?
- How far had the Liberals moved away from strict *laissez-faire* ('old liberal') principles?
- As a working class person living in poverty before 1914, what thoughts and responses might you have had to the Liberal social reforms?

I *P. Thane in an article in the Economic History Society Journal* ReFresh *(1988)*
The earliest reforms enacted at the time of the Liberal ministry owed relatively little to the New Liberalism. The first enactment – the provision of free school meals in 1906 – was in fact introduced by a Labour M.P. And the introduction of medical inspection in schools in the following year was essentially the work of civil servants making the first moves towards a national free medical service. (This illustrates the importance of civil servants in welfare policy-making; in this case a constructive role was played, although in other instances they were sometimes obstructive.) The Liberals themselves initiated old age pensions in 1908. This was the product of a long campaign and was the first cash benefit to be paid by the state outside the poor law. Nonetheless it at first imposed on claimants means and character tests not far removed in spirit

from the poor law. The Children Act of the same year was a response to thirty years of lobbying for the comprehensive state protection of children. The Trades Board Act of 1909 introduced a minimum wage and improved conditions for some of the lowest paid, and largely female occupations. The Housing and Town Planning Act of the same year sought to limit existing and future urban overcrowding and pollution. Successive Lloyd George budgets rendered the system of direct taxation somewhat more progressive. National insurance, introduced in 1911, provided health and unemployment benefits for the regularly employed, in return for compulsory weekly contributions that were designed to relieve the Treasury of a considerable burden. Social insurance was also intended to build long-established values into a state venture; the regular payment reminded the worker of the obligation of self-help and saving, and established for him – or more rarely her – a contractual right to benefit.

2 *W.H.B. Court:* British Economic History 1870–1914 – Commentary and Documents *(1965)*
The Poor Law, the product of an earlier society, more authoritarian, socially and politically, than late Victorian Britain could be, began to fall into disrepute from the 1890's onwards. This way of dealing *en bloc* with the economic risks of life no longer satisfied. The royal commission on the Poor Law of 1905–9 failed to pull off the major reform which many people by that time desired. One by one, the chief risks of working life were isolated and dealt with in other ways. They left the Poor Law standing side by side with what was substantially a new system of social policies run on different principles. Industrial accident was handled through employer's liability law (1894, 1897); old age by State pensions, non-contributory (1908); sickness, by national insurance, contributory (1911).

This process of transforming or supplementing incomes went beyond the beginning of a break up of the Poor Law and its replacement by social services. The State recognized for the first time since 1813 a certain responsibility for the level of wages. This was clearly implied in the Trade Boards Act of 1909. It was aimed at the sweated

trades but provided an object lesson for the coal and the farming industries, which were far larger employers.

The further the State travelled along this road, the more clear it became that to undertake responsibility for income was also to take it for the employment by which income was earned. Unemployment provided the biggest problem of all. Its mere existence challenged the basic Victorian assumption that employment was always there for those who wanted it. The devastating effect of unemployment on incomes was approached indirectly by legislation in 1905, 1909 and 1911 on unemployment and public works, labour exchanges and unemployment insurance. The 1911 National Insurance Act brought unemployment within the new insurance scheme.

3 The Illustrated Dictionary of British History *ed. A. Marwick (1980)*
People's Budget 1909. Introduced by Lloyd George, who had to find cash to pay for old age pensions and the Dreadnought programme. He did so by increasing income tax and death duties, taxing luxuries and attempting to set up a road fund. But also imposed new taxes on high incomes, on undeveloped land and on the unearned increment resulting from land sales. This enraged the Conservatives and the aristocracy, led to the House of Lords throwing out the budget and precipitated the constitutional crisis.

4 *M. St. J. Parker and D.J. Reid:* The British Revolution 1750–1970 – A Social and Economic History *(1972)*
This was the situation which a new Liberal government set about changing in 1905. Among the factors which influenced it were two very disturbing and widely read Reports about social conditions in London and York (by Charles Booth and Seebohm Rowntree respectively). These revealed that over one-third of the population of these cities was living below the 'poverty line'. Agitation by the 'New Unions' and the emerging Labour Party at this time showed the growing anger which working people felt about their conditions, and the success in Germany of a limited scheme of state assistance (started in the 1880s) was carefully

Lloyd George and Winston Churchill

noted. Most important, the Liberal government included two dynamic men – David Lloyd George and Winston Churchill – who felt strongly that more urgent state action was needed to solve the social problems of the country.

As a result, several important measures were passed. One was the Old Age Pensions Act of 1908, under which the state paid 5s. a week to people over 70 years old. In 1909 Labour Exchanges were set up, making it much easier for the unemployed to find work. The National Insurance Act of 1911 established a scheme whereby small unemployment benefits and some medical treatment could be obtained in return for insurance contributions paid each week, in part by employees, in part by employers, and the remainder made up by the state out of general taxation.

5 *P. Thane:* Foundations of the Welfare State *(1982)*
The costs of the Boer War increased Treasury reluctance to countenance social expenditure by the state. However, under the post-war Conserva-

tive government they were under little pressure to do so. Balfour, as Prime Minister from 1902, and his Cabinet colleagues showed no passionate concern for social reform. Joseph Chamberlain resigned from the Cabinet and from active politics in 1903 after a serious accident. Tory philanthropy on the Disraelian model, if not dead, was not prominent.

The exception to Balfour's disinterest in social issues was education. The Education Act 1902 was largely the work of R. L. Morant, the chief civil servant at the Board of Education, one of a number of policy-innovating civil servants in his generation. But without Balfour's active support such a controversial piece of education reform would not have passed.

6 *D. Read:* Edwardian England *(1972)*
The depression of 1904–5 had stimulated the Balfour Government to appoint a Royal Commission on the Poor Laws and Relief of Distress. Its majority report appeared in February 1909, also a minority report signed by four socialist members headed by Beatrice Webb. (Their report was largely written by Sidney Webb). The majority wished to reform and retain (even though to rename) the Poor Law: the Webbs wanted to abolish it. Both reports agreed on the need for thorough reform of the Edwardian machinery for controlling poverty and unemployment.

7 *E. J. Evans:* Social Policy 1830–1914 *(1978)*
Between 1895 and 1914 the functions of the state continued to grow. Many of the ideas germinating in the minds of progressive politicians in the 1880s and 1890s came to fruit during the Liberal Government of 1905–14. A non-contributory old-age pensions scheme was begun in January 1909. Care of children, the lifeblood of the nation, was vastly improved by the provision of school meals, by regular medical inspection, and by the 'Children's Charter' of 1908. Lloyd George introduced a controversial and wide-ranging compulsory insurance scheme against both sickness and unemployment. The sickness scheme involved limited free medical treatment for the head of the family and more access to hospitals. Conditions of work were also brought under stricter treatment. Workers in the

'sweated' trades – tailoring, lace-making and the like – predominantly women, were protected by legislation enabling minimum wages to be paid. The miners won a similar concession in 1912, though plans for a national minimum fell on deaf ears. Labour exchanges were instituted in 1909 to facilitate movement of labour and prevent unnecessary unemployment. Perhaps most far-reaching of all, the Liberals committed themselves to paying for many of these reforms by redistributive taxation. The principle that the rich should help to provide the necessities of the poor by compulsory deductions ran counter to every tenet of Gladstonian Liberalism, and Lloyd George persuaded his party to face the most serious constitutional crisis of the century in defence of it. The role of the State was thus much more positive, and its range of social responsibilities far wider, in 1914 than in 1895. In 1891 government expenditure on education, science, salaries and other administrative costs of public departments amounted to 5s.3d. per head of the population. In the next twenty years, it more than doubled to 10s.11d. Most of this increase was accounted for by provision and administration of social welfare schemes.

H ISTORIANS' VIEWS & OPINIONS

EVALUATING THE LIBERAL SOCIAL REFORMS

The activities in this section are based on assessments of the Liberal social reforms made by seven historians. The extracts have been deliberately selected to give you some contrasting opinions on the reforms.

Activity I

a Study the views of the different historians given here and decide which, on balance, are favourable to, and which are unfavourable to or more critical of the Liberal governments and their reforms. You should find as you do this that you are familiar with most of the ideas and details discussed by the historians – if not, go back to the beginning and start again!

b Working in pairs, you should now carry out the following tasks of analysis which are concerned with getting you to break down the secondary extracts into distinct ideas and arguments.
- Make a list of the different motives for the reforms passed by the Liberal politicians, as put forward by the seven historians (some extracts are more relevant for this than others).
- Draw up a table of the various arguments used by the historians showing those which are, in general, for and those which are against the Liberal achievement. This will inevitably overlap with your list of motives.

Discussion

You should now be in a position to make your own informed evaluation of the social reform record of the Liberals from 1906 to 1914. Were the reforms a 'good' or 'bad' thing? Did they reflect a genuine concern for, or fear of, the working class? Could the reforms have been taken much further? To what extent had the Poor Law and *laissez-faire*/'old liberal' attitudes been abandoned and replaced by a Welfare State? Using the lists you've drawn up, hold a general discussion of these questions – in groups and/or as a class.

Further Reading and Research

Find out what the views of the author of your textbook for this course are on these issues. Perhaps your teacher might be persuaded to give an opinion . . . To complete this final section of the main theme you should write a paragraph entitled 'An Evaluation of the Liberal Social Reforms'. This paragraph should include a consideration of the views of historians along with some of your own ideas, suggestions and criticisms.

1 *C. Cross:* The Liberals in Power *(1963)*
Two men, for politicians young men, David Lloyd George and Winston Churchill, were responsible both for reviving the Liberal government from the doldrums of 1908 and for launching a great social programme which laid the foundations of the future Welfare State.

2 *K. Aikin:* The Last Years of Liberal England 1900–1914 *(1972)*
G.D.H. Cole and Raymond Postgate have suggested that the Liberal reforms were essentially a conservative measure aimed at preserving the existing economic order against socialist attack, and that the cost of the new health and unemployment service established under the National Insurance Act, so far from effecting a transfer of wealth, fell on the workers themselves. This is an interesting point of view, but unreasonable since the Liberals, working with limited funds and facing severe political difficulties, were forced to adopt a realistic approach. Something had to be done, and social insurance was the way to do it. Half a loaf was surely better than no loaf at all. In the end, baulked by the outbreak of war from further reforms and destroyed as a political force soon after the war ended, the Liberal Party had nonetheless left a memorial that time would not deface – the Welfare State.

3 *G. Williams:* The Coming of the Welfare State *(1967)*
The period from 1906 to the beginning of the First World War was one of great activity in the field of social legislation. In fact, it would be true to say that most of the developments that we now think of as part of the Welfare State are built on the foundations laid during that exciting time. The opportunity was provided by the rise to power of the Liberal Party which was pledged to many reforms; but one must be careful not to lay too much stress on these party changes for the anxiety to improve the lot of the masses of the population was not confined to any one political group. Indeed it is worth remembering that Charles Booth, who did more than anybody else to open people's eyes to the extent and causes of poverty and who fought so hard for a State Old Age Pension free of a

means test, was a Conservative. Yet on the whole it is true that at the time of which I am now speaking the Liberal Party showed a much greater readiness than the Conservatives to bring in the help of the State in the protection of the weaker sections of society, and their success in the election of 1906 enabled them to begin a great series of legislative experiments.

4 *E.J. Evans:* Social Policy 1830–1914 *(1978)*
Given that the response was essentially pragmatic, we should beware of grandiloquent claims that the Liberal Party created the Welfare State between 1906 and 1914. This hypothesis is shaky on two main grounds. First, the legislation was piecemeal; second, permissive enactments were still the main order of the day. Lloyd George introduced much of his legislation as avowedly experimental. Unemployment insurance related only to the most vulnerable trades; sickness benefits applied only to the insured, not their families; pensions were only available to the non-pauperized over-seventies; medical provision was grudging and limited; secondary education was available only to a small, though growing, minority of poor children. One could go on, but the point seems clear that these reforms hardly instituted a system of welfare which aimed to provide 'from the cradle to the grave'. The Liberals did not even dismantle the poor law, with its hated associations of degradation and humiliation. Rather the new services were expected to operate alongside the old. Liberal legislation certainly provided a basis for future initiatives; but the way was hardly so clearly charted, in insurance, education, or other fields, that post-war developments were pre-ordained.

5 *J.R. Hay:* The Origins of the Liberal Welfare Reforms *(1975)*
There were many participants in the creation of the Liberal reforms who had no thought of creating a 'welfare state' of the type which developed in Britain after 1945. Indeed many of the Liberals of 1906–14 would have been appalled by that prospect. Moreover the measures adopted always had a tactical significance in the parliamentary struggle between the parties: each was a response to a specific electoral situation, as was the case with the

decision to proceed with labour exchanges and unemployment insurance in 1908–9. But this does not mean that social reform can be completely explained in such terms. Key figures, like Lloyd George and Churchill, looked beyond individual pieces of legislation towards the creation of a society in which the worst ravages of poverty would be eliminated. They saw the strategic importance of welfare measures which would, at one and the same time, act as an antidote to socialism and hinder the polarisation of the electorate between Labour and Conservatives in Britain, contribute to the efficiency of the British economy by preventing the physical and mental deterioration of the workers, and provide a measure of social justice which would help to attract working-class votes without alienating the middle classes.

6 *M.E. Rose:* The Relief of Poverty 1834–1914 *(1972)*
It is of course difficult to assess the value of the Liberal reforms in terms of their effect on poverty before the outbreak of the First World War. The Old Age Pension Act, confined as it was to the very poor, since only those with an income of less than £21 a year received the full pension of 5s. a week, drastically reduced the numbers of old people in receipt of outdoor relief from the boards of guardians. It did little, however, to reduce the numbers in workhouses and other institutions, such aged inmates being largely incapable of caring for themselves even if given an independent source of income. The Insurance Act of 1911 was not brought into operation until 1913, and therefore could have had little impact on poverty or pauperism before 1914. Unemployment insurance was in

any case confined at first to a few skilled trades, whose members were unlikely except in periods of extreme distress to come on the poor law. The health insurance sickness benefit of 10s. a week alleviated to some extent the disaster which the illness of the bread-winner spelt for a poor family. But the medical benefits of the system were severely limited since they were confined to free G.P. treatment for the insured person only, and thus did nothing to improve the health of the wives and children of the poor. The fall in the numbers on poor relief between 1911 and 1914 owed more to the economic boom of the immediate pre-war period than it did to welfare legislation.

7 *P. Thane:* The Foundations of the Welfare State *(1982)*
However, the labour movement was divided as to the extent and type of provision they desired from the state. Many still felt that the chief need was for full employment and adequate pay, which would enable the working class to provide for their own needs and to retain their independence of state control; though they were prepared to accept immediate state help for those whose needs could not be met in this way, such as the aged. Many also were prepared to accept state welfare reform if it was to be truly redistributive from rich to poor, rather than financed by taxes on the poor themselves. There was also widespread hostility to measures which entailed closer control over, and intrusion upon, the lives of the working class by those of other classes. . . . Fear of Labour remained the motive for the promotion of social refom among non-Labour politicians, but equally important were military and economic fears.

S PECIAL TOPIC

THE HOUSE OF LORDS CRISIS 1906–11

This Special Topic involves first finding out something about the role of the House of Lords before 1906. Then, on the basis of a sample of short primary source extracts you will be involved in your own reconstruction of the history of this controversial issue.

Reading and Research

Use reference books to find out a little about the origins, powers and purposes of the House of Lords before 1906. See if you can discover what the constitutional role of the House of Lords was supposed to be and how this was changing, and also some examples of important decisions made by the Lords in the nineteenth century. Why could it be argued that the House of Lords was out of date by 1900?

Discussion

Move into small discussion groups or committees and work out your own set of proposals for reforming the House of Lords. Consider in your deliberations both the powers and the composition of the Lords, and also the issue of whether there should be a second chamber at all in Parliament. Come together as a class to discuss each other's set of proposals and see if the class as a whole can agree on a programme for reforming the Lords. You could take votes to resolve any disagreements.

Activity

The various pieces of primary material presented here are designed to be clues for unravelling the events and ideas of 'The House of Lords Crisis 1906–11' for yourselves. Working in small groups you should use these clues to carry out the following tasks:

a Reconstruct the narrative of the Lords Crisis – what happened when and why? Ensure that each member of the group has their own copy of the narrative.
b Make a note of the main points at issue in the Lords Crisis in terms of democracy, the balance of the Constitution, party conflict, the right of taxation and social reform.
c Jot down all those references and points which, for whatever reason, you are not clear about at this stage.

Discussion

In class discussion compare each other's version of the Lords Crisis and the other notes you have made. With the guidance of your teacher try to agree upon a definitive account and explanation of events – as far as this is possible. Now discuss the following: Were the Conservatives at all justified in the way they used the House of Lords? Did the reform of the Lords go far enough? How skilful was Asquith's handling of the whole situation?

Further Reading and Research

Using textbooks etc, information from your teacher and the work you have done so far, assemble an additional set of brief notes explaining 'The House of Lords Crisis 1906–11'. Make sure you find out about those things which you have not understood up to now – for instance, those more obscure references previously identified in the activity above.

---

1 *Lord Lansdowne, Leader of the Conservatives in the House of Lords, in a Memorandum to Balfour in 1906*
The Opposition is lamentably weak in the House of Commons and enormously powerful in the House of Lords. It is essential that the two wings of the army should work together, and that neither House should take up a line of its own without carefully considering the effects which the adoption of such a line might have upon the other House...

Mr. Balfour might like to call a few of us together after the holidays in order to consider the procedure which might be adopted.

2 *Balfour, Leader of the Conservative Party and defeated Prime Minister, in reply to Lansdowne's memorandum in 1906*

I do not think the House of Lords will be able to escape the duty of making serious modifications in important Government measures, but, if this is done with caution and tact, I do not believe they will do themselves any harm.

3 *Lloyd George in a speech in 1907*

The House of Lords has long ceased to be the watch-dog of the Constitution. It has become Mr. Balfour's Poodle. It barks for him. It fetches and carries for him. It bites anybody that he sets it on to.

4 *Balfour in a speech in 1907*

... power was vested in the House of Lords, not to prevent the people of this country having the laws they wished to have, but to see that the laws were not the hasty and ill-considered offspring of one passionate election. ...

5 *Dr John Clifford, Liberal and Nonconformist, in a speech July 1909*

The rejection of the London Elections Bill is another indication that 'Britons will be slaves' as long as the Veto of the Lords is allowed to exist. ... Where is the Plural Voting Bill? Slain by the Lords. What became of the Licensing Bill? Slain by the Lords. Where is the Education Bill? Slain by the Lords. Who destroyed the Irish Land Bill? Again the Lords. And the murderous weapon they use is the Veto. ...

6 *Lloyd George, Chancellor of the Exchequer, in a speech July 1909*

We are raising money to pay for the new road (cheers), aye, and to widen it so that 200,000 paupers shall be able to join in the march. (Cheers) There are many in the country blessed by Providence with great wealth, and if there are amongst them men who grudge out of their riches a fair contribution towards the less fortunate of their fellow-countrymen they are shabby rich men. (Cheers) We propose to do more by means of the Budget. We are raising money to provide against the evils and the sufferings that follow from unemployment. (Cheers) We are raising money for the purpose of assisting out great friendly societies to provide for the sick and the widows and orphans. We are providing money to enable us to develop the resources of our own land. (Cheers) I do not believe any fair-minded man would challenge the justice and the fairness of the objects which we have in view in raising this money.

7 *Balfour in a speech in November 1909*

No man who looks at the world in which we live thinks, at all events in November 1909, that there are before the country other than these two alternatives – the Budget or fiscal reform ... you may say truly of this Budget that it is a combination of bad finance and muddle-headed Socialism. ...

The object of a second Chamber is not, and never has been, to prevent the people, the mass of the community, the electorate, the constituencies determining what policy they should pursue; it exists for the purpose of seeing that on great issues the policy which is pursued is not the policy of a temporary majority elected for a different purpose, but represents the sovereign conviction of the people for the few years in which it carries their mandate.

Cartoon from the Westminster Gazette

8 *Lord Lansdowne's amendment in the House of Lords to the 'People's Budget', November 1909*
'That this House is not justified in giving its consent to the Bill until it has been submitted to the judgment of the country.'

9 *Lord Lansdowne on the Lord's vote effectively rejecting the Budget, November 1909*
When the division was taken, 350 voted for Lord Lansdowne's motion and 75 against. In the majority were many unfamiliar figures who might perhaps have been included in Mr. Lloyd George's well known uncomplimentary designation of 'backwoodsmen'.

10 *Asquith, Liberal Prime Minister, in a speech in the House of Commons December 1909*
2nd December: Mr Asquith … We are living under a system of false balances and loaded dice. When the democracy votes Tory we are submitted to the uncontrolled domination of a single Chamber. When the democracy votes Liberal, a dormant Second Chamber wakes up from its slumbers and is able to frustrate and nullify our efforts, as it did with regard to education, as it did with regard to licensing, as it has done again this year with regard to measures for Scotland, and with regard to finance. I cannot exhaust the list; it would be too long. They proceed to frustrate and nullify the clearest and most plainly expressed intention of the elective House. The House of Lords have deliberately chosen their ground. They have elected to set at nought in regard to finance the unwritten and time-honoured conventions of our Constitution. In so doing, whether they foresaw it or not, they have opened out a wider and a more far-reaching issue. We have not provoked the challenge, but we welcome it. We believe that the first principles of representative government, as embodied in our slow and ordered but ever-broadening constitutional development, are at stake, and we ask the House of Commons by this Resolution to-day, as at the earliest possible moment we shall ask the constituencies of the country, to declare that the organ, the voice of the free people of this country, is to be found in the elective representatives of the nation.

11 *Viscount Simon, leading Liberal at the time, in his memoirs:* Retrospect *(1952)*

Asquith was resolved that there should be no possible doubt as to what the country wanted. The Election of January, 1910, might have been regarded as turning principally upon the Lords' rejection of the Budget. Therefore, after the Parliament Bill had been introduced and its provisions made known, the Prime Minister decided that there must be yet another General Election in the same year. The verdict of the country was unaltered and it may fairly be claimed that this verdict was given upon the crucial issue. It now remained to get the Parliament Bill on to the Statute Book and, as matters then stood, the veto of the Lords might prevent this.

12 *Election results in 1910*

	Total votes	MPs Elected	Candidates
1910 14 Jan–9 Feb			
Conservative	3,127,887	273	600
Liberal	2,880,581	275	516
Labour	505,657	40	78
Irish Nationalist	124,586	82	104
Others	28,693	—	17
Elec. 7,694,741 Turnout 86·6%	6,667,404	670	1,315
1910 2–19 Dec			
Conservative	2,420,566	272	550
Liberal	2,295,888	272	467
Labour	371,772	42	56
Irish Nationalist	131,375	84	106
Others	8,768	—	11
Elec. 7,709,981 Turnout 81·1%	5,228,369	670	1,190

Adapted from D. Butler and A. Sloman British Political Facts 1900–1979 *(1980)*

13 *J.R. Clynes, Labour MP during these events:* The Right Honourable J.R. Clynes Memoirs 1869–1924 *(1937)*
On my return from America I found the new Parliament of 1910 in a state of uneasy expectancy. Lloyd George's rejected Budget was sent once more to the Lords, and was passed by them this time in scared silence. Then Mr. Asquith's Government introduced a Bill reducing the life of Parlia-

ment from seven years to five, and providing that the Lords should never be able in future to interfere in any way with national finance.

One of the arguments used by certain elements in the country at this time, to frighten the House of Commons off any endeavour to curb the powers of the Upper House, was the specious one that the King, whose health had been failing, was being worried and made ill by the conflict between the two Houses.

In May 1910, Edward VII died. By common consent the Lords *v.* Commons issue was suspended for the time being, as a gesture of respect to a ruler who had been admired by all alike.

But things could not go on as they were. Government and Opposition were too nearly of the same power; no real work was done; and in November another General Election was held, in an endeavour to give one Party or other a working majority.

14 *Margot Asquith, wife of Prime Minister Asquith:* The Autobiography of Margot Asquith *(1922)*
With the accession to the Throne of King George – whom my husband and I had known and loved since boyhood – the Constitutional question dealing with the House of Lords became much more difficult. Rather than embarrass the new King, my husband decided to refer the subject to a round-table Conference, over which he held high hopes; but after six months of deliberation the negotiations broke down; and on the 10th of November, I received a telegram while I was staying with the children in Scotland, in which he wrote:
    'Tout est fini.'
It was clear to me that there was nothing for it but for us to have another General Election and as quickly as possible before the discontent of our party could become vocal.

15 *Parliamentary Bill for reforming the House of Lords – first introduced into the House of Commons in April 1910*
Whereas it is intended to substitute for the House of Lords as it at present exists, a Second Chamber constituted on a popular instead of a hereditary basis, but such a substitution cannot immediately be brought into operation . . .

1. That it is expedient that the House of Lords be disabled by law from rejecting or amending a Money Bill . . .
2. That it is expedient that the powers of the House of Lords . . . be restricted by law, so that any [non-Money] Bill which has passed the House of Commons in three successive Sessions and, having been sent up to the House of Lords at least one month before the end of the Session, has been rejected by that House in each of those Sessions, shall become law without the consent of the House of Lords on the Royal assent being declared; Provided that at least two years shall have elapsed between the date of the first introduction of the Bill in the House of Commons and the date on which it passes the House of Commons for the third time . . .
3. That it is expedient to limit the duration of Parliament to five years . . .

16 *George V in his diary about a meeting with Asquith, 16 November 1910*
After a long talk, I agreed most reluctantly to give the Cabinet a secret undertaking that in the event of the Government being returned with a majority at the General Election, I should use my Prerogative to make Peers if asked for. I disliked having to do this very much, but agreed that this was the only alternative to the Cabinet resigning, which at this moment would be disastrous.

17 *Viscount Simon in his memoirs, 1952*
I witnessed the final scene on August 9th, 1911, sitting side by side with Alec Murray in the M.P.s' Gallery overlooking the Lords' Chamber. The concluding exchanges in the debate made for a climax not to be forgotten. Lord Lansdowne and Lord St. Aldwyn were for bowing to the inevitable. Old Lord Halsbury led the die-hards, who professed even at this last moment that the prospect of a further creation of peers was a mere bogey. What added immensely to the sense of excitement was that no-one knew how the division would go . . . Ultimately the Bill was carried by 131 to 114, a majority of 17. Thus the creation of a new *bloc* of peers was avoided and the Parliament Act became the law of the land.

B ACK TO TI E ᵖRESENT

At the time of writing this book the problem of poverty is still with us, although the exact nature of this problem is hotly disputed by different political groupings. Recently, Conservative politicians in government have actually denied the existence of poverty and, significantly, have compared the 'improved' standards of living of 'the poor' today with the much lower standards of 'the poor' a hundred years ago. Labour and Liberal politicians, however, claim that there is still an unacceptable level of poverty in Britain today and use this claim to attack the record of Tory governments. In certain ways the arguments about poverty in society and what the state's responsibility should be in dealing with it have not changed all that much since 1914. The following questions can be used to bring the historical controversies you have been investigating 'up to date':

1 What is an appropriate definition of poverty for making an assessment of standards of living in Britain today?

2 To what extent does society have an obligation to help the poor through the state? How great should this help be?

3 What exactly are the different ways in which the 'Welfare State' today tries to ensure that people are guaranteed a minimum standard of existence? Are you generally for or against these kinds of welfare provision?

4 To what extent is it still the responsibility of individuals to look after themselves without having to look to the state for support?

5 What should the role of charity be in alleviating poverty?

6 Can inequalities between rich and poor ever be eradicated? Is it even desirable to try to eradicate these inequalities?

2 BRITISH FOREIGN POLICY AND THE COMING OF WAR

1900-14

INTRODUCTION

On 28 July 1914 the leaders of the Austro-Hungarian Empire declared war on Serbia. Austria-Hungary's intention was to curb the power of the leading Slav nation in the Balkans and thus to limit the threat of Slav nationalism within the Empire itself. The assassination of Archduke Franz Ferdinand a month or so earlier in Sarajevo merely provided the pretext for this assault on the independence of Serbia. By August 1914 this localised dispute had turned into a major European war in which Austria-Hungary, supported by their more powerful ally, Germany, found themselves in conflict with Russia, France and Britain. By the end of 1918 this European war had become a world war and almost ten million people had lost their lives. Of this ten million dead, one million were accounted for by soldiers from Britain and her empire.

On the face of it, British involvement in a war started by a dispute thousands of miles away in South East Europe seems most unlikely. To understand Britain's entry into the war we need to understand the course of British foreign policy in the decades leading up to August 1914. Did our diplomacy contribute to the coming of the war in any way? Did our policies make sense in terms of British interests in the world before 1914? What exactly were British interests before 1914? It is these problems and issues with which this theme is concerned. The Special Topic – 'The Decision For War 1914' – concentrates on the decisions made by the British government in the weeks leading up to our actual entry into the war.

KEY QUESTIONS

1 How and why did British diplomacy 1900–14 change from a policy of 'isolation' to one of commitment to other powers?

2 Why did Britain go to war in 1914 on the side of France and Russia against Germany and Austria-Hungary?

3 To what extent did Britain and its governing classes help bring about war in 1914?

4 Should Britain have gone to war at all in 1914?

OUTLINING THE EVENTS I

'SPLENDID ISOLATION' TO 1902

The collection of brief extracts in this section taken from a variety of textbooks provides you with evidence about the principles and some of the events of British foreign policy before 1900. It is crucial to understand Britain's role in the world and the nature of our international policies and relationships before 1900 in order to appreciate how these policies changed in subsequent years.

Activity

Study the extracts carefully (including the map) and think about what they tell you about Britain's relations with the rest of the world. Now, working individually or in pairs answer the following questions:

a What is meant by 'splendid isolation' in describing British foreign policy up to 1902?
b What do the extracts suggest were the reasons for 'splendid isolation'?
c What challenges to British power were emerging by the 1890s and which powers seemed to pose the greatest threats?
d Why did these challenges and threats make it difficult for politicians to maintain isolation?

Make sure each of you have readable copies of the deductions you have made in answer to these questions.

Discussion

As a class, discuss your answers to the questions above in order to make sure you all have a clear understanding of the issues involved. Make additional notes where appropriate.

Further Reading and Research

Using textbooks and materials indicated by your teacher put together a set of notes on 'Splendid Isolation to 1902'. The questions you investigated above should provide you with ideas for headings and with much of the material you will need. In your reading check up on names and events mentioned in the sources which you feel you need to find out more about. Here are some important references: Lord Salisbury; the Boer War; the Franco-Russian alliance; the German-Austro-Hungarian alliance; the Fashoda incident.

I *A.W. Palmer:* A Dictionary of Modern History *(1962)*
'Splendid Isolation'. British foreign policy during the Salisbury Governments of 1895–1902 has frequently been described as being based upon the principle of 'splendid isolation'. While the other European Great Powers tended to line up in two rival camps, Britain was able, because of her naval strength, to remain without an ally until 1902 – when a treaty limited to Far Eastern waters was made with Japan.

2 *K.D. Cornwell:* World History in the Twentieth Century *(1980)*
The deliberate policy of Britain until about 1896 was one of 'splendid isolation'. Thereafter, for a variety of reasons, a sense of insecurity developed. Relations with France had become increasingly bitter because of colonial disputes in Siam (Thailand) and at Fashoda. British influence in the Middle East and the security of the Indian frontiers seemed to be threatened by Russian expansion in Persia and Afghanistan and the growing German interest in the Turkish Empire. It appeared that Germany, hitherto a land power, was trying also to rival British naval power, for in 1898 and 1900 two Navy Laws provided for a large programme of shipbuilding.

3 *E.A. Carter and R.A. Mears:* A History of Britain *(1960)*
'Splendid isolation' was the term coined to describe the position of mighty and complacent Britannia at the end of the nineteenth century – until it was seen that this isolation was more dangerous than splendid. The unfriendly attitude of most European countries during the Boer War – their scarcely

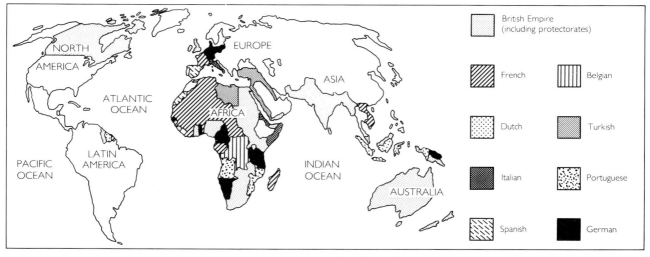

British Empire (including protectorates)

French   Belgian

Dutch   Turkish

Italian   Portuguese

Spanish   German

The British Empire and other empires of Western Europe in 1910

veiled hope that the British Empire would lose in this colonial struggle – did something to shake British complacency ... The Naval Defence Act (1889) had laid down that the British Navy should be superior to the combined strength of any two other Powers.

4 *L.C.B. Seaman:* Post-Victorian Britain 1902–1951 *(1966)*
In the closing years of the nineteenth century almost all these advantages were ceasing to operate. Britain's industrial monopoly was passing away, and this indicated that both the United States and Germany would sooner or later possess the means, even if they did not acquire the will, to challenge Britain as a world Power. The fragmentation of Europe had been ended by the events of the 1860s, with the emergence of a united German State and a united Italy. The first major consequence of this revolution in the European State-system was the creation by 1894 of the Franco-Russian alliance as a defensive reaction to the Bismarckian system of alliances. This system, by binding together the German Empire, the Austro-Hungarian Empire, Italy, Roumania (and, for a time, Serbia) had placed Central Europe, from the Baltic to the Adriatic and the Black Sea, under the domination of Berlin.

5 *R.K. Webb:* Modern England *(1980)*
On balance, down to the nineties, Russia still seemed to pose the major threat, while France was the persistent nuisance in the foreground, squabbling, demanding compensation, and repeatedly

changing front with changes of ministries ... Most of Britain's diplomatic involvement with Continental nations in the last two decades of the century grew out of conflicts originating in competition for overseas empire.

6 *Percentage distribution of world manufacturing production*

Year	United Kingdom	United States	Germany
1870	31.8	23.3	13.2
1913	14.0	35.8	15.7

From A.E. Musson: The Growth of British Industry *(1981)*

7 *Colonial possessions of the great powers (million square km and million inhabitants)*

	1900 No. of Colonies	Colonies 1876 Area Pop.	1914 Area Pop.	Home Countries 1914 Area Pop.	Total 1914 Area Pop.
Gt Britain	50	22·5 251·9	33·5 393·5	0·3 46·5	33·8 440·0
Russia	3	17·0 15·9	17·4 33·2	5·4 136·2	22·8 169·4
France	33	0·9 6·0	10·6 55·5	0·5 39·6	11·1 95·1
Germany	13	— —	2·9 12·3	0·5 64·9	3·4 77·2
USA	6	— —	0·3 9·7	9·4 97·0	9·7 106·7
Japan	6	— —	0·3 19·2	0·4 53·0	0·7 72·2
Total		40·4 273·8	65·0 523·4	16·5 437·2	81·5 960·6

Based on V.I. Lenin: Imperialism: The Highest Stage of Capitalism *(1916) from J. Wroughton and Denys Cook:* Documents on World History 1870–1918 *(1976)*

OUTLINING THE EVENTS II

BRITISH FOREIGN POLICY 1900–14

The further set of textbook extracts in this section have been selected to embrace the key events and issues in British foreign policy to 1914. The activities below are devised to help you grasp the basic narrative of events. You need to establish a knowledge of the facts of the topic before you can start analysing and interpreting with any confidence. You should bear in mind that the governments in power in the period were Conservative 1900–05 and Liberal 1905–15.

Activity I

a Working in pairs, use the secondary evidence to construct a chronology of events in British foreign policy from 1900 to 1914. When you have sorted out a comprehensive list of dates and events, try to work out exactly what the main events were about. Jot down a sentence or two for each entry in your chronology summarising what happened – at least according to the versions of history presented here.

b You should now check the accuracy of your chronology by comparing it with the work of other students in the class. Your teacher will help you to resolve any difficulties and confusions in understanding what is going on.

Activity II

At this point you should have a fair appreciation of the basic changes and developments in British foreign policy in the period. Using your chronologies and the secondary source extracts, answer the questions below. Your responses can form a written piece of work and/or an exercise for class discussion.

a What was the significance of the Anglo-Japanese alliance?
b How and why did Britain's relations with France change in the period 1900–14?
c Similarly, in what ways did the relationship between Britain and Russia change?

d How and why did relations change with Germany in the period?
e What had happened to the policy of 'splendid isolation' by 1914?
f What do you understand by the idea of Britain pursuing a 'balance of power' policy in Europe in the period (see Extract 1)?
g Had British security and interests been improved or diminished by the foreign policies of both Conservative and Liberal governments in the period?

If these questions have been the basis of class discussion, make sure you take notes of any important points or pieces of information that are significant.

Further Reading and Research

Make sure your chronology of events is full and accurate. This might mean making a revised copy. Now, using your textbooks and other relevant works of history, make additional notes on the main episodes outlined in your chronology. Alternatively, your teacher might prefer to provide you with a detailed set of notes to accompany the work you have carried out so far.

---

1 *K. Robbins:* The Eclipse of a Great Power *(1983)*
Two men bear the responsibility for the conduct of British foreign policy between 1902 and 1914, though we can only speculate on the importance of their individual contribution to the course of events – Lord Lansdowne (1902–05) and Sir Edward Grey (1905–16). The war, whose course and conclusion has just been discussed, inevitably conditions our consideration of their diplomacy. We know that they failed and are tempted, at each turn, to discover a way in which war might have been avoided. There can be little doubt that they did seek to avoid it. Both would have agreed that Britain had two basic interests; that the rival alliance systems should remain antagonistic but they should not go to war. The 'balance of power' would prevent any state or group of states from dominating Europe.

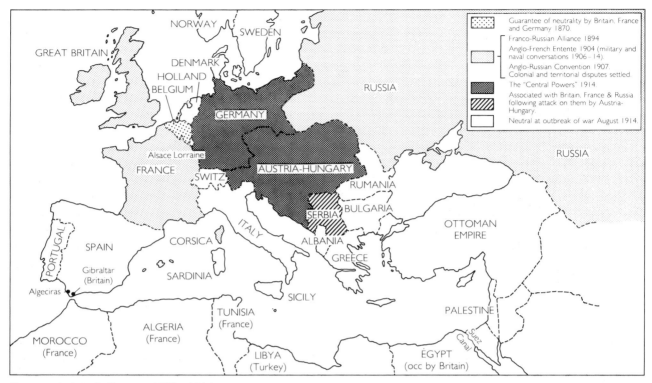

The legend of the map reads:

- Guarantee of neutrality by Britain, France and Germany 1870.
- Franco-Russian Alliance 1894
- Anglo-French Entente 1904 (military and naval conversations 1906 – 14).
- Anglo-Russian Convention 1907. Colonial and territorial disputes settled.
- The "Central Powers" 1914.
- Associated with Britain, France & Russia following attack on them by Austria-Hungary.
- Neutral at outbreak of war August 1914.

Power relations in Europe 1900–1914

2 Dictionary of British History *ed. J.P. Kenyon* (*1988*)

Anglo-Japanese alliance. A defensive treaty concluded between Great Britain and Japan in 1902 and renewed twice thereafter (1905, 1911). The treaty aimed to prevent Russian expansion in the Far East and ensured Japan's participation in World War I on the allied side. The alliance was terminated in 1921 at the Washington conference.

3 *D. Read:* England 1868–1914 (*1979*)

The Germans eventually moderated their demands; but the Agadir crisis stimulated the renewal of Anglo-French military staff talks, and the beginning of naval staff discussions. Only now did the whole cabinet hear of the 1906 contacts.

4 *K. Robbins:* The Eclipse of a Great Power (*1983*)

The Franco-British *entente* (for it was not a formal alliance) was concluded, not without difficulty, in April 1904. The bargaining had centred on colonial questions. In the event, the French agreed to accept the British position in Egypt and, in effect, the British withdrew opposition to French designs on Morocco. Other lesser colonial matters were also resolved. Lansdowne's primary objective was to improve relations with France. He had no wish to exacerbate relations with Germany. Nevertheless, there was acrimony and suspicion between London and Berlin and the new agreement did nothing to lessen this tension.

5 *J.A.S. Grenville:* A World History of the Twentieth Century (*1980*)

The British government knew that they possessed the resources to keep pace with any increase in Germany's naval construction. By 1914 Britain had twenty new super-battleships of the *Dreadnought* class, against Germany's thirteen; in older battleships Britain's superiority was even greater – twenty-six to Germany's twelve. By making arrangements with France to concentrate this fleet in home waters, leaving the Mediterranean to be defended by the French fleet, British naval superiority over Germany was assured and, also significantly, her ties with France were strengthened.

Still trying at the same time to assure Germany of Britain's general goodwill, Grey concluded two agreements with Germany in 1913 and 1914. The first, a rather dubious one, divided up two Portu-

Sir Edward Grey, 1910

guese colonies in Africa, Mozambique and Angola, allowing Germany a good share should Portugal choose to dispose of these possessions. The other agreement helped Germany to realize plans for the final sections of the Berlin–Baghdad railway project and so facilitated German commercial penetration of Asia Minor and Mesopotamia. It was concluded on the very eve of the outbreak of war in Europe.

6 *E.J. Feuchtwanger:* Democracy and Empire – Britain 1865–1914 *(1985)*
In 1905 the Germans decided to put the Moroccan understanding between Britain and France to the test by pressing their own interests in Morocco, signalled by the Kaiser's visit to Tangier in March. It was not a well thought-out step, though at that moment the Russian defeats in the Far East and the outbreak of revolution at home had created a favourable situation for Germany in Euope. The Germans were working to clinch an alliance with the hard-pressed Russians. The ups and downs of the Moroccan affair caused some misunderstandings between London and Paris but in the end the German pressure strengthened the *entente cordiale* rather than weakened it.

7 *J. Joll:* Origins of the First World War *(1984)*
The crisis over Morocco died down after the Algeciras conference; and although France's in-

fluence in Morocco was confirmed at the conference and Germany suffered a diplomatic defeat, nevertheless the two countries were able to cooperate in various economic enterprises over the next few years and it was not until 1911 that their rivalry in Morocco led to a second acute crisis. But the consolidation of the Anglo-French *Entente* continued, though perhaps not as fast as some of the French leaders would have liked. In 1907 the apparent division of Europe into two rival camps was carried a stage further. On 31 August 1907 the British and Russian governments signed an agreement which was intended to settle old differences between them on the borders between their two empires, particularly in Persia, Afghanistan and Tibet.

8 *R.K. Webb:* Modern England *(1980)*
In 1905, the Kaiser intervened dramatically in the Moroccan question as a response to the Anglo-French understanding, but got nothing from the Algeciras Conference, called in 1906 at Germany's insistence to settle the problem she had created . . .

9 *T.O. Lloyd:* Empire to Welfare State – English History 1906–1967 *(1970)*
The international situation seemed better in 1914 than for some time; in 1911 there had been some tense weeks when the German government had sent a warship, the *Panther*, to Agadir to demonstrate the seriousness of German claims to a position of influence in Morocco, and for a few years after 1908 Germany had been building battleships at a rate which seemed to be threatening Britain's maritime supremacy. But by 1914 the race was virtually over; after a moment of anxiety in 1909 Britain had settled down to building two battleships a year more than Germany, and the British preparations for additional ships were further advanced.

10 *Z.S. Steiner:* Britain and the Origins of the First World War *(1977)*
Although individual members of the Cabinet had serious doubts about the bargain which was finally concluded, the Anglo-Japanese treaty was signed on 30 January 1902.

At the time, it was assumed that this treaty represented a sharp departure in British policy. Britain had 'given up her fixed policy of not making alliances'. Lansdowne admonished his fellow peers to forget old-fashioned superstitions as to the desirability of a policy of isolation. Britain had incurred an obligation to go to war which was conspicuously absent from agreements made in the post-1830 period.

11 Dictionary of British History *ed. J.P. Kenyon (1988)*
Algeciras conference (16 Jan–7 April 1906). An international meeting in Algeciras, Spain, held at Germany's insistence, which regulated intervention by France and Spain in the internal affairs of Morocco. It confirmed the Anglo-French *entente cordiale* and marked a stage in the division of Europe before World War I into opposing camps.

12 *R.K. Webb:* Modern England *(1980)*
Then, in 1898, Germany began to build up her navy. To this new threat from abroad, made worse by her now apparent diplomatic isolation, Britain responded by a third building program, launched in 1904 by the able and controversial first sea lord, Sir John Fisher, a program that created the modern battleship; the *Dreadnought* was the first of them and gave its name to its class. Such naval building plans had not only important diplomatic repercussions but profound effects on government finance and, through that, on politics.

13 *E.J. Hobsbawm:* The Age of Empire 1875– 1914 *(1987)*
The third great international crisis, over Morocco in 1911, admittedly had little to do with revolution, and everything to do with imperialism – and the shady operations of free-booting businessmen who recognized its multiple possibilities. Germany sent a gunboat ready to seize the south Moroccan port of Agadir, in order to gain some 'compensation' from the French for their imminent 'protectorate' over Morocco, but was forced into retreat by what appeared to be a British threat to go to war on the side of the French. Whether this was actually intended is irrelevant.

The Agadir crisis demonstrated that almost any confrontation between two major powers now brought them to the brink of war.

14 *R. Rhodes James:* The British Revolution – British Politics 1880–1939 *(1978)*
But – and this was particularly true of the public awakening to the softly developing crisis – it was the building of a modern North Sea Fleet which provided a direct challenge that could not be ignored. All attempts to end the naval race by negotiation failed; the last ones were in 1912, when Haldane proposed to the Kaiser a lowering of the British superiority rate, and in March 1913, when Churchill proposed a 'naval holiday' in battleship construction. The German Government proceeded relentlessly on its course.

15 *D. Read:* Edwardian England *(1972)*
The term 'splendid isolation' had been coined in 1896 to describe a situation in which the isolation was already coming to be more felt than the splendour. An Anglo-Japanese alliance was hesitantly concluded in 1902 to protect British interests in the Far East, followed in 1904 by the Anglo-French Entente, on paper simply the settlement of long-standing colonial differences but increasingly in practice something more. In 1907 Grey concluded a similar entente with Russia. This was neither so successful nor so popular; but it did mean that Britain had come to terms with both partners (the Dual Entente) on one side of the European balance, yet not with the Triple Alliance of Germany, Austria and Italy on the other. As early as 1906 Grey sanctioned secret military conversations with France. Most members even of the Cabinet knew nothing of these until 1912. Grey felt that conversations were necessary so that Britain *could* (not necessarily *would*) support France if she were attacked by Germany. He always insisted in public and in private that there was no formal commitment, an entente was not an alliance. But, especially after naval discussions had led in 1913 to the withdrawal of the French fleet to the Mediterranean, Britain's moral obligation was hard to deny.

CONTEMPORARY VIEWS & OPINIONS

ANGLO-GERMAN RELATIONS 1900–14

It is obviously important to understand Anglo-German relations in the years up to 1914 if we are to appreciate why the two countries went to war with each other. The contemporary source extracts in this section give an indication of the ways in which Germany was perceived by influential opinion in Britain in the period – and also some indication of how Germany perceived Britain.

Activity I

a Study the extracts carefully. Pay attention to the date of each source, who the author is and, where appropriate, to whom the view is directed. Also, make sure you understand the references in the sources to things like Tangier, Agadir, and so on. Your chronologies and notes will help you with this.

b Extract 3 gives two alternative views of German ambitions in the world. Write down in your own words what these two views are. Which of these views is reflected in many of the extracts in this section? Make a note of which ones in particular.

Activity II

a Working individually or in small groups, use the pieces of evidence here and other work you have done on the theme to make a list of reasons explaining the suspicion of Britain towards Germany. Don't forget to look at the cartoons which are also of significance.

b Read extracts 10 and 11 which express rather different views about the relationship between Britain and Germany. What exactly are the alternative views expressed in each of the passages? In what ways do the two views reinforce each other? Make a note of your observations.

Discussion

Discuss as a class the answers and ideas you have come up with in the work above. The following questions can be used as the basis for further discussion: Were British fears of Germany justified? Did Germany have any grounds to be afraid of British power and policies in the period up to 1914? What further kinds of evidence would you need to examine in order to fully answer these questions?

---

1 *An article in the* Daily Mail, *1897*
Let us make no mistake about it. It is natural to deplore the unfriendship of the two nations, but it is idle to ignore it. *Hostility to England is the mission of young Germany.*

It is idle to ignore it, but we need be neither furious nor panic-stricken. It is as much Germany's right to seek after the good things of the earth as it is ours. It is proper that we should be plain with ourselves, and admit that for the time Germany is our chiefest rival in all fields. We can be competitors without being enemies. Only in the honest effort to avoid enmity we need not cease to compete. Be very sure, at least, that methodical, patient, unresting Germany will make no such mistake. So, for the next ten years, fix your eyes very hard on Germany.

2 *Grey, the future Liberal Foreign Secretary (1905–16) describing Germany in 1903*
... our worst enemy and our greatest danger. I do not doubt that there are many Germans well disposed to us, but they are a minority; and the majority dislike us so intensely that the friendship of their Emperor or their Government cannot be really useful to us.

3 *Eyre Crowe, leading Foreign Office diplomat, in a memorandum in 1907*
If it be considered necessary to formulate and accept a theory that will fit all the ascertained facts of German foreign policy, the choice must lie between the two hypotheses here presented: Either Germany is definitely aiming at a general political hegemony and maritime ascendancy, threatening the independence of her neighbours and ultimately the existence of England. Or Germany, free from

any such clear-cut ambition and thinking for the present merely of using her legitimate position and influence as one of the leading powers in the council of nations, is seeking to promote her foreign commerce, spread the benefits of German culture, extend the scope of her national energies and create fresh German interests all over the world wherever and whenever a peaceful opportunity offers, leaving it to an uncertain future to decide whether the occurrence of great changes in the world may not some day assign to Germany a larger share of direct political action over regions not now part of her dominions without that violation of the established rights of other countries which would be involved in any such action under existing political conditions. In either case Germany would clearly be wise to build as powerful a navy as she can afford.

4 *Foreign Secretary Grey's views in the minutes of the Committee of Imperial Defence, May 1911*
... the cause of anxiety now in public opinion here as regards Germany arises entirely from the question of the German naval expenditure, which is very considerable, which may be increased, and which, if it is increased, will produce an impression on the world at large that the object of Germany is to build a fleet which shall be bigger than the British fleet ... if she had a fleet bigger than the British fleet, obviously she could not only defeat us at sea, but could be in London in a very short time with her army.

'Let Germany be careful now' – *a British cartoon of the* entente cordiale

5 *Tyrell to Hardinge – a communication between Foreign Office diplomats, July 1911*
It is depressing to find that after six years' experience of Germany the inclination here is still to believe that she can be placated by small concessions ... What she wants is the hegemony of Europe. The French game in Morocco has been stupid and dishonest, but it is a vital interest for us to support her on this occasion in the same way in which the Germans supported the Austrian policy of 1908 in Bosnia. It is going to be a narrow shave and we may pull it off again but that is about all that I feel about it at present.

6 *Lloyd George, Chancellor of the Exchequer, warning Germany in his Mansion House speech, July 21st 1911*
But I am bound also to say this – that I believe it is essential in the highest interests, not merely of this country, but of the world, that Britain should at all hazards maintain her place and her prestige amongst the Great Powers of the world. Her potent influence has many a time been in the past, and may yet be in the future, invaluable to the cause of human liberty.... But if a situation were to be forced upon us in which peace could only be preserved by the surrender of the great and beneficent position Britain has won by centuries of heroism and achievement, by allowing Britain to be treated where her interests were vitally affected as if she were of no account in the Cabinet of nations, then I say emphatically that peace at that price would be a humiliation intolerable for a great country like ours to endure. National honour is no party question. The security of our great international trade is no party question; the peace of the world is much more likely to be secured if all nations realize fairly what the conditions of peace must be.

7 *Memorandum by the General Staff, August 1911*
In this paper it has been assumed that the policy of England is to prevent any one or more of the Continental Powers from attaining a position of superiority which would enable it or them to dominate the other Continental Powers. Such domination or control would place at the disposal of the Power or Powers concerned a preponderance of naval and military force which would

menace the independence of the United Kingdom and the integrity of the British Empire.

This policy, if correctly defined, may possibly be held to apply to Germany at the present time, just as it applied to France in our struggle with Napoleon. It is proposed to examine what course of action England should adopt if, in pursuance of a policy of continental domination, Germany, with the support of Austria, were to attack France. England can either remain neutral or become the active ally of France.

8 *McDonagh, a newspaper journalist on* The Times, *writing in his diary on 3 August 1914*
Germany has always been disliked and distrusted for her bullying policy of sabre-rattling, the mailed fist, the goose-step, and the spiked helmet – symbols of violence and brute force. Indeed she has been suspected for years of looking forward to a war with Great Britain.

9 *Hardinge, Foreign Office diplomat, writing to Grey in 1915*
I often think of the five years I spent with you at the F.O. and wonder if any mistake was then made in our policy, and if anything we might then have done could have possibly staved off this war. I think not. It seems as though there can be no doubt that the careful preparation for war was then in full swing, and that the ideal of German hegemony in Europe and of worldwide domination had already sunk too deep into the convictions of the governing class in Germany to make it possible that war should be averted. Everything points to this now, though to some it may have been obscure in the past.

10 *The German Chancellor, Bethmann-Hollweg, in a speech to the Reichstag in December 1914*
The world is wide; it offers, if only no one tries to hinder the free development of our powers, room enough for both nations to measure their strength in peaceful competition. That was the principle which our policy had always adopted. (Very true!)

But, gentlemen, while we were negotiating in this way, England was unceasingly intent upon making her relations to Russia and France closer and closer. The determining factor in this was that,

beyond the domain of politics, further military agreements were always being made to provide for the event of a Continental war. England carried on these negotiations as secretly as possible. When any hint of them leaked out, their significance was represented in the press and in Parliament as thoroughly innocent. They have not remained hidden from us, as you know from the publications that I have been responsible for. The whole position, gentlemen, was simply this: England was ready, indeed, to come to an understanding with us on isolated questions, but the supreme and first principle of English policy remained with her: Germany must be kept in check in the free development of her energies by means of the "balance of power." That is the extreme limit for friendly relations with Germany. With this object, strengthening of the Triple *Entente* to the uttermost!

11 *Edward Carpenter, writer, in* The Healing of Nations *(1916)*
What, indeed, shall we say of England? Germany has for years maintained that with her own growing population and her growing trade she needs a more extended seaboard in Europe, and coaling stations and colonies in other regions of the globe, but that England, jealous of commercial supremacy, has been determined to deny her these, and, if possible, to crush her; that she (Germany) has lived in perpetual fear and panic; and that if in this case she has been the first to strike, it has only been because to wait England's opportunity would have been to court defeat. Allowing for the exaggerations inseparable from opposed points of view, is there not some justification for this plea? England, who plunged into the Crimean War in order to *prevent* Russia from obtaining a seaboard and her natural commercial expansion, and who afterwards joined with Russia in order to plunder Persia and to prevent Germany from getting her railways along the Persian Gulf; who calmly appropriated Egypt, with its valuable cottonlands and market; who, at the behest of a group of capitalists and financiers, turned her great military machine on a little nation of Boer farmers in South Africa ... – what trust can be placed in her?

SIMULATION

THE BRITISH CABINET ON THE BRINK OF WAR, 1914

Introduction

The aim of the simulation is to encourage you to think about and discuss the problems which the Liberal government faced in July and August 1914 in relation to the crisis in Europe. Putting yourself in the position of Asquith's Cabinet at this time will help you to appreciate the dilemmas and difficulties of the government as it decided how best to preserve British interests. Also, by having the opportunity to make different decisions from those actually taken in 1914 you may be able to understand more fully the reasons and motives behind the decisions actually taken.

The Situation

You are the British Cabinet facing an escalating European crisis in the summer of 1914. You are responsible for making a vital series of 'life and death' decisions about what Britain is going to do and say with respect to the other Great Powers of Europe as they move, seemingly inexorably, towards full-scale war. Your overriding aim in making your decisions is to preserve British interests. These interests are considerable, given that Britain is one of the greatest economic powers in the world and has the largest empire. The two main areas of decision-making will be as follows:

- To decide how you will bring British influence to bear on the other European powers in order to avert war altogether or at least to keep the conflict localised.

- If you fail in the above aim you will then have to decide whether Britain will herself take part in the war or stay neutral.

Background Information

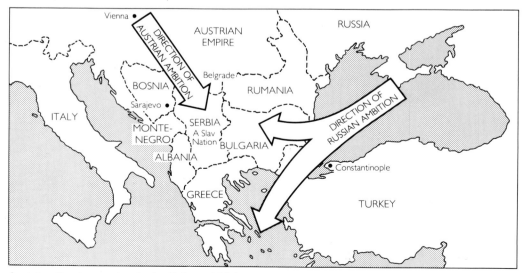

Austrian-Russian tension in the Balkans 1914

The relationships between the powers, and their individual ambitions and fears, are as you understand them from your study of British foreign policy thus far. Here is a summary:
— Germany and Austria-Hungary have a military alliance.
— France and Russia have a military alliance.
— Britain has ententes (understandings) with both France and Russia but has no formal military obligations to either.
— British military officials have, however, consulted in the past with French military officials. As a result, plans have been drawn up as to how the British navy and the small British army might assist France in the event of a war with Germany. The extent of these plans has not been fully disclosed to the Cabinet, apart from the Prime Minister and the Foreign Secretary.
— Germany fears encirclement by France, Russia and Britain.
— Austria-Hungary believes that Slav nationalism led by Serbia will lead to the collapse of her empire.
— Russia fears that Austro-Hungarian influence in the Balkans will undermine her power.
— France fears German strength, but, on the other hand, would like to recover Alsace-Lorraine taken from her by Germany in the Franco-Prussian war of 1870–1.
— Britain fears Germany's growing economic might, and her attempt to build up a navy to rival that of Britain.

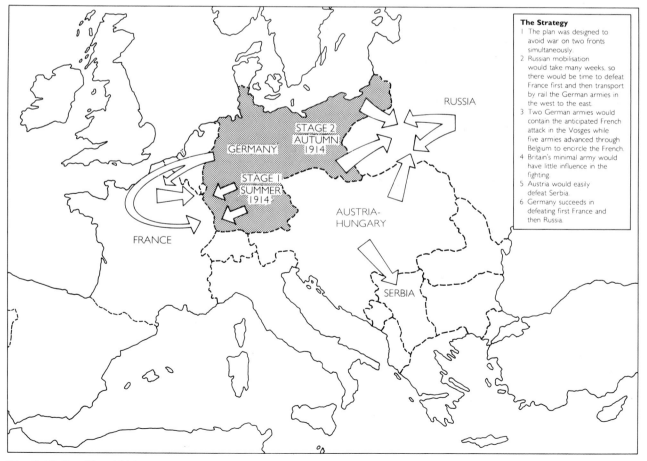

The Strategy
1 The plan was designed to avoid war on two fronts simultaneously.
2 Russian mobilisation would take many weeks, so there would be time to defeat France first and then transport by rail the German armies in the west to the east.
3 Two German armies would contain the anticipated French attack in the Vosges while five armies advanced through Belgium to encircle the French.
4 Britain's minimal army would have little influence in the fighting.
5 Austria would easily defeat Serbia.
6 Germany succeeds in defeating first France and then Russia.

The Schlieffen Plan 1914

Procedure

1 Read through the material in 'Background Information' above and study the two maps to remind yourself about the historical context of the simulation.

2 Groups of four or five students should each form a British Cabinet. You should select a Prime Minister, a Foreign Secretary, and someone to act as a secretary.

3 Examine the information given for the relevant phase of the simulation. Your Cabinet must identify British interests and responsibilities in the given situation. You must then issue appropriate written communications to the other powers. These communications might involve proposals, warnings, requests for further information or clarification of intentions.

4 Your teacher will play the parts of all the other powers. He or she will read your communications and issue plausible replies – in the role of France, Germany or whoever – based on his/her detailed knowledge of the actual historical situation.

5 Having selected responses to your communications from the relevant governments you must then make further decisions and issue further communications based on the changing situation.

6 Each phase should last between 30 and 45 minutes.

7 When each phase is deemed to be at an end the teacher will hold a discussion about the decisions which have been taken and how successful the different groups have been.

PHASE 1

AIM – To try to avert or localise war.

July 30 Austria-Hungary has declared war on Serbia.

Russia seems determined to support Serbia.

Germany is certain to support Austria.

France is likely to back Russia.

France, Russia and Germany have all requested the British government to indicate where it stands in the present situation.

What is the British Cabinet going to do? And why?

PHASE 2

AIM – To decide whether Britain will go to war or not.

Aug 2 Russia has mobilised its armed forces.

Germany has declared war on Russia and is about to declare war on France.

France will support Russia and has appealed to Britain to use its navy to keep the German navy out of the Channel – as discussed in previous military consultations.

Germany has appealed to Britain to stay neutral, and in return has promised that if she defeats France she will not annex any of her European territory. It seems very likely that Germany will attack France through Belgium.

Belgium's neutrality is guaranteed by the powers acting *collectively*, though not necessarily *individually*.

What is the British Cabinet going to do now? And why?

S PECIAL TOPIC

THE DECISION FOR WAR, 1914

This Special Topic contains a range of primary source extracts set out in roughly chronological order. It is designed to enable you to investigate the thinking and the decisions of the Liberal government, led by Prime Minister Asquith, in the week or so before war was finally declared against Germany on 4 August 1914. More generally this section is concerned with examining contemporary arguments for and against war, and considering the issue of whether the government was right or wrong in taking Britain into the conflict.

Activity

a Read through the different pieces of evidence. Use textbooks and other works of reference to check up on people and events you feel you need to find out more about. Also, keep an eye on the date of each extract. The chronology included in the section should be of some assistance.

b Use the evidence to make a detailed record of the changes which took place in the attitude of the Liberal Cabinet between 31 July and 4 August over whether Britain should fight in a general European war, or not. Write a short paragraph on why you think these changes took place.

c Examine the source material once again and decide which passages are definitely in favour of fighting a war, which are definitely against, and which are neither clearly for or against (or seem totally incomprehensible!). Now, draw up a list of the reasons and explanations given by those who were in favour of going to war against Germany, and a list for those who were against.

Discussion

Working in small groups, compare each others' lists of reasons for and against war. Within your group discuss the validity of the different explanations given by politicians and other commentators at the time. If you took part in the simulation exercise earlier in this theme, think about the views you expressed then. See if you can reach agreement in your group as to who was right – those who were, by August 1914, in favour of intervention, or those who believed Britain should remain neutral in the war. As a class, discuss the views reached by different groups and find out if there is any overall consensus in the class about this issue. Finally, consider the following question: 'To what extent should historians make moral judgements about the past?'

---

1 Manchester Guardian *editorial, 27 July 1914*
The best hope of our success in the part of mediators, which we have very properly assumed, is that our impartiality should be above suspicion. . . . We have no . . . commitments. Not only are we neutral now, but we could and ought to remain neutral throughout the whole course of the war. It is strange that Sir E. Grey should not have referred to this fact, which is the chief source of our moral authority in Europe . . . the whole future of England depends on the suppression of the spirit that if Russia, Germany and France start fighting we must start too. It is war to the knife between it and Liberalism. Either it kills us or we kill it.

2 Manchester Guardian *editorial, 30 July 1914*
We have not seen a shred of reason for thinking that the triumph of Germany in a European war in which we had been neutral would injure a single British interest, however small, whereas the triumph of Russia would create a situation for us really formidable.

3 *Asquith, the Prime Minister, writing to his close friend Venetia Stanley, 31 July 1914*
Of course, everybody longs to stand aside, but I need not say that France thro' Cambon is pressing strongly for a reassuring declaration. E. Grey had an interview with him this afternoon wh. he told me was rather painful. He had of course to tell Cambon (for we are under no obligation) that we could give no pledges, and that our action must depend upon the course of events – including the

Belgian question, and the direction of public opinion here.

Kitchener whom I met at lunch at Winston's is very strong that if we don't back up France when she is in real danger, we shall never be regarded or exercise real power again. But the general opinion at present – particularly strong in the City – is to keep out at almost all costs.

4 *Lord Loreburn, ex-Liberal Minister and 'pacifist' in a letter to C. P. Scott, editor of the* Manchester Guardian, *31 July 1914*
I send a line to express my most hearty sympathy and admiration of the line you are taking about this threat of war. It is the time of trial which we have thought of as possible after the worship of the 'Entente'.

I have come back today from London. The Cabinet is I believe, by a majority, quite against our intervening. You know what are the elements on the wrong side.

5 The Times *editorial, 1 August 1914*
We dare not stand aside with folded arms and placidly watch our friends placed in peril of destruction. Should we remain passive, should the fortune of war go against those whose interests march with ours, we know full well that it would be our turn next. None would then raise a hand to save us. Peace is not, at such a moment, our strongest interest, however dear it may be to us, and however earnestly we may strive to maintain it. Our strongest interest is the law of self-preservation which is common to all humanity. The armies now marshalling against our friends challenge in reality our security not less than theirs.

6 *Asquith to Venetia Stanley, 1 August 1914*
There was really no fresh news this morning. We had a Cabinet wh. lasted from 11 to ½ past 1. It is no exaggeration to say that Winston occupied at least half of the time. We came, every now & again, near to the parting of the ways: Morley & I think the Impeccable are on what may be called the *Manchester Guardian* tack – that we shd. declare now & at once that *in no circumstances* will we take a hand. This no doubt is the view for the moment of the bulk of the party. Ll. George – all for peace – is more sensible & statesmanlike, for keeping the

position still open. Grey, of course, declares that if an out & out & uncompromising policy of non-intervention at all costs is adopted, he will go. Winston very bellicose & demanding immediate mobilisation. Haldane diffuse (how clever of you to retrieve the second 'f') and nebulous. The main controversy pivots upon Belgium & its neutrality. We parted in a fairly amicable mood, & are to sit again at 11 to-morrow (Sunday) an almost unprecedented event.

I am still *not quite* hopeless about peace, tho' far from hopeful. But if it comes to war I feel sure (this is entirely between you & me) that we shall have *some* split in the Cabinet. Of course, if Grey went I should go, & the whole thing would break up.

7 *Asquith to Venetia Stanley, 2 August 1914*
I had a visit at breakfast time from Lichnowsky, who was very *émotionné*, and implored me not to side with France. He said that Germany, with her army cut in two between France & Russia, was far more likely to be 'crushed' than France. He was very agitated poor man & wept. I told him that we had no desire to intervene, and that it rested largely with Germany to make intervention impossible, if she would (1) not invade Belgium, and (2) not send her fleet into the Channel to attack the unprotected North Coast of France. He was bitter about the policy of his Government in not restraining Austria & seemed quite heartbroken . . .

Happily I am quite clear in my own mind as to what is right & wrong. I put it down for you in a few sentences.

(1) We have no obligation of any kind either to France or Russia to give them military or naval help.

(2) The despatch of the Expeditionary force to help France at this moment is out of the question & wd. serve no object.

(3) We mustn't forget the ties created by our long-standing & intimate friendship with France.

(4) It is against British interests that France shd. be wiped out as a Great Power.

(5) We cannot allow Germany to use the Channel as a hostile base.

(6) We have obligations to Belgium to prevent her being utilised & absorbed by Germany.

8 *Charles Hobhouse, Liberal Minister, in a diary entry relating to 2 August 1914*

When we met at 6.30 to continue the pros and cons of neutrality or intervention we the majority came to an understanding that E.G. should tell the H. of C. that we could not stand aside if Belgium were invaded, and that we would give France maritime protection, and so inform Germany.

9 *Arthur Ponsonby, Liberal MP, in a speech to the House of Commons, 3 August 1914*

I feel that I cannot remain seated at what I feel to be the most tragic moment I have yet seen. We are on the eve of a great war, and I hate to see people embarking on it with a light heart. The war fever has already begun. I saw it last night when I walked through the streets. I saw bands of half-drunken youths waving flags, and I saw a group outside a great club in St. James's Street being encouraged by members of the club from the balcony. The war fever has begun, and that is what is called patriotism! I think we have plunged too quickly, and I think the Foreign Secretary's speech shows that what has been rankling all these years is a deep animosity against German ambitions. The balance of power is responsible for this – this mad desire to keep up an impossibility in Europe, to try and divide the two sections of Europe into an armed camp, glaring at one another with suspicion and hostility and hatred, and arming all the time, and bleeding the people to pay for the armaments. Since I have been in this House I have every year protested against the growth in the expenditure upon armaments. Every year it has mounted up and up, and old women of both sexes have told us that the best way to prepare to maintain peace is to prepare for war. This is what they have led us to – those who were foolish enough to believe it. It was inevitable that if Europe continued to arm, if every nation bled the people in order to furnish new ships and new guns, to grind all the people who devote their energy, their labour, and their enterprise to one sole object, the preparation for war, war will take place.

10 *Asquith to Venetia Stanley, 4 August 1914*

We had an interesting Cabinet, as we got the news that the Germans had entered Belgium, & had announced to 'les braves Belges' that if necessary they wd. push their way through by force of arms. This simplifies matters, so we sent the Germans an ultimatum to expire at midnight, requesting them to give a like assurance with the French that they wd. respect Belgian neutrality.

11 *'Neutrality League' advertisement in the* Manchester Guardian, *4 August 1914*

The facts are these:

1. If we took sides with Russia and France, the balance of power would be upset as it has never been before. It would make the military Russian Empire of 160,000,000 the dominant Power of Europe. You know the kind of country Russia is.

2. **We are not bound to join in a general European war to defend the neutrality of Belgium.** Out treaties expressly stipulate that our obligations under them **shall not compel us to take part in a general European war** in order to fulfil them. And if we are to fight for the neutrality of Belgium, we must be prepared to fight France as well as Germany.

3. The Prime Minister and Sir Edward Grey have both emphatically and solemnly declared in the House of Commons that we have no undertaking whatever, written or spoken, to go to war for France. We discharged our obligations in the Morocco affair. The *Entente Cordiale* was a pact of peace and not an alliance for war.

4. If Germany did attempt to annex any part of Belgium, Holland or Normandy – and there is no reason to suppose that she would attempt such a thing – she would be weaker than she is now, for she would have to use all her forces for holding her conquests down. She would have so many difficulties like those arising out of Alsace that she would have to leave other nations alone as much as possible. But we do not know in the least that she would do these things. It would be monstrous to drag this country into war on so vague a suspicion.

12 *Bertrand Russell, philosopher: letter to the* Nation, *15 August 1914*

Sir,

Against the vast majority of my countrymen, even at this moment, in the name of humanity and civilization, I protest against our share in the destruction of Germany.

A month ago Europe was a peaceful comity of nations; if an Englishman killed a German he was hanged. Now, if an Englishman kills a German, or if a German kills an Englishman, he is a patriot, who has deserved well of his country. . . .

And all this madness, all this rage, all this flaming death of our civilization and our hopes, has been brought about because a set of official gentlemen, living luxurious lives, mostly stupid, and all without imagination or heart, have chosen that it should occur rather than that any one of them should suffer some infinite rebuff to his country's pride. . . .

And behind the diplomatists, dimly heard in the official documents, stand vast forces of national greed and national hatred – atavistic instincts, harmful to mankind at its present level, but transmitted from savage and half-animal ancestors, concentrated and directed by Governments and the Press, fostered by the upper class as a distraction from social discontent, artificially nourished by the sinister influence of the makers of armaments, encouraged by a whole foul literature of 'glory', and by every text-book of history with which the minds of children are polluted.

13 *C.P. Scott: diary entry recording a conversation with Lord Loreburn, 23 October 1914*
He thought the war could have been prevented by a resolute policy of co-operation with Germany and a plain warning to France and Russia that they would not receive our support in a war with Germany. There were the two parties in Germany – the military and the civil. By alarming and irritating Germany we played into the hands of the first.

14 *Lloyd George speech, 28 February 1915*
All the same, national honour is a reality, and any nation that disregards it is doomed. Why is our honour as a country involved in this war? Because, in the first instance, we are bound by honourable obligations to defend the independence, the liberty, the integrity of a small neighbour that has always lived peaceably. She could not have compelled us; she was weak; but the man who declines to discharge his duty because his creditor is too poor to enforce it is a blackguard. We entered into a treaty – a solemn treaty – two treaties – to defend Belgium and her integrity. . . .

15 *Sir Edward Grey, in his autobiography* Twenty Five Years – 1892–1916 *(1926)*
The real reason for going into the war was that, if we did not stand by France and stand up for Belgium against this aggression, we should be isolated, discredited, and hated; and there would be before us nothing but a miserable and ignoble future. The speech was directed to presenting this consideration in the way that would convince and make the strongest appeal to the House, and which was, in fact, the way this issue presented itself from the first to some of us, and in the end to all the Cabinet, except the two, John Morley and John Burns.

Chronology

28 June	Assassination of Archduke Franz Ferdinand in Sarajevo.
5 July	Germany promises Austria-Hungary full backing in actions against Serbia.
23 July	Austro-Hungarian ultimatum to Serbia.
24 July	First Cabinet meeting in Britain on the European situation.
25 July	Russia determined to back Serbia against Austria-Hungary.
26 July	Grey puts forward idea of a four-power conference of Britain, Germany, France and Italy to resolve the growing crisis. This idea comes to nothing.
28 July	Austria declares war on Serbia.
30 July	Russia begins a general mobilisation of her armed forces. It seems that the French will back Russia by the terms of their military alliance with her.
1 August	Germany declares war on Russia. Britain mobilises her navy.
2 August	Germany invades Luxemburg and sends ultimatum to Belgium.
3 August	Germany declares war on France.
4 August	Germany invades Belgium. British ultimatum to Germany followed by declaration of war. The Labour Party, having been against war, supports the call to arms.

H ISTORIANS' VIEWS & OPINIONS

INTERPRETATIONS OF BRITAIN'S ENTRY INTO THE WAR

The theme is completed with a glance at the views of five historians concerning Britain's entry into the First World War and the policies that preceded it.

Activity

a Read through the extracts carefully.
- What are the major reasons given by the five historians for Britain's entry into war against Germany?
- In what ways do the interpretations taken by Steiner and Gilbert about the tensions between Britain and Germany differ from those of Hayes and Wilson?
- To what extent do the reasons given by the historians differ (if at all) from the explanations given by politicians at the time?
- Make notes of your responses.

b There is another major contradiction in the views taken by two of the historians here, concerning Britain's actions in the days before Europe was engulfed by war. Can you spot what this is and the historians concerned? Which evaluation do you support and why?

c What is the key point being made by Gilbert in the extract from his biography of Lloyd George? If Gilbert is right, how does this affect our outlook on the debates in the Liberal Cabinet about whether Britain should fight Germany or not in the week before 4 August?

Class Debate

The motion is: 'There was no justification for Britain's entry into the war against Germany in August 1914.'

1 *Z. Steiner:* Britain and the Origins of the First World War *(1977)*
In concrete terms, the options available to an Edwardian foreign secretary were limited. No government could ignore the German challenge. In so far as this situation was due to internal conflicts within Germany, the British were relatively helpless. If the German leaders were determined to alter the European balance, it was difficult to believe that without a coalition of powers against them, this bid would fail. If Germany controlled the continent, British security would be menaced ... It was never clear what Germany would see as her proper place in Europe. It was never apparent where German ambitions would find their proper outlets. Who knew what the Germans wanted? An African empire? A controlling position in the Balkans and in Turkey? A Central European Customs Union? Control of the seas? As the Germans themselves were divided, no foreign secretary, however acute, could have accurately read the German riddle. Moreover, even if Grey had made it perfectly clear where Britain stood, the Germans would have moved. She was too strong to accept a final check on her ambitions without at least trying to break out of her enclosed position unless that check was powerful enough to make all hope of success futile. Britain, even in alliance with France and Russia, could not pose that kind of threat.

2 *P. Hayes:* Modern British Foreign Policy – The Twentieth Century 1880–1939 *(1978)*
The immediate factors were not, then, the most significant; important though they were. Britain might claim that war was declared in 1914 to protect freedom (though this did not prevent conscription and censorship during the war) and the rights of small nations (to whom little regard was paid in the post-war settlement), but the truth was that Britain became involved because it was the consensus of opinion that her interests and the balance of power were threatened by Germany. In fact, German power was probably over-estimated, but the reasons for this misjudgment stemmed too from the errors of the past. For two decades public opinion had been moving in a direction hostile to Germany, fanned by a generally Germanophobe press. It was widely believed that Germany would easily defeat France and Russia and then impose a

new hegemony on Europe. The public had become imbued with Social Darwinist theories about vigorous and decaying nations and it was believed that the choice lay between third-rate obscurity and fighting Germany.

3 *L.C.B. Seaman:* Post-Victorian Britain 1902–1951 *(1966)*
The only way in which war might have been avoided would have been to make it clear well in advance to the Germans that there would be an immediate British military contribution effective enough to make the Schlieffen Plan obviously unworkable; and to have made it abundantly clear that the whole resources of Britain and its Empire in manpower, industry and finance would swiftly be invoked. Only in this way could the civilian elements in Germany be provided with a strong enough basis for opposing the military leaders. Indeed, it would probably have given the military themselves to pause.

4 *K.M. Wilson:* The Policy of the Entente *(1985)*
Without the ententes, it was not that Europe would have been more vulnerable to Germany. It

Men in the trenches

was that Britain would have been vulnerable to everyone. What was really at stake in their preservation was the fate of the British Empire at the hands, in the first place, of France and especially of Russia.

That the power of Germany frightened and overawed her neighbours in Europe was only to be expected. The British Foreign Office, however, embellished the clumsiness of German diplomacy that merely represented in many cases her nervousness and anxiety and sense of *amour propre* and legitimate grievance to such an extent that they effectively invented for her designs of a hegemonial character upon Europe. They did so because 'the German menace' served to conceal British weakness. It served to divert attention from the British Empire's vulnerability and to rivet it upon Germany. It provided the ententes, which had been made because Britain was unable any longer to maintain unaided her position in the world against the competition which she faced, with a more respectable *raison d'être* than that of merely trying desperately to hang on to what she had.

5 *B. Gilbert:* David Lloyd George *(1987)*
Taken together, the secret planning sessions and the Cabinet changes of August, September and October of 1911 are of far greater significance than the public international confrontation between France and Germany in July. One cannot avoid the impression that some of Britain's foremost politicians, Grey in the lead strongly supported by Churchill and Haldane with Asquith trailing more reluctantly behind, all driven along by Henry Wilson, came at this time to the conclusion that in the event of a German attack upon France Britain would have to act whether or not the Germans invaded Belgium. The implications for Britain of a defeated, bloodied, and pauperized France, reduced in size and stripped of her colonies, were too terrible to contemplate. Britain would face alone a German-dominated and organized Europe. What would the dreadnought competition be like then? Who would secure the seas? What would become of free trade and Britain's commercial predominance? Could the empire, indeed the home islands, be defended? In all of this the question of Belgium was hardly raised except amid speculation that she

might be afraid to resist the German armies. As a consequence, during the gloomy Bank Holiday weekend at the end of 1914, although many members did not know it, the Cabinet was debating a decision that for practical purposes had already been made and in which Lloyd George had participated. His behaviour at that time, his reluctance to commit himself publicly until the Germans had in fact invaded Belgium, his willingness to consort with the pacifists in the Cabinet, need to be judged against the fact that he knew and accepted the assumption that although the Germans would indeed attack France through Belgium, Britain would have to intervene in any case.

B ACK TO THE PRESENT

In many respects the international status and role of Britain today is vastly different from that of Britain before 1914. Britain is no longer a Great Power with an empire covering more than a quarter of the world's territory. It is no longer one of the world's strongest economies – capable of supporting a great navy and paying for extensive administrative systems in its colonies – as it was before 1914. Indeed, by the end of the First World War Britain was already too weak to pursue its traditional 'balance of power' policy in Europe and thus sustain its self-appointed role as chief arbiter in world affairs. In fact we were probably too weak to do this before 1914 and this, perhaps, partly accounts for both our failure to prevent European war and our involvement in it. Furthermore, the establishment of a more democratic society in the 1920s meant that the making of foreign policy could no longer be carried out behind closed doors by an aristocratic élite, confident in its right and in its power to rule the world with little reference to the British people.

Yet, though Britain has irrevocably declined as a power in the world, in other respects some of the features and elements of international relations before 1914 still exist today. The arms race between the European powers before 1914, especially the naval race between Britain and Germany, has been mirrored in the nuclear arms race since 1945 between America and the Soviet Union. The concept of a 'balance of power' keeping the peace in the world before 1914 has been reflected in the deterrence effect achieved, it is argued, through the balance of infinitely destructive nuclear weapons held by capitalist NATO and the Soviet-dominated Warsaw Pact. Nationalism continues to be a major force in international relations, as reflected in the efforts of countries and peoples such as Israel, Vietnam, Iran, Nicaragua and the Palestinian Arabs either to attain or maintain their freedom as sovereign states. And in Britain, patriotism as an idea and an emotion continues to influence the politics of the country – the feelings generated by the Falklands War which helped the Conservative Party win the 1983 General Election is evidence of this. Here are some general political and moral questions for you to consider as relevant to international politics both before 1914 and the 1990s:

1 In what circumstances is nationalism a healthy idea and emotion, and in what circumstances can it be harmful? Are you patriotic? Why, and in what kinds of ways?

2 Are power struggles between nations inevitable? Are arms races which achieve a balance of forces between opposing power blocs more likely to keep the peace or make war a certainty?

3 Has Britain really declined as a power in the world as much as has been suggested?

4 To what extent do you agree with the statement that 'the need for a government to make quick and effective decisions in foreign policy requires a measure of secrecy and the freedom to act without immediate reference to Parliament or the people'? Are there instances where 'national security' demands absolute secrecy? What is 'national security'?

3 LLOYD GEORGE AND THE DECLINE OF THE LIBERAL PARTY

1914–35

I NTRODUCTION

The Liberal Party evolved in the 1860s from an amalgam of political groupings – Whigs, Radicals, Peelites and other sundry reformers. What united these groupings and enabled them to work together in Parliament, albeit on a very precarious basis, was a concern with extending freedom in society. This concern with extending freedom was closely associated with the aim of limiting the powers of the landed gentry and advancing those of the middle classes. In fact, many Liberals were very suspicious of extending 'freedom in society' to include the working classes or women. In the country the Liberal Party was supported by a diverse range of interest-groups, including nonconformists, political reformers, free traders, industrialists and trade unionists. These disparate elements were held together partly by a common commitment to the ideas of liberalism, and up to the 1890s by the impassioned and charismatic figure of William Gladstone.

In 1914 the Liberal Party was in government and was therefore still a major political force in society. Indeed, the Liberals had been in office for more than half of the period between 1859 and 1914. By the Second World War, however, the Liberal Party had been reduced to virtual insignificance: the Labour Party had become the alternative political grouping to the Conservatives in a two-party electoral system. Up to the present time the Liberal Party has aspired to regaining a position of political influence – with little success, although it has maintained a significant popular vote in elections. In 1988 the name 'Liberal Party' disappeared from view with the establishment of a new centre party – now known as the Liberal Democrats.

This theme, then, is concerned with exploring the

Herbert Asquith, 1914

decline of the Liberal Party in the years 1914 to 1935. To reach an understanding of Liberal decline we will be examining such factors as leadership, the relevance of liberal ideas, changing class relationships, the extending electorate, economic problems and the rise of the Labour Party. The Special Topic within the theme is 'Lloyd George and the Coalition Government 1918–22'. The record of the Coalition government from 1918 to 1922 will act as a focus for looking at the personality and politics of Lloyd George – one of the most controversial and colourful figures of twentieth-century liberalism.

David Lloyd George speaking in 1924

K EY QUESTIONS

1 What are the key historical moments and events central to an understanding of the decline of the Liberal Party in the period 1914–35?

2 What are the different ways in which this decline can be explained and which interpretation do you support?

3 What were the achievements of Lloyd George as a major Liberal figure in the period 1906–22?

SIMULATION

LIBERALISM AND TOTAL WAR 1914–18

Introduction

The aim of this exercise is to encourage you to think about some of the dilemmas and difficulties which the *laissez-faire* Liberal government had to face after 1914 in fighting a 'total war'. This should help you appreciate some of the issues and ideas which underpin the story of the Liberal Party in British politics after 1914.

The Situation

A major European war is underway and you are the British Liberal government faced with organising the resources and population of your country in order to defeat Germany. As with previous simulations, the situation you will find yourself in roughly reflects that which existed at the time – namely, the critical problems which Asquith's Liberal government was facing after August 1914.

The Problem of Liberalism and 'Total War'

A 'total war' requires a nation to mobilise and reorganise the whole of its manpower and resources if it is to have any chance of victory against the enemy powers. This entails creating vast armies and enormous quantities of munitions and armaments. This in turn creates the need for the economy and the labour force to be radically re-organised to meet these unprecedented demands. Furthermore, given the massive amount of disruption which all this involves (not least of which is the high loss of life) the presiding government will be faced with the additional problem of how it is going to maintain the morale and loyalty of the population during 'total war'.

Liberalism (*laissez-faire*) is a doctrine which says that society should be founded on the principle of the freedom of individuals to pursue their own self-interest. This idea is associated with the view that the efficiency and prosperity of a society are best achieved through a free enterprise economy – a capitalist economy – where individuals freely pursue wealth and profit in competition with each other. Liberalism therefore implies a minimal role for the state and government in society. Broadly speaking, this doctrine was supported by both Liberal and Conservative parties in the period from 1850 to 1914.

The major problem which your government faces, then, is how to win a 'total war' whilst preserving the principles of liberalism. Or will one of these aims have to be sacrificed?

Background Information

Political Position
- Your Liberal government only has a small majority over the Conservatives in the House of Commons.
- The Labour Party is small but becoming increasingly significant – it believes in socialism.
- The Labour Party holds the balance of power in the House of Commons.
- Only two in three men have the vote at the moment.
- An election is due by the end of 1915.

Economic Position
- Britain is a capitalist economy and all business is privately owned.
- The major industries – coal, iron and steel, shipbuilding and textiles have been experiencing problems since 1870.
- An important part of Britain's income comes from exports.
- Britain is dependent on imports for food, chemicals, iron ore and some steel.
- Before 1914 America and Germany have been catching up with Britain in economic power.
- Taxes are low.
- Inflation is very low.

Industrial Relations Position
- 25 per cent of workers are in trade unions, but this proportion is increasing all the time.
- Unions are very strong in the coal, iron and steel, engineering and railway industries.
- The years 1911–14 witnessed many strikes, particularly over falling real wages.
- Some workers before the war were becoming attracted to using unions to bring about socialist changes.
- The standards of living of over a quarter of the working class are extremely low.

Military Position
- Stalemate has set in all along the Western Front and it is clear that the war is not going to be over quickly.
- All countries are experiencing huge losses of men without territorial gains.
- So far in the conflict against Germany working people are patriotic and loyal to the government.

Procedure

1 Groups of three to five people should form separate Liberal Cabinets.

2 The simulation should consist of several decision-making phases of perhaps 15–20 minutes in duration.

3 In each phase your government should discuss and agree upon what decisions need to be taken in order to fight the war effectively and eventually win it. You will also need to think through some of the details of your decisions.

4 Decisions and details of decisions should be recorded on the 'Decisions and Scoring Sheet' (format given below).

5 At the end of each phase your group or government should present its decisions to the teacher for assessment. This will involve further explanation of your ideas to the teacher in answer to his/her questions.

6 Your teacher will award marks according to how well he/she thinks you are doing in running the war effort. He/she will also indicate areas of concern, continuing problems, and the likely consequences of your actions (or lack of them) in the 'Comment' section of the 'Decisions and Scoring Sheet'.

7 The weighting of the marks is at the discretion of your teacher who will have worked out a scoring system beforehand relating to the four areas in the 'Background Information' above.

8 At an appropriate point in the simulation your teacher will announce what score you need to reach in order to win the war. This will give you a rough indication of how far short you are of making the right kinds of decisions to win the war.

9 The simulation should continue until one of the groups or Cabinets has achieved the winning score, or until the teacher decides that the exercise should come to an end, in which case the group with the highest score wins.

Decisions and Scoring Sheet			
Decision	Details	Comment	Score

Further Advice

- You should bear in mind that policies initiated in one area – 'Industrial Relations', for example – may have important implications in another area. The logic of your decisions therefore needs to be fully considered.
- The failure to take certain decisions at the right time may, in the judgement of your teacher, lead to disastrous consequences – economic chaos, strikes, military defeats or revolutionary uprisings. These may result in your group or Cabinet scoring negative marks.
- Don't forget that your main aim is to solve the dilemma of winning a 'total war' whilst retaining the credibility of your liberal beliefs which many in the Liberal Party hold dear. If you feel the necessity of abandoning these beliefs you will have to provide certain explanations and justifications.

O UTLINING THE EVENTS

THE DECLINE OF THE LIBERAL PARTY TO 1935

You can discover a great deal about the narrative of Liberal Party decline through an analysis of the election results for the period. The activity below is based on these election results and one or two other snippets of information which provide additional clues for your investigation. In examining this data, you should follow through the performance of the Liberal Party in all its manifestations: any party with the name 'Liberal' in its title is of relevance. Also, keep an eye on the fortunes of the other political parties.

Activity

The following tasks are probably best carried out in pairs:

a Illustrate what happened to the Liberal Party from 1906 to 1935 by compiling your own selection of key pieces of information from the data provided. These key pieces of information should represent what you think are (or might be) the significant moments and turning points in the history of the Party in the period. Write a sentence or two to explain the information in your selection.

b Put together a list of possible explanations or hypotheses accounting for Liberal decline. Astute guesswork is as relevant here as careful scrutiny of the sources.

c Write down a list of unresolved questions and problems which you feel you need to investigate further if you are going to develop a better understanding of the whole issue.

Discussion

Come together as a class to compare and discuss each

other's observations and ideas in response to the tasks above. Take the opportunity to clear up any major misunderstandings at this stage of the theme.

1 General Election results 1906–35

	Total Votes	M.P.s Elected	Candidates	Un-opposed Returns	% Share of Total Vote
1906 12 Jan–7 Feb					
Conservative	2,451,454	157	574	13	43·6
Liberal	2,757,883	400	539	27	49·0
Labour	329,748	30	51	—	5·9
Irish Nationalist	35,031	83	87	74	0·6
Others	52,387	—	22	—	0·9
Elec. 7,264,608	5,626,503	670	1,273	114	100·0
Turnout 82·6%					
1910 14 Jan–9 Feb					
Conservative	3,127,887	273	600	19	46·9
Liberal	2,880,581	275	516	1	43·2
Labour	505,657	40	78	—	7·6
Irish Nationalist	124,586	82	104	55	1·9
Others	28,693	—	17	—	0·4
Elec. 7,694,741	6,667,404	670	1,315	75	100·0
Turnout 86·6%					
1910 2–19 Dec					
Conservative	2,420,566	272	550	72	46·3
Liberal	2,295,888	272	467	35	43·9
Labour	371,772	42	56	3	7·1
Irish Nationalist	131,375	84	106	53	2·5
Others	8,768	—	11	—	0·2
Elec. 7,709,981	5,228,369	670	1,190	163	100·0
Turnout 81·1%					
1918 14 Dec					
Coalition Unionist	3,504,198	335	374	42	32·6
Coalition Liberal	1,455,640	133	158	27	13·5
Coalition Labour	161,521	10	18	—	1·5
(Coalition)	(5,121,359)	(478)	(550)	(69)	(47·6)
Conservative	370,375	23	37	—	3·4
Irish Unionist	292,722	25	38	—	2·7
Liberal	1,298,808	28	253	—	12·1
Labour	2,385,472	63	388	12	22·2
Irish Nationalist	238,477	7	60	1	2·2
Sinn Fein	486,867	73	102	25	4·5
Others	572,503	10	197	—	5·3
Elec. 21,392,322	10,766,583	707	1,625	107	100·0
Turnout 58·9%					
1922 15 Nov					
Conservative	5,500,382	345	483	42	38·2
National Liberal	1,673,240	62	162	5	11·6
Liberal	2,516,287	54	328	5	17·5
Labour	4,241,383	142	411	4	29·5
Others	462,340	12	59	1	3·2
Elec. 21,127,663	14,393,632	615	1,443	57	100·0
Turnout 71·3%					
1923 6 Dec					
Conservative	5,538,824	258	540	35	38·1
Liberal	4,311,147	159	453	11	29·6
Labour	4,438,508	191	422	3	30·5
Others	260,042	7	31	1	1·8
Elec. 21,281,232	14,548,521	615	1,446	50	100·0
Turnout 70·8%					
1924 29 Oct					
Conservative	8,039,598	419	552	16	48·3
Liberal	2,928,747	40	340	6	17·6
Labour	5,489,077	151	512	9	33·0
Communist	55,346	1	8	—	0·3
Others	126,511	4	16	1	0·8
Elec. 21,731,320	16,639,279	615	1,428	32	100·0
Turnout 76·6%					
1929 30 May					
Conservative	8,656,473	260	590	4	38·2
Liberal	5,308,510	59	513	—	23·4
Labour	8,389,512	288	571	—	37·1
Communist	50,614	—	25	—	0·3
Others	243,266	8	31	3	1·0
Elec. 28,850,870	22,648,375	615	1,730	7	100·0
Turnout 76·1%					
1931 27 Oct					
Conservative	11,978,745	473	523	56	55·2
National Labour	341,370	13	20	—	1·6
Liberal National	809,302	35	41	—	3·7
Liberal	1,403,102	33	112	5	6·5
(National Government)	(14,532,519)	(554)	(696)	(61)	(67·0)
Independent Liberal	106,106	4	7	—	0·5
Labour	6,649,630	52	515	6	30·6
Communist	74,824	—	26	—	0·3
New Party	36,377	—	24	—	0·2
Others	256,917	5	24	—	1·2
Elec. 29,960,071	21,656,373	615	1,292	67	100·0
Turnout 76·3%					
1935 14 Nov					
Conservative	11,810,158	432	585	26	53·7
Liberal	1,422,116	20	161	—	6·4
Labour	8,325,491	154	552	13	37·9
Independent Labour Party	139,577	4	17	—	0·7
Communist	27,117	1	2	—	0·1
Others	272,595	4	31	1	1·2
Elec. 31,379,050	21,997,054	615	1,348	40	100·0
Turnout 71·2%					

Adapted from D. Butler and A. Solman: British Political Facts 1900–1979 (1980)

2a *Biographies*

Asquith, Herbert Henry. 1st E of Oxford and Asquith (1925)

b. 1852. *Educ.* City of London School; Oxford. Barrister, 1876, practised M.P. (Lib.) for E. Fife, 1886–1918. M.P. for Paisley, 1920–24. Home Sec., 1892–95. Chanc. of Exch., 1905–8. P.M. and Leader of Lib. party, 1908–1916. Sec. for War, 1914. Formed Coalition Govt., 1915. Resigned as P.M., became Leader of Opposition, 1916. Resigned Leadership of Lib. party, 1926. d. 1928.

Lloyd George, David. 1st Earl Lloyd George of Dwyfor (1945)

b. 1863. *Educ.* Church School. Solicitor, 1884. M.P. (Lib.) for Caernarvon Boroughs, 1890–1945 (Ind. L., 1931–35). Pres. of Bd. of Trade, 1905–8. Chanc. of Exch., 1908–15. Min. of Munitions, 1915–16. Sec. for War, 1916. P.M., 1916–22. Leader of Lib. party, 1926–31. d. 1945.

b *The Representation of the People Act, 1918,* reduced the residence qualification to six months and enfranchised some categories of men who had not previously had the vote. It also enfranchised women over 30. In 1928 the *Equal Franchise Act* lowered the voting age for women to 21.

Electorate

Year	Population	Population over 21	Electorate	Electorate as % of Adult Population[a] Male	Total
1900	41,155,000	22,675,000	6,730,935	58	27
1910	44,915,000	26,134,000	7,694,741	58	28
1919	44,599,000	27,364,000	21,755,583	—	78
1929	46,679,000	31,711,000	28,850,870	—	90
1939	47,762,000	32,855,000	32,403,559	—	97
1949	50,363,000	35,042,000	34,269,770	—	98
1959	52,157,000	35,911,000	35,397,080	—	99
1965	54,606,000	36,837,000	36,128,387	—	98
1970	55,700,000	40,784,000[b]	39,153,000	—	96
1979	55,822,000	42,100,000[b]	41,769,000	—	99

[a] This percentage makes allowance for plural voting. In the period before 1914 this amounted to about 500,000. After 1918 the business vote reached its peak in 1929 at 370,000. The university electorate rose from 39,101 in 1900 to 217,363 in 1945.

[b] Population over 18.

c *Prime Ministers*

1900		M of Salisbury (3rd)
12 Jul	02	A. Balfour
5 Dec	05	Sir H. Campbell-Bannerman
5 Apr	08	H. Asquith
6 Dec	16	D. Lloyd George
23 Oct	22	A. Bonar Law
22 May	23	S. Baldwin
22 Jan	24	R. MacDonald
4 Nov	24	S. Baldwin
5 Jun	29	R. MacDonald
7 Jun	35	S. Baldwin
28 May	37	N. Chamberlain

Adapted from D. Butler and A. Sloman: British Political Facts 1900–1979 *(1980)*

3 *Social and Educational Composition of British Cabinets 1895–1935*

Date	Party	P.M.	Cabinet Size	Aristo-crats	Middle Class	Working Class	Public school All	Eton	University educated All	Oxbridge
Aug 1895	Con.	Salisbury	19	8	11	—	16	7	15	14
Jul 1902	Con.	Balfour	19	9	10	—	16	9	14	13
Dec 1905	Lib.	Campbell-Bannerman	19	7	11	1	11	3	14	12
Jul 1914	Lib.	Asquith	19	6	12	1	11	3	15	13
Jan 1919	Coal.	Lloyd George	21	3	17	1	12	2	13	8
Nov 1922	Con.	Bonar Law	16	8	8	—	14	8	13	13
Jan 1924	Lab.	MacDonald	19	3	5	11	8	—	6	6
Nov 1924	Con.	Baldwin	21	9	12	—	21	7	16	16
Jan 1929	Lab.	MacDonald	18	2	4	12	5	—	6	3
Aug 1931	Nat.	MacDonald	20	8	10	2	13	6	11	10
Jun 1935	Con.	Baldwin	22	9	11	2	14	9	11	10

Adapted from W.L. Guttsman: The British Political Elite *(1963)*

HISTORIANS' VIEWS & OPINIONS

DIFFERENT EXPLANATIONS OF LIBERAL PARTY DECLINE

At this point you should have a grasp of the statistics of the decline of the Liberal Party, and one or two ideas about why it happened. The next piece of investigation is designed to introduce you to some of the historiography of the theme – the arguments and interpretations of historians. The extracts in this section provide a cross-section of views on why the Liberal Party declined and whether or not this decline was inevitable. A chronology is included to help you find your way around the historical details. You will also find it useful to keep an eye on the election statistics as you carry out the activities.

Activity

Read through the secondary source extracts and think carefully about what each historian is saying. Talk over any initial difficulties in understanding with your partner and/or your teacher. Working individually or in pairs carry out the following tasks:

a Examine extracts 1–5. These extracts contain two differing views about the condition of the Liberal Party on the eve of the First World War.

- What are these two views exactly?
- What reasons can you find in the extracts supporting these two views?
- What does Wilson suggest is the real reason accounting for the break-up of the Liberal Party?

b Look at the historians' views in extracts 4–8. What is the nature of the disagreement between these historians over the role of the emerging Labour Party in the decline of the Liberal Party? In what way do the views taken by McKibbon, Pelling and Thompson contradict the explanation of Liberal decline put forward by Wilson?

c Read extract 8 carefully and make sure you understand (i) the reasons for the formation of a Liberal-dominated coalition in May 1915 and (ii) the role of

Bonar Law, the leader of the Conservatives. Why does Pugh consider the formation of a coalition as a 'triumph for Asquith' – at least in the short term? Why does Pugh nevertheless see these political events as 'a crucial point in the disintegration of the Liberal Party'?

d The secondary sources 10–13 contain two differing interpretations of the role of Lloyd George in the removal of Asquith from power in December 1916 and the consequent division of the Liberal Party. Explain these views in detail.

e The remaining four extracts 14–17 reflect on the continuing problems of the Liberal Party after the end of the First World War. What are the important points which each of the authors of these accounts make?

f Return to the work you did in **b** and **c** of the 'Outlining the Events' section and see to what extent you have now established answers to the problems and hypotheses identified there.

Discussion

As a class, discuss the work you have just been doing. With your teacher, ensure that you have a reasonable understanding of the different ideas and arguments examined. Which of the historians' views are you inclined to go along with at this point?

Further Reading and Research

You should now have reached the stage where you have an understanding of the basic narrative of the decline of the Liberal Party, and an appreciation of different historians' interpretations of this decline. It is now essential to dig out more detailed historical evidence concerning the events of the theme. You should therefore compile a set of notes with the assistance of textbooks, teacher's notes/handouts, plus the work you have carried out so far. The chronology will be of some assistance. It should be obvious by now what kinds of headings you should use for your notes – relating them to the distinct phases in Liberal Party history at this time.

Class Debate

The motion is: 'The decline of the Liberal Party was inevitable.'

1 *C. Cook:* A Short History of the Liberal Party (*1976*)
But of the debate on the downfall of Liberalism a few points can be said. In 1914 the Liberal Party was certainly not dead, nor indeed dying, despite the arguments propounded by George Dangerfield, who saw in the political and industrial crisis prior to 1914 symptoms of the oncoming 'Strange Death of Liberal England'.

2 *G. Dangerfield:* The Strange Death of Liberal England (*1935*)
The year 1910 is not just a convenient starting point. It is actually a landmark in English history, which stands out against a peculiar background of flame. For it was in 1910 that fires long smouldering in the English spirit suddenly flared up, so that by the end of 1913 Liberal England was reduced to ashes. From these ashes, a new England seems to have emerged.

I realize, of course, that the word 'Liberal' will always have a meaning so long as there is one democracy left in the world, or any remnant of a middle class; but the true pre-war Liberal – supported, as it still was in 1910, by Free Trade, a majority in Parliament, the ten commandments and the illusion of Progress – can never return. It was killed, or it killed itself, in 1913. And a very good thing too.

3 *G.D.H. Cole and R. Postgate:* The Common People 1746–1946 (*1949*)
Coming on top of suffragette outrages and widespread strikes which the Government was powerless to settle or to repress, the Irish events of 1914 had reduced the Liberal Party to the last gasp. The great Liberal experiment, begun so glamorously with the electoral victory of 1906, was ending in ignominious rout.

4 *T. Wilson:* The Downfall of the Liberal Party 1914–35 (*1966*)
The outbreak of the First World War initiated a process of disintegration in the Liberal party which

by 1918 had reduced it to ruins. As Liberals were often the first to recognise, the onset of war jeopardised the existence of a party whose guiding principles were international conciliation, personal liberty, and social reform. . . . The real danger to the Liberals was that in seeking to retain their "whigs" they might lose contact with Labour. Yet in 1914 this was not happening. The social reforming wing of the Liberal government was making the running. "Advanced" thinkers were still looking to Liberalism to implement their ideas. And Labour had put forward no major policy items which the Liberal party was unable to implement.

Nor in purely electoral terms was there any sign that Labour was supplanting the Liberals. In the general elections of 1910, and in by-elections from 1911 until the outbreak of war, Labour fared abysmally in contests with the Liberals.

5 *M. Pugh:* The Making of Modern British Politics 1867–1939 (*1982*)
The traditional view that Edwardian politics was characterized by a Liberal Party too ideologically rigid and rooted in middle-class radicalism to avoid being outflanked by a socialist party or to survive the emergence of a working-class electorate has proved to be virtually untenable. Yet the evidence that has destroyed the old view has also generated an alternative interpretation . . .

Thus the 'Progressive' interpretation amounts to much more than the view that Liberalism survived the Edwardian elections; it suggests that it adapted to the chief trends of twentieth-century politics, flourishing on the basis of its social-economic appeal to the working class. The implication is that there was nothing inevitable in the rise of Edwardian Labour as a governing party . . .

The more the Edwardian evidence underlines the fact that the Liberals were in no imminent danger of decline, let alone eclipse, the more importance must, apparently, be attached to the First World War as the decisive factor in their downfall.

6 *R. McKibbon:* The Evolution of the Labour Party 1910–24 (*1974*)
I have argued here that the Labour Party cannot be seen as a declining force before 1914, but that, on the contrary, it was already successfully mobilizing working-class support at the expense of the Liber-

als, and that this was happening almost regardless of what went on in parliament . . .

But the 1918 Act, all at once, gave Britain for the first time an electorate in which the industrial working class was now unquestionably predominant. The 'Liberal' vote, indeed, may even have survived more or less intact, but after 1918 was overwhelmed by voters who could not be enrolled by official Liberalism. Much of this new electorate voted Labour in 1918; but had it been enfranchised it probably would have done so in 1914 as well.

7 H. Pelling: Popular Politics and Society in Late Victorian Britain (1968)

We may conclude, therefore, that the decline of Liberalism was not due to a sordid intrigue between Lloyd George and a few Conservative leaders and press lords, as many widely-read historians of the present day would have us believe. Nor was it due solely or predominantly, as Dr Wilson has suggested, to the impact of the war upon Liberal values and upon the unity of the parliamentary Liberal Party. Rather it was the result of long-term social and economic changes which were simultaneously uniting Britain geographically and dividing her inhabitants in terms of class; enabling the population to achieve the full dimensions of political democracy but condemning it to years of bitter strife owing to the forced contraction of the staple industries which had prospered so remarkably in the later Victorian era – an era politically as well as socially distinct from that of the inter-war period.

8 P. Thompson: Socialists, Liberals, and Labour – The Struggle for London 1885–1914 (1967)

There has been a recent tendency to think of the Liberal revival in the 1900s as a genuine recovery which was only interrupted by the First World War and the personal split between Lloyd George and Asquith. This view is not supported by the situation in London. The Liberal recovery was not based on a solution of its problems, but on the temporary revival of Nonconformist and trade union support and of old radical political issues. The Liberal Party in the 1900s still lacked a coherent political standpoint, a firm electoral basis in working class enthusiasm, and a secure financial backing. Its disastrous decay in local politics antici-pated its national eclipse after 1918. It is especially striking that this was so in London, where the Labour Party was late to emerge as an obvious rival.

9 M. Pugh: The Making of Modern British Politics 1867–1939 (1982)

By the spring of 1915 Bonar Law faced three unpalatable courses of action. He could simply join his followers in attacking the Liberals, which would have led to the general election due in December, and probably a Conservative government. He ruled this out because it would push much of the Liberal and Labour forces into opposition to the war as in 1899–1902 but with far more serious consequences; also the Edwardian industrial revolt seemed to compound Conservative doubts about their ability to handle an organized working class in a crisis. An alternative was to form a coalition with the Liberals, but this was rejected by Law and virtually all leading Conservatives as calculated to silence necessary criticism. Thus Bonar Law stuck to the third option, the 'party truce', until May 1915. At this point the split between Churchill and Admiral Sir John Fisher, First Sea Lord, at the Admiraty combined with the launching of the 'shells scandal' in the press created pressure that was too powerful for Law to resist. Anxious to avoid being driven to censure the government he was pleasantly relieved to discover that Lloyd George and Asquith himself were offering him a coalition. However, because Law accomplished this largely in isolation from and against the wishes of many of his colleagues, the Conservatives failed to confront Asquith with agreed terms either on policy or offices. Asquith retained in Liberal hands all the key posts except the Admiralty, and Law, despite his obvious claim to a major role, was relegated to the Colonial Office because it suited his own rivals in the party to devalue his status. Yet this underlined for the Conservatives that it was not a genuine coalition but a triumph for Asquith.

In the short run the coalition served to put off the election which the Liberals expected to lose and kept Asquith in office until the end of 1916. In a longer perspective, however, it proved a crucial point in the disintegration of the Liberal Party.

10 *D. Thomson:* England in the Twentieth Century *(1950)*
At the end of 1916 Asquith was ousted from power by a complex intrigue, conducted by Lloyd George with ruthless skill.

11 *T. Wilson:* The Downfall of the Liberal Party 1914–35 *(1966)*
In short, the war having placed Lloyd George in a position to displace Asquith, he did not scruple to seize this opportunity for his advancement . . .

Had Lloyd George really been reluctant to occupy the premiership, he would have shown it during the long period when Asquith was being subjected to unprecedented attacks on his behalf. Far from doing so, he craved for power so blatantly that he aroused the distrust of nearly all the leading Conservatives. Indeed it required an incipient rebellion of Conservative back-benchers late in 1916 before Bonar Law was finally driven to align with him against Asquith.

What happened thereafter has been described in considerable detail, and with no little controversy, by a number of historians. In essentials the story is straightforward enough. As their price for remaining in the government, Lloyd George and Bonar Law called on Asquith to establish a 'War Council' which would take over direction of the war. Asquith, after initial hesitation, rejected this scheme on 4 December 1916, and Lloyd George and the Conservatives resigned, precipitating the break-up

'*In the wash*' – Daily Graphic *13 December 1916*

of the government. Two days later Lloyd George became Prime Minister.

It is hard to doubt that this was the unexpressed, and perhaps unacknowledged, object for which Lloyd George and Bonar Law were working. For the scheme they offered Asquith was so humiliating and unworkable that at best it made his departure from office only a matter of time.

12 *J. Grigg in* Lloyd George, Twelve Essays *ed. A. J. P. Taylor (1971)*
Until the final crisis, Lloyd George believed Asquith must remain prime minister. What Lloyd George desired was better, more effective government. He did not force a crisis earlier because he was not aiming at the premiership. Lloyd George was regarded with distaste and distrust by many: the speed with which his mind worked, his readiness to criticize others – a quality in which he was never deficient – accentuated by his mysterious relations with the press, all caused suspicion and enmity. Thus these traits partly cancelled out the favourable impression given by his arduous work. Lloyd George became prime minister because the war was going badly and distrust of him was outweighed by disillusionment with Asquith. There were doubts among many but the feeling that however Lloyd George performed, he could scarcely be worse than Asquith was common by December 1916.

13 *K.O. Morgan:* Lloyd George *(1974)*
Behind this brief narrative lies a complex skein of political imponderables. No aspect of his career has done more to cloud Lloyd George's reputation than the events of the first week of December 1916. It has often been alleged that he gained power through a sordid conspiracy with the Unionists, with the aid of Northcliffe and other press lords, and that Asquith was the honourable and hapless victim of treachery. Lloyd George is portrayed as 'the envious Casca', Asquith as 'the noblest Roman of them all'. But, now that we have the advantage of an immense range of new material, including latterly the papers of Lord Beaverbrook, a very different version of these critical events can be put forward.

First of all, the discussions between Lloyd George, Bonar Law and Carson were no conspiracy: Asquith was kept fully informed about them from 20 November onwards. Secondly, there is no evidence, direct or indirect, that Lloyd George was trying to build up an anti-Asquith faction within the Liberal Party, or that he thought of doing so. It was only after he took on the premiership on 7 December that Addison, David Davies and other Liberal backbenchers tried to rally Liberal support behind him. Thirdly, it was Asquith, not Lloyd George, who broke off negotiations.

14 K.O. Morgan: The Age of Lloyd George (1971)

The 'coupon election' marked a political revolution. Over 520 supporters of the government were returned, over 470 of them with the 'coupon', while the 'un-couponed' Liberals numbered less than thirty. Indeed, most of these few at first claimed to be supporters of the government also, as did many Labour members. The Liberal Party

A FORLORN APPEAL.

Mr. Asquith. "COALITION, ERE WE PART, GIVE, O GIVE ME BACK MY—ER—PARTY!"

Punch *4 December 1918*

emerged from the election shattered in morale. They had indeed 136 'couponed' representatives at Westminster, but many of these had been forced upon hostile local associations, and the extent to which they still remained Liberals in anything but name was far from clear. At the party level, the electoral triumph belonged to the Unionists – and also to the Labour Party whose small tally of fifty-seven seats masked a notable electoral breakthrough in terms of votes, despite the adverse circumstances in which the election was fought.

15 C.L. Mowat: Britain Between the Wars (1955)

The greater part, which had followed Lloyd George into the Coalition, had become prisoners of the Conservative majority. The non-Coalition Liberals, with almost all their leaders defeated from Asquith downwards, were a mere rump, and considered disbanding altogether, but held together under the leadership of Sir Donald Maclean. Subsequently, the party recovered a good deal of its strength, and for a time also its unity; but never again was it anywhere near to obtaining a parliamentary majority. Not that the coupon election was more than a milestone on the road of its decline. The split between Asquith and Lloyd George, dating from 1916, was fatal, and it was never healed, in spite of several attempts, particularly in 1918. Even further back, the party had showed mortal weakness, when its formula of discussion and compromise had failed to meet the prewar tests of the Tory revolt over Ulster, the suffragettes' campaigns, and the great strikes of 1910–13. The rise of the Labour party had ended its claims to Radicalism; and the middle ground which was all that remained to it proved no more than a sand spit.

16 R. Douglas: The History of the Liberal Party 1895–1970 (1971)

By the end of 1920, the Liberal Party seemed to be dissolving in utter chaos. Not only were the Asquithians and Lloyd Georgeites almost constantly at each other's throats, but each of the two groups included a very wide range of opinions on matters both of policy and administration. No war is as debilitating as civil war, and it was becoming increasingly evident that the common enemies of Liberalism – but particularly the Labour Party –

were deriving more and more advantage from the contest.

17 *C. Cook in* Lloyd George, Twelve Essays *ed. A. J. P. Taylor (1971)*

The essay is not an attempt to deny that, with the emergence of a firmly-based Labour Party, and with the combined effects of the war and of the party split, the former position of the Liberal Party had been eroded. It does, however, seek to question the *degree* of erosion: in particular, it will be argued that, although the party in industrial England was perhaps already in irreversible decline, in rural England the Liberal Party remained the major opposition party to the Conservatives, and could, with a reform of the voting system, as the party of rural radicalism, have remained a major party in a system of three-party politics.

The vital distinction drawn in this essay is between the *decline* of the Liberal Party and its *downfall*. In the last resort, the decline of the Party was transformed into its downfall between December 1923, when the party held 159 seats, and October 1924, when it retained only 40.

Prior to 1923, the Liberal Party, though facing all the obstacles of a third party, was still thought of as a party which might again form a government.

Chronology of Important Events

1914
4 Aug	Britain declares war on Germany. Party truce agreed. Kitchener appointed as Secretary of State for War.
Dec	Military stalemate reached on Western Front.

1915
Mar	Treasury Agreement with the unions.
Jan–May	Various military failures at Ypres, Aubers Ridge, Neuve Chappelle and Gallipoli.
13 May	Conservative backbenchers threaten debate on the issue of 'shells shortage'.
15 May	Fisher resigns as First Sea Lord.
26 May	Asquith announces the formation of a Coalition government with the Conservatives (and Labour).

Oct	McKenna, Chancellor of the Exchequer, introduces limited protection.

1916
Jan	Conscription for unmarried men introduced after much internal debate in the Liberal Party.
Apr	'Easter Rising' in Ireland.
May	Conscription for all.
Jun	British fleet fails to defeat the German fleet at Jutland. Lloyd George replaces Kitchener as the Secretary of State for War.
Jul-Nov	400,000 casualties at the Battle of the Somme.
8 Nov	Many Tory backbenchers vote against the government on the Nigerian property debate. Lloyd George, Bonar Law and Carson put forward executive War Committee idea to Asquith at the end of the month.
5 Dec	Asquith resigns.
7 Dec	Lloyd George forms a new Coalition government.

1917
Jan-Dec	Ministries of Agriculture, Shipping, Pensions, Labour and Reconstruction set up.
May	Convoy system established.
Aug-Nov	Military 'failure' at the Third Battle of Ypres – Passchendaele.

1918
Feb	Representation of Peoples Act.
May	'Maurice Debate'.
Nov	German surrender and 'Coupon' election results in a renewed mandate for the Lloyd George Coalition.

1922
19 Oct	Carlton Club meeting sees the Conservatives bring the Lloyd George Coalition to an end.
15 Nov	General Election produces a Conservative victory.

1923
6 Dec	Liberal Party is reunited for the election which produces a hung parliament and a minority Labour government.

S PECIAL TOPIC

LLOYD GEORGE AND THE COALITION GOVERNMENT OF 1918–22

This Special Topic is approached by means of two different secondary source extracts. In both extracts the historians provide some kind of general appraisal of Lloyd George's leadership as a whole and the record of the Coalition government 1918–22. The extracts have been selected to provide a coverage of the main details of the topic and a sample of historians' interpretations.

Activity I

Working individually and/or in pairs, study the secondary pieces of evidence and make a list of the various problems, events and policies which constitute the record and experience of the Coalition in the four years after the end of the First World War. Make sure your list is in roughly chronological order. To carry out this activity effectively you will need to cross-reference the two extracts.

Further Reading and Research

You should now have a very general (if a little confused) idea of what happened in the period 1918–22. To obtain a clearer understanding you will need to flesh out the bare outline of events with further historical detail. Using your textbook and other sources of information, construct a set of notes for each of the following areas: Foreign Policy, Domestic Policy, Industrial Events, Ireland and Lloyd George's Style of Leadership.

Activity II

You should at this stage have a much clearer idea of the events and the possible interpretations which this topic involves. Using the historians' accounts and the notes you have just completed, draw up a balance sheet of the 'good points' and 'bad points' of Lloyd George's administration. Remember that invariably the same policies and events can be interpreted in different ways, and thus might appear in both columns of your balance sheet. Provide a little piece of explanation for each entry. Again, this work can be done individually or in pairs, but everyone should end up with their own balance sheet.

Discussion

Now hold discussions, either in larger groups of four or five people, or as a class, of the different appraisals represented by your balance sheets. What are the agreements and disagreements in the group or class over the record of the Coalition? At this point (if it hasn't happened already) you should be putting forward your own ideas and opinions – having mastered some of those of the historians.

Activity III

For this activity the spotlight moves onto the political partnership between the Conservatives and the Liberals which was the main basis of the Coalition government. Before going any further, remind yourself of the details of the 'Coupon' election of November 1918 which extended Lloyd George's wartime coalition into peacetime. Now, use the historians' views and your notes to answer the questions below. Your answers should consist of short paragraphs containing specific references to the ideas of the historians and other relevant details.

a Given the composition of the Coalition, why might you have expected it to experience internal political difficulties after the war?

b How did the partnership between the Conservatives and Liberals within the Coalition develop between 1918 and 1922?

c Why did Lloyd George's Coalition government come to an end in October 1922?

Further Discussion

Before embarking on this discussion it would be a good idea to go back over previous notes to check up on all the achievements (and failures) of Lloyd George since

1906. Make a rough list of the relevant details. The question for discussion is: 'How significant was Lloyd George's contribution to Britain in the period 1906–1922?'

Here are a series of supplementary questions to consider:

- Did Lloyd George's dynamism outweigh his destructive tendencies?
- Was he a principalled man of the people or a power-seeking opportunist?
- Is it valid at all to look at history from the point of view of one man?

---

1 *K.O. Morgan:* The Oxford Illustrated History of Britain *ed. K.O. Morgan (1984)*

The election seemed to confirm, too, that socio-economic normality in many respects was being rapidly restored. Many of the wartime controls and the apparatus of state collectivism disappeared as if they had never been. Major industries were returned to private hands – the railways, shipping, even the coal mines whose owners were perhaps the most hated group in the entire capitalist world. The government also began a consistent financial policy to ensure an eventual return to the gold standard; this would entail a deflationary approach, with a steady contraction of the note issue expanded so rapidly during the war. The City of London, the class system, private capitalism appeared destined to continue their unchallenged reign. To indicate that this was capitalism with a human face, the government also began with a flurry of reforming activity in 1919–20. Indeed, Lloyd George had campaigned far more vigorously at the election as a social reformer anxious to build a 'land fit for heroes', than as a chauvinist determined to hang the Kaiser or 'squeeze Germany till the pips squeaked'. So there followed a vigorous, if shortlived, programme to extend health and educational services, to raise pensions, and spread universal unemployment insurance. Most spectacular of all was the subsidized housing programme launched by the Liberal minister Dr Christopher Addison which, with reluctant treasury support, achieved a total of over 200,000 publicly-built houses in the 1919–22 period, a limited but valuable start in dealing with one of the major social scandals in the land . . .

A series of challenges were launched which gradually undermined the coalition's claim to govern. New patterns were being formed which would shape the course of British history for the next twenty years. On the left, Lloyd George was bitterly attacked by many Liberals over his casualness towards old and hallowed principles such as free trade. His policy in Ireland appeared even more shocking since the British government pursued war against the IRA in 1919–21 with an unrestrained policy of retaliation which led to bloody atrocities being committed by the auxiliary forces that were maintained by the Crown to back up the army and the constabulary. In December 1921, Lloyd George, always by instinct a negotiator, eventually made peace with the Sinn Fein leaders, Arthur Griffith and Michael Collins. From January 1922, an Irish Free State, consisting of the twenty-six Catholic counties of southern Ireland, was created, with just the six Protestant counties of Ulster in the north-east left within the United Kingdom. But this volte-face was too late to repair Lloyd George's tarnished image amongst liberal opinion. In the Labour Party and trade union world, the Prime Minister totally lost the reputation he had long enjoyed as a patron of labour. His government used tough methods, including emergency powers and the use of troops as strike-breakers, in dealing with national strikes by miners, railwaymen, and many other workers (including even the police) in 1919–21. Thereafter, the government failed to prevent massive unemployment (soon rising to over a million workers) from growing up and casting a blight over the older industrial areas. Episodes like the apparent deceiving of the coal-miners over the Sankey report and the proposed nationalization of the mines in 1919, and the further undermining of the 'Triple Alliance' to frustrate the miners again on 'Black Friday' (15 April 1921) sank deep into the consciousness of the working class. A government elected to promote national solidarity and social unity had made the class divide wider than ever before. If the coalition was attacked on the left, it was increasingly under fire on the right as well. Conservatives longed for the return of a healthy system of independent party politics, freed from the buccaneering methods of an autocratic Prime

Minister and his retainers. Although the coalition hung on for almost four years, it was in dire straits and Lloyd George himself a Prime Minister at bay.

Above and beyond all this, there was a wider mood of disillusion with the peace treaties and the 'system of Versailles'. The peace settlement was increasingly unpopular. It was linked with covert secret treaties concluded during the war between Britain and its allies, and with unjust terms, for financial reparation and frontier arrangements, imposed on the defeated Germans... The final blow for Lloyd George's coalition came in October 1922 when it seemed that Britain was on the verge of war with Turkey over the defence of the Greek position in Asia Minor and protection of the Straits. Conservatives as well as the British left revolted against this rekindling of jingoism. The right-wing basis of the government collapsed. Lloyd George fell from power on 19 October 1922, a political pariah for the rest of his life.

2 *P. Rowland:* Lloyd George *(1975)*

He could reckon on being remembered, first and foremost, as the man who had won the war, but he was also the man who had settled the Irish problem – and, for that matter, the man who had settled the Welsh problem, for a Disestablishment Bill (with very generous terms of compensation) had reached the Statute Book in 1920 and came into force the following year. The suffragette problem had also been solved. Beyond this, however, what did his achievements actually amount to? There was the Education Act of 1918 but this was Fisher's handiwork rather than his own – and most of its provisions had, in any case, been effectively demolished by the Geddes axe. There had been, similarly, several spasmodic efforts at agricultural reform, which would be on record as evidence of good intentions, but these too had been nullified by the drive for economy. There had been the extensions to the original National Insurance Act of 1911, but these had been brought about by the pressure of events rather than a genuine desire for reform: the dole was simply regarded as the best available means of staving off revolution. All things considered, however, Lloyd George was not dissatisfied with his record. "I cannot accept", he would tell C. P. Scott on December 6th, "the part often

'The wizard who can't finish his tricks' – Lloyd George in 1921, as seen by David Low

proposed to me of a traitor to Liberalism who can only be taken back as penitent. As a matter of fact the record of Liberal measures passed by the Coalition Government is a fine one – the greatest measure of Irish self-government ever proposed or thought of, a very great measure of franchise extension, a remarkable temperance measure, a not insignificant measure of land reform which accepts my land valuation survey as its basis, an important international agreement as to disarmament."

It is doubtful whether he ever appreciated the extent to which he was generally regarded, by this time, with an impatience not far removed from contempt. The audience had cheered him at Manchester, and he would be cheered elsewhere during the forthcoming election campaign, but the by-elections were a more accurate guide to his popularity than the cheers, and the by-election results were, in the main, pretty awful. Lloyd George may or may not have been the man who won the war, but he was most definitely the man who had failed to provide a land fit for heroes to live in and the man who had presided over the destinies of the nation while the unemployment level soared to, and surpassed, the two million mark. The homes had not materialised and neither had the jobs. It had been generally agreed, since the end of 1919, thanks to J. M. Keynes and *The Economic Consequences of the Peace*, that he personally had been responsible for the punitive terms and crippling reparations imposed upon Germany and that this short-sighted policy of revenge had been directly responsible for creating havoc in Europe. By 1922 Keynes himself was beginning to realise just how wide of the mark his earlier condemnations had been but the damage had been done and Lloyd George would continue to be regarded as the man who had promised to hang the Kaiser, and squeeze Germany until the pips squeaked, in order to curry favour with the electorate. His Bristol speeches, in particular, would be cited as appalling examples of the depths to which a politician would sink in order to obtain power and his later utterances – such as the speech at Manchester – would be seen as further instances of the demagogue and rabble-rouser at work. The Khaki election of 1918 had been a confidence trick, and woe betide any attempt to stage a repeat performance!

By the autumn of 1922 everyone was on to Lloyd George. His slapdash methods, his blatant opportunism, his attempts to manipulate the Press, his network of spies and personal contacts – radiating outwards from the much-despised Garden Suburb – and lastly, but very far from least, the stench of the Honours scandal, had given rise to a widespread and very real repugnance. Everyone knew about them. Had he retired earlier in the year, after securing the Irish settlement, he could perhaps have salvaged something of his reputation and returned to power a few fears later with a strong party organisation behind him. As it was, however, he hung on to office, hoping that the Genoa conference would provide him with the huge success he needed – and, when that failed, hoping something else would turn up to give him a boost. The crisis at Chanak had seemed, at first, a reasonable platform – but the wood had proved rotten and he had fallen to his fate, dragging most of his colleagues with him. Nothing succeeds like success and nothing fails like failure: the Welsh wizard, having produced one glittering achievement after another in a dazzling display of pyrotechnics, and after eluding his critics for so long by keeping three jumps ahead of them, had struck a singularly bad patch. None of his tricks would work in 1922, although the conjuror's patter went on just as cheerfully as before, and the audience left the theatre as the footlights dimmed and the critics closed in for the kill. The star performer had ceased to amuse.

B ACK TO THE PRESENT

As was indicated in the introduction, the Liberal Party in its new guise as the Liberal Democrats is still a political force today. More significantly, the values of the doctrine of liberalism are pervasive throughout society. The freedom of the individual is accepted by most as a fundamental principle in our political, economic, religious and cultural life. However, people on the Left of the political spectrum argue that we are not as free as we like to think we are. They say that the economic freedom embodied in the capitalist system results in major inequalities of wealth – implying that 'poorer' people are much less free than 'richer' people. The Liberal Democrats, in fact, believe that without an election system based on proportional representation we are not as politically free a country as we could be. Of course, proportional representation would give the Liberal Democrats much greater representation in our House of Commons. The following questions for discussion link the events of Liberal history you have been studying in this theme with present-day controversies:

1 How free are people in Britain today? Could we be more free? If so, how?

2 Is there anything wrong with inequality? Should we be seeking to pursue greater social and economic equality in this country?

3 What exactly is proportional representation? Should we reform our electoral system on the basis of proportional representation?

4 What do you see as the relationship between social class and political representation in society today?

5 To what extent is it still possible for a charismatic leader like Lloyd George to dominate politics in a way which perhaps goes against the idea of democracy?

4 BALDWIN AND THE CONSERVATIVES

1922–37

I NTRODUCTION

There is a thesis which argues that in 1914 the Liberal Party was already in terminal decline because it was fundamentally incapable of dealing with the new democratic, nationalist and industrial forces of the age. This thesis further contends that it was only a matter of time before the Liberal Party was replaced by an emerging Labour Party as the main progressive party in the country. This view has now, to a certain extent, been discredited. However, a more plausible argument might be that it was the Conservative Party (or Unionist Party, as it was then known) which was facing political oblivion in the period. Between 1906 and 1914 the Conservatives had lost three elections in a row. Since 1906 they had set themselves firmly against the democratic spirit of the times by using the House of Lords – dominated by Tory hereditary peers – to block important legislation of a Liberal government with a majority in the House of Commons. Between 1912 and 1914 the Conservatives used distinctly underhand methods to resist Home Rule for Ireland – in spite of the Liberal government's mandate for carrying out such reform. Bound by a strong commitment to the ideas of economic liberalism and therefore limited government expenditure, they had singularly failed to introduce any major social reforms in their last period of office between 1895 and 1905. Finally, in their one main attempt at a major departure from *laissez-faire* economics – the issue of tariff reform – the Tories had fallen into disunity.

On the face of it the Conservative Party was more radically out of tune with the times than the Liberals in 1914. The rise of a Labour Party, it could be argued, might just as easily have led to two party politics based on a Liberal/Labour rather than a Tory/Labour axis. However, the experience of the First World War dramatically transformed the political scene: the Liberal Party became fatally divided and the Conservative Party was given a new lease of life as the dominant partner in the Lloyd George Coalition which won the war in 1918. In the inter-war period, politics was dominated by Conservative governments or 'national' governments in which the Conservatives held overwhelming majorities. Leader of the Conservative Party for much of this time was Stanley Baldwin, who was Prime Minister on three separate occasions and the key figure in a fourth government. The pre-eminence of the Tories in this period is in sharp contrast to their parlous condition on the eve of the First World War, and yet the economic, social and political problems facing Britain at this time were more acute than they had been before 1914.

This theme is concerned with understanding how Baldwin and successive Conservative governments coped with, and adapted to, the challenges they faced between 1922 and 1937, what their substantial achievements were, and why they were able to stay in power for so long. In the Special Topic – 'Stanley Baldwin and the General Strike 1925–26' – you will have the opportunity to examine the major industrial crisis of the period and assess Baldwin's handling of the situation.

K EY QUESTIONS

1 What were the aims and principles of Baldwin and the Conservatives in the period 1922–1937?

2 How successful were Baldwin and the Conservative governments in meeting the challenges of the period? What were their main policies and achievements?

3 What in particular was Baldwin's contribution to both the Conservative Party and the well-being of the nation?

4 Why was the Conservative Party so successful in electoral terms in the inter-war years?

C ONTEMPORARY VIEWS & OPINIONS

BALDWIN AND THE PRINCIPLES OF CONSERVATISM

This theme begins with a look at the principles of Conservatism as expressed by four Conservative representatives, including Baldwin, before the Second World War. Your understanding of the 'theory' of Conservatism will assist you in assessing the actual practice of Baldwin and Conservative governments in the inter-war period.

Activity

a Study the extracts carefully and working individually or in pairs make a note of all the differing ideals and aims of Conservatism that you can discover. Also, make a note of any significant differences you can detect between these versions of Conservatism. Discuss with other members of the class and your teacher the meaning of some of the more difficult ideas and concepts contained in the extracts.

b Now try and work out your own 'perfect' definition of Conservatism in two or three sentences. This definition should knit together the elements you have identified in the previous exercise. This will be difficult, but do your best.

c Finally (if you haven't considered this already) what do these passages reveal about the way Conservatives viewed the ideas of socialism in the inter-war years? Make a note of your deductions.

Discussion

As a class, go over the work you have just done and see if you have reached similar conclusions about what Conservatism meant before the Second World War. Now hold a discussion around the following questions:
- What do you think of the Conservative ideas you have been examining?
- Was (is?) the Conservative critique of Socialism fair?
- Is the argument between Conservatives and Socialists any different nowadays?
- In what ways and why?

1 *F.J.C. Hearnshaw:* **A Survey of Socialism** *(1928)*
For the unjust and unreasonable attack which socialism makes upon the rich tends to make them hard and unsympathetic. Those who assail and abuse them can scarcely expect to be loved by them: those who mulct them of all they can, and threaten to rob them of the whole of their possessions, can hardly hope to be relieved by their benevolence.

It is, in short, difficult to overstate the injury which socialist propaganda has done to social peace and industrial prosperity.

Hence the sum of the whole matter is that I entirely agree with those who see in socialism one of the main causes of our industrial troubles during the past half-century, and one of the gravest of existing menaces to the future peace and prosperity of the world in general, and of Britain and the Empire in particular. I agree with Lord Rosebery when he says: 'The great danger is socialism.... Socialism is the end of all – the negation of faith, of property, of the monarchy, of the Empire.'* I agree with Mr. Boris Brasol when he contends that 'both labour and industry must be protected against socialist agitation which threatens to ruin not only the existing order but also every attempt to improve it and to ensure social progress and general prosperity.'†

*Raymond, E. T., *The Man of Promise* (1923), p. 228.

†Brasol, B., *Socialism versus Civilisation* (1920), p. 59.

2 *Sir Alfred Mond:* Why I Become A Conservative – *the* Saturday Review *(1926)*

There are definite limits, well determined and easily defined, beyond which the application of State control or State intervention can do no good, but rather may achieve tremendous harm. In view of the evolution of the political theory to which parties or political leaders have recently subscribed, I have come to the conclusion that the Conservative Party, under its present direction, is the national anti-Socialist Party.

3 *Stanley Baldwin in a speech, 1926*

If you look at a doctrine which is being preached to-day in certain parts of the Continent, and even here, the teaching of communism, you will find that, whatever else may be said about it, it is a system in which there can be no freedom as we understand that word in England. It is a system that can only be ordered by an iron discipline, and no system that requires an iron discipline is adapted to our people. I want to put that thought into your minds to-night, particularly that thought of freedom, personal liberty and individual freedom. It was the battleground of long, hard struggles in this country many generations ago, and after we believed that the principle was safe in our country, people took it for granted. But do not fail to notice the sinister signs of a campaign against that liberty in those doctrines of which I have been speaking.

'Much ado about next to nothing' – Low, 1924

4 *Stanley Baldwin in a speech, 1930*

Over the vast tracts of the Empire the indigenous population can only judge of Great Britain by their knowledge of the character of the one or two white men who live among them, or even by the demeanour of the passing visitor. And if they see truth and loyalty, fair play and self-control exhibited in such individuals, that will be their conception of the nation; and the nation's work in governing, controlling and advising is to that extent made more easy instead of more difficult. The day that we cease to be worthy of respect, that day the foundations of the Colonial Empire crack.

I have used the word patriotism on purpose because, rightly used, it is a potent force for good. At its best it is a noble virtue. It derives strength from the fact that it is a fundamental primitive instinct, an instinct common to higher and lower civilizations, attaching itself to the earliest memories of childhood, to the fields and woods and streams amongst which we grew up. The highest form of human altruism has been inspired by patriotism. Not only with soldiers and sailors, but with scholars, engineers and business men, service of their country has been the deepest motive of their work.

5 *Stanley Baldwin in a speech, 1933*

Kindliness, sympathy with the under dog, love of home! Are not these all characteristics of the ordinary Englishman that you know? He is a strong individualist in this, that he does not want to mould himself into any common mould, to be like everybody else; he likes to develop his own individuality. And yet he can combine for service.

Some of the best things in this country have originated among our own common people with no help from governments – friendly society work, our trade unions, our hospitals and our education before the State took it in hand. Then the Englishman has a profound respect for law and order – that is part of his tradition of self-government. Ordered liberty – not disordered liberty, nor what invariably follows, tyranny; but ordered liberty, at present one of the rare things of this topsy-turvy world.

6 *Harold Macmillan:* The Middle Way *(1938)*
I reject the Fascist and the Communist theories of violent change because (a) they are politically impossible, and (b) the revolutionary seizure of power would be, and must be, followed by a political tyranny in which man's cultural freedom (which is the prerequisite of human progress) would be sacrificed. I reject the constitutional Socialist approach because, even if their 'economic totalitarianism' would work without political

tyranny, it would sacrifice the beneficial dynamic element that private enterprise can give to society when exercised in its proper sphere, and because it would not provide the scope for human diversity which is essential if men are really to be free. But the most important reason for the rejection of these theories is that they are remote from what is immediately practicable in the circumstances of our time. . . .

But I do not propose to employ this defence of private enterprise in the fields for which it is best suited in order to condone or excuse the poverty and insecurity in the basic necessities of life, which we have today as a legacy of unrestrained competition and uneconomic waste and redundancy. I shall advocate all the more passionately on grounds of morality, of social responsibility, as well as of economic wisdom, a wide extension of social enterprise and control in the sphere of minimum human needs. The satisfaction of those needs is a duty which society owes to its citizens.

O UTLINING THE EVENTS

BALDWIN AND THE CONSERVATIVES 1922–37

It is important to establish an outline appreciation of the events of the theme before looking at the deeper levels of argument. The eight extracts here, taken from books written by various historians, tell us something about the main episodes and issues in this period when politics were dominated by Baldwin and the Conservative Party. It is important that these pieces of evidence are used in conjunction with the election statistics on page 51.

Activity I

Study the secondary source extracts and the election statistics carefully. Working individually or in pairs draw up three different lists containing the following information:

- The election victories and defeats of the Conservative Party in the period 1922–37 with figures for the number of seats won in the House of Commons. You should also write down the names of the different positions in government which Baldwin held throughout the period.
- The main challenges and problems which Conservative governments faced between 1922 and 1937.
- As many policies, Acts of Parliament and other political actions as you can find mentioned in the extracts for which Baldwin and Conservative governments were in some way responsible in the period.

Activity II

a Re-examine the sources and identify any debating points or opinions outlined by the authors concerning Baldwin's record as a leader. Draw up a provisional 'balance sheet' of points for and against Baldwin. Where a particular point of view is clearly supported by one of the authors represented in this selection, write down that author's name next to the relevant point.

b What do you think might be the reasons for the electoral success of the Conservative Party in the period? Again, careful examination of the extracts and statistics will reveal more than you think. Make a note of the reasons you have identified.

Discussion

Hold a class discussion to review the various pieces of work carried out so far, in order to make sure you are on the right lines in your investigation of this topic.

Further Reading and Research

You ought to have some ideas about what problems Baldwin and Conservative governments faced in the 1920s and 1930s, how they dealt with these problems and some of the verdicts historians have reached about the Conservative record. On the basis of the work you have done so far you must now extend your understanding of the theme by reading and noting from relevant history texts. Your teacher will point out areas of historical importance not really touched on in the sources and may provide you with his or her own additional notes.

***

I Dictionary of British History *ed. J. P. Kenyon (1981)*
Baldwin of Bewdley, Stanley Baldwin, 1st Earl (1867–1947). Prime minister (1923–24, 1924–29, 1935–37). A Conservative MP from 1908 to 1937, when he was created an earl, in 1917 he was parliamentary private secretary to Lloyd George's chancellor of the exchequer, Bonar Law, and then (1917–21) financial secretary to the Treasury. His opposition, while president of the board of trade (1921–22), to Lloyd George's coalition government was supported by the majority of Conservative MPs and helped bring about its downfall. Baldwin served as chancellor of the exchequer (1922–23) in Bonar Law's government, succeeding him as prime minister in May 1923. In the subsequent election (Dec 1923) the Conservatives lost their majority

and resigned in Jan 1924. Returned in Dec 1924, Baldwin in his second ministry was faced by the general strike (1926); he announced a state of emergency and passed the retaliatory Trade Disputes Act (1927). Defeated in the election of 1929, he served as lord president of the council (1931–35) in the national government and became prime minister for the third time, in succession to MacDonald, in 1935. His government negotiated the Hoare-Laval pact (1935), widely condemned for its proposal to permit Italy to annex Ethiopia, and negotiated the abdication of Edward VIII (1936). He retired in 1937. He was a writer, his books including *England*.

2 *R. Blake:* The Conservative Party from Peel to Churchill *(1979)*
But what did the party do with the power it secured? In the inter-war years there were three great problems. These were the condition of the people, the future of the empire, the rise of Germany.

On the first the Conservatives failed to deal with unemployment although there *were* alternative policies which might have solved it or softened it – policies not the monopoly of cranks or even of voices crying in the wilderness. On the other hand, Neville Chamberlain by his social reforms, and Baldwin by his genuine kindliness, generosity and goodwill did something to soften the stark confrontation of the classes and the masses, something too in the case of Baldwin (not Chamberlain whom they hated for his blunt contemptuousness) to bring the Labour party towards constitutionalism and ease it into the parliamentary system.

On the second problem – the empire – the party's policy was much more successful. Ireland was a lesson never forgotten. The Statute of Westminster and the India Act were both in their contemporary setting notable advances. Baldwin deserves much of the credit for this, but he could not have done it if the party's outlook had remained crystallised in the climate of 1914.

On the third problem – resurgent Germany – the Conservative leadership has a record that is hard to defend. It is true that rearmament went a good deal further from 1935 onwards than has always been appreciated.

3 *K. Young:* Stanley Baldwin *(1976)*
Men will long debate whether he deliberately provoked the general strike. It is certain that he defeated it and yet averted a legacy of bitterness. In foreign affairs, too, his record is disputed. Did he, as Churchill alleged, put party before country? Or did he initiate a policy of deterrence towards Hitler, which Chamberlain then neglected?

Some things can be set indisputably to his credit. Baldwin more than any other political leader pursued a policy of constitutional concession towards India. The attempt failed, but it is thanks to Baldwin that India achieved her freedom and preserved much of the British political heritage until just the other day. Unwittingly Baldwin prepared the national unity which the British displayed during the Second World War. Despite the dark years of unemployment, he softened the asperities of the class war.

4 *C.L. Mowat:* Britain Between the Wars *(1955)*
Few reputations have faded as quickly as Baldwin's. When Britain's military unpreparedness was revealed by the ordeal of war, Baldwin, living in retirement, was given much of the blame, partly because of his 'appalling frankness' speech about the general election of 1935, of which the public was reminded by *Guilty Men* in 1940. This was unfair. Certainly he was not a great man, nor a

master in the part of leadership in which he was strangely cast. He was also unfortunate. The India Act might have been a monument to him had fate not given it so short a life. He intended to preserve national unity and industrial peace; yet he must be held partly responsible for the general strike of 1926 and for the Trade Disputes Act. If rearmament was too slow, he shared the blame with Chamberlain and with the rest of the government – and with the nation which followed the lead he gave it. *There* is his final defence: that he was tolerated for so long.

5 *R. Jenkins:* Baldwin *(1987)*
Baldwin's reputation cannot be equally detached from the economic performance during his years of power. Until recently this was generally held to be a substantial count against him. A man who fought the general election of 1929, when unemployment was over 1 million, on a slogan as static as 'Safety first', and who then held power for over half of the 1930s years of distressed areas, basic industries without orders, and men without work, must surely have been guilty of a complacency verging upon discreditable negligence.

Baldwin presided over a vastly unequal society and somewhat stagnant economy disfigured by pockets of appalling poverty (but so, it must be said, did Lloyd George and Asquith before him

'You know you can trust me' – Evening Standard *20 December 1935 (David Low)*

and MacDonald alongside him) and did so with some complacency. But his record on unemployment was incomparably better than Mrs Thatcher's, and he witnessed no such precipitate decline of Britain's relative wealth as occurred between 1958 and 1973.

6 *T. Lindsay and M. Harrington:* The Conservative Party 1918–1979 *(1979)*
In other fields the domestic policy of the Government was by no means unconstructive. The reform of local government, the abolition of the Poor Law and the derating of industry were important and substantial reforms. There is justice in the claim of Baldwin's defenders that the 1924–9 Government made an outstanding contribution to the development of the social services and social security.

7 *R.K. Webb:* Modern England *(1980)*
In general, the thirties were a period of gradual but steady recovery. As Britain had never fallen so far into depression as other industrial countries, her recovery was easier. Leaving aside the grim conditions in the special areas, the decade was marked by a rise in real wages and living standards. Protection got much of the credit, but it is doubtful that protection deserved it, and the various government measures were at best a minor contribution. The economy lifted itself by its own bootstraps – not so far or so intelligently as it might have done with more systematic encouragement and direction. Probably the most important single factor in the expansion of the thirties was the boom in house-building.

8 *A. Ball:* British Political Parties *(1981)*
Part of this image bears some resemblance to reality; he was patriotic, uninterested in foreign affairs, centrist in his policies and adverse to change whether it was suggested by the left or the right, and therein may lie the answer to the accusations of policy failure. But this picture ignores the ruthlessness in Baldwin's character. This aspect was clearly illustrated by his conduct and direction of his government during the General Strike of 1926; contrary to many views, Baldwin was in firm control, not directed by his subordinates. His firmness was fully illustrated years later when he secured the abdication of Edward VIII. Yet Baldwin's main claim to fame is his role as party leader. His main aim was the protection of the interests of his party. Before becoming leader he was one of the main factors in the rescue of the party from the clutches of Lloyd George in 1922; he was not too perturbed by the accession to power of Labour in 1924, seeing Asquith dig the Liberals' electoral grave much to the advantage of the Conservative Party; he was ultimately convinced of the need to make either the Labour Party or the Labour leadership responsible for the harsh economic cuts after the 1931 crisis; he risked the accusation of putting party before country in his refusal to re-arm with full vigour in the 1930s. His strength as party leader resulted partly from a warm personality and partly from a lack of extreme partisanship. His greatest claim to fame was that in spite of losing two elections as party leader he maintained his leadership and he chose his moment to retire accompanied by the fulsome praise of his followers.

SIMULATION

INDUSTRIAL CONFLICT AND THE MINING INDUSTRY 1926

Introduction

This simulation is designed to help you think about the problems and decisions which different interest groups in Britain were faced with over the crisis in the coal-mining industry in the mid-1920s. In the simulation the class will divide up into groups representing the Conservative government, the TUC, the colliery owners, representatives of the miners' union – the Miners Federation of Great Britain – and journalists. You will be involved in making decisions and negotiating with other groups to secure the interests of the particular people you represent.

The Situation

The date is 1 May 1926 and the coal industry is facing serious economic problems. The employers have instigated a lock-out of the miners starting on 1 May. The miners will not be allowed to work and therefore will not be paid until they accept the employers' demands for cuts in wages, a longer working week and regional rather than national wage agreements. These requirements are designed to produce a more profitable mining industry. The TUC, in response, is thinking seriously about organising a general strike in support of the miners to begin at midnight on 3 May. In this context the aim will be for each of the four main groups to try to produce a settlement of the short-term and long-term problems of the coal industry which favours its particular interests and ideology. Also, each organisation has certain political objectives which it wants to achieve. All four groups show some willingness to resolve the dispute through negotiation, although there are elements within each group who believe, for different political reasons, that industrial conflict would be a good thing.

The background information given below is very approximately based on the actual economic and political situation as it was at the time. The specific procedures for the simulation are outlined further on.

Background Information

Profiles of the Relevant Groups

The Conservative Government

The Conservative government – led by its Prime Minister, Stanley Baldwin – wants, on the whole, to avoid the confrontation of a general strike and to produce a negotiated settlement to end the coal dispute. Indeed, Baldwin himself has made it clear that one of his aims is to maintain harmony between the social classes. On the other hand, the government believes in *laissez-faire* economics and is not all that willing to accept a solution to the dispute which involves major state intervention to improve the workings of the coal industry. More especially the government seeks to uphold the capitalist system and therefore believes in the owners' right to manage as they wish. The Conservative government also wants to uphold the rule of law as they see it.

The Coal-Owners

The capitalists in the coal industry believe that the immediate problem of loss of profits can only be dealt with by cutting the wages of miners, increasing the length of the working day and returning to regional rather than national rates of pay. They see this as sensible economics. For the coal-owners nothing can be achieved through strikes, which the owners attribute to the influence of dangerous communist revolutionaries in unions. There is, however, some acceptance amongst coal-owners that more radical long-term solutions are needed to improve the coal industry. Finally, the coal-owners are rich enough to sustain a lengthy lock-out of the miners while they wait for their terms to be accepted.

The Miners' Union

The miners do a dirty and difficult job and do not see why their living standards should be sacrificed in order to make the coal industry more profitable in the short-term. They believe that the only way in which the performance of the coal industry can be improved is through massive modernisation, and this is really only possible through major state intervention – even through nationalisation. To this end the miners can point to the successful state management of the industry during the First World War and the support of a government commission for nationalisation in 1919. Also, many miners influenced by socialist and communist ideals believe it is their duty to confront the employers and the government – with the support of other workers – in a general strike in order to change the capitalist system.

The TUC

As the representative body of the majority of unions in the country, the TUC is worried about increasing unemployment in British industry. In general it believes that if the miners are defeated over the issue of worsening wages and conditions of service, then this will be a signal for employers in other industries to reduce workers' living standards in the same kind of way. Many TUC leaders have a vague belief in socialism and think that increased state management of the economy might solve some of the problems which are unsolvable under pure capitalism. For these reasons many in the TUC are willing to call a general strike on behalf of the miners. On the other hand, some of the TUC leadership fear that industrial confrontation might provide an opportunity for communists and other 'hot-heads' to promote revolution. so the TUC is in two minds about what to do.

The Journalists

The journalists' role (as more fully described in the 'Procedures' section) is to bring news of the dispute to the public. The way in which they do this can, of course, influence the development of the dispute.

General Information

The Economy in the Mid-1920s

The economy is going through a period of difficulty in the mid-1920s. Due to the failure to modernise in competition with foreign rivals and the loss of export markets, Britain's primary industries (including coal, textiles, iron and steel and shipbuilding) are suffering from declining rates of production. Unemployment, concentrated in these industries, is over one million people – ten per cent of the possible working population. The Conservative government believes in *laissez-faire* and minimum state intervention; they think the economy will improve only if businesses are left to sort out their own problems according to the workings of market forces. However, there are exceptions to this philosophy and in 1926 the government is proposing to nationalise the BBC and the electricity industry. The Labour Party and other groupings on the political Left believe that some kind of state management of the economy is necessary in order to improve the performance of failing industries and indeed to reduce the misery created by unemployment.

The Problems of the Coal Industry by the Mid-1920s

In 1913 the coal industry had accounted for one tenth of Britain's export trade and employed over one million miners, but was already experiencing problems. By 1925 and 1926 production has fallen below the 1913 level. This is due to a number of factors (historians do not agree on which were the most important).

The coal industries of rival countries such as America, Belgium and Poland are more efficient. They use a much higher percentage of mechanical coal-cutting equipment than we do. Whereas there are over 1,400 small-sized mining concerns in Britain, firms in competing countries are much bigger and therefore more economically powerful. British coal-owners seem reluctant to invest in new technologies and better forms of organisation in order to improve the industry. In home markets, new fuels are being used to replace coal such as gas, oil, and electricity. By 1925 many pits are running at a loss and employers are determined to improve profits – not through modernisation, but through cutting the wages of the workforce (by between ten per cent and 27 per cent according to the area) and lengthening their hours (from seven to eight hours a day). Only a reluctantly-conceded government subsidy prevented industrial conflict and a general strike breaking out in 1925 over the employers' proposal to worsen the position of their workers.

The Political Position in the Mid-1920s

In 1924 a Conservative government with a large majority replaced a minority Labour government in power – the first ever Labour government. The right-wing of the Tory Party are afraid of the rise of organised labour and the ideas of socialism. They want to crush any socialist challenge to capitalism. But the Prime Minister, Baldwin, and others are more inclined to conciliate labour and the trades unions, and in particular to give the Labour Party a fair chance of power: in this way socialism might be neutralised. Within the labour movement itself there are those who believe socialism can only be achieved very gradually through an elected Labour Party majority in the House of Commons, and there are those who believe in using confrontation through something like a general strike to achieve radical change. Therefore the possibility of a general strike raises all sorts of problems within the labour movement and the politicised working class about the best way to achieve socialism.

Procedure

1 The teacher should divide the class into the five main organisations with appropriate numbers in each (no more than two journalists). The TUC should contain a miners' representative who will therefore be a member of two groups. This person can be elected by the miners' union. These groups should be located in different rooms if possible or in separate parts of the room.

2 How the situation develops will be very much determined by the decisions made by the different parties concerned. But, remember the aim of each organisation is to achieve an eventual settlement which is as favourable as possible to the interests of that organisation. What a 'favourable settlement' and an 'organisation's interests' actually are will be up to each group to determine using the background information.

3 Each group will therefore be involved in a number of activities: discussing with its own members its immediate and long-term aims; establishing its negotiating strategies in relation to the other organisations and issuing press handouts to clarify its position to the public. It will be involved in actual negotiations/unofficial talks with other organisations or combinations of other organisations (although any organisation can refuse to have any kind of discussion with another). The phases given below provide a basic structure for these activities.

4 Any organisation, at almost any time, can initiate negotiations and discussions with another organisation. This must be done through the teacher. In addition the teacher can set up negotiations at his/her discretion. In general, the role of the teacher is to help each group grasp the key issues explained in the 'Background Information' section and to keep the simulation moving.

5 The role of the journalists is to interview the different organisations and their representatives and to issue short news bulletins giving their interpretation of what is going on. Of course, these actual articles will have a substantive effect on the dispute as it unfolds. The journalists will be free to report also, by word of mouth, what they know of one group's intentions to another group. In this way rumour and mis-information will begin to influence the situation.

PHASES

Phase 1 – Last-Minute Negotiations

Each organisation should spend up to 20 minutes sorting out what its immediate and longer-term aims, beliefs and interests actually are. A thorough grasp of the relevant 'Background Information' is essential here. It should then spend further time agreeing on a set of negotiating proposals, and who it actually wants to try to negotiate with and in what order.

When an organisation is ready it can initiate negotiations through the 'good offices' of the teacher. After a while (up to an hour) the teacher should set up a full round table discussion between all four groups and the journalists to see if any common ground has emerged for a compromise settlement.

At various points any group can issue a press statement or the journalist/teacher might ask for a press statement to be issued. The press statement can be used as a tactic in the negotiations.

This basic format should continue until there is an agreed settlement, or a general strike is called.

Optional Phase 2 – The General Strike

For this phase the government, the coal-owners, the TUC and the Miners Union representatives should join together.

Each side should then produce a list of proposals about how they intend to organise against the strike or how they intend to run the strike to achieve the ends they desire. These should be presented to the teacher who will assess the merits of each set of proposals and, working with the journalists, will issue an account of who is actually 'winning' the conflict and any relevant consequences of the submitted proposals.

Any group is free to initiate continuing talks with another group. This may mean individual organisations acting independently of the main bodies.

This phase continues until something happens to bring everything to an end or until everybody is exhausted and has had enough.

S PECIAL TOPIC

BALDWIN AND THE GENERAL STRIKE 1925–26

The General Strike of 1926 was a pivotal moment in the history of inter-war Britain – the fundamental character of power and politics in this country seemed to depend on the outcome of the Strike. Inevitably its exact historical significance has been argued over by both the participants themselves and historians. In particular there has been much controversy about the part played by Stanley Baldwin as Prime Minister of the Conservative government at the time.

The short extracts in this section are taken from the speeches, newspapers, diaries, official letters, autobiographies and memoirs of people involved in the events. The activities are concerned with helping you begin to understand the events and issues of the General Strike and, in particular, the role of Baldwin. If you carried out the simulation in the previous section then you will already be familiar with many of the main ideas and arguments.

Activity

a Using the extracts as your evidence, reconstruct the 'story' of 'Baldwin and the General Strike 1925–1926'. Your account should describe and explain the dispute in the coal-mining industry, its culmination in the General Strike (including details of negotiations, 30 April–3 May), the outcome of the Strike and the miners' return to work by the end of 1926. Your account should be brief, yet at the same time include what you consider to be the essential pieces of historical detail and explanation. This should be an individual piece of work.

b Compare your narrative of events with that of someone else in the class and assess each other's versions of what happened. Discuss whether you feel either of your accounts has omitted or misunderstood important aspects of the General Strike – as far as you can tell. Talk over any difficulties in understanding you have at this stage. When discussions have been satisfactorily completed, each of you should make any necessary corrections or additions to your accounts.

c Now, as a class, review the whole narrative of events to ensure there is general agreement about the facts of the topic. This will be an opportunity for your teacher to begin to clear up any misunderstandings and provide you with further details of the story. At this stage you are still concerned with the facts rather than the interpretations of the General Strike, although, as you no doubt might be aware, the distinction between the two is rather artificial.

d Working individually or in small groups and returning to the evidence in the sources, identify more clearly the attitudes and motives of each of the following in the period: Baldwin and the government; the TUC; the miners; the colliery owners. Did the approach of any of these groups change in the period of the coal-mining dispute and during or after the Strike itself? Make a note of your observations.

Further Reading and Research

You should now have some grasp of the details and issues of this Special Topic, but it will be obvious that the extracts in this selection provide only a rather sketchy and provisional view of the General Strike events. You need to deepen your knowledge with additional reading and note-making from textbooks, other history books and/or notes and handouts from your teacher. The work you have done so far should act as a guide to your research.

Discussion

You ought now to be ready to make some well-informed evaluations of the Strike. As a class, hold a discussion around the following questions and issues:

- Was the General Strike a 'good thing' or a 'bad thing'?
- How would you assess Baldwin and his government's handling of the whole dispute 1925–6?
- What do you think of the TUC's handling of the dispute?
- Do you think the miners were betrayed when the TUC ended the strike in the way they did on 12 May 1926?

- In general, do you support the miners' or the employers' case with regards to improving the coal-mining industry at this time?
- What economic alternatives were there?
- What do you think might have happened if the TUC had continued the Strike in support of the miners?

---

1 Stanley Baldwin in a speech, 1923

... I want to see in the next year or two the beginning of a better unity between all classes of our people. If there are those who want to fight the class war we will take up the challenge, and we will beat them by the hardness of our heads and the largeness of our hearts. I want to leave this country, when my term ends, in better heart than it has been for years. I want to be a healer and I believe that as these things have to be done through the intrumentality of parties, the Unionist party is the one upon which the country must lean if it desires these ends.

2 Philip Snowden, leading Labour Party politician: An Autobiography (1934)

A serious crisis in the industry was only averted in July 1925 by the offer of the Government to grant a subsidy to the mine-owners which cost the tax-payers about £25,000,000. At the same time it was decided to set up a Royal Commission to enquire into the state of the mining industry. The Report of this Commission was made in March 1926, and during the month of April the recommendations of this Report were considered by the Government and by joint committees of the owners and the miners.

The main matters in dispute centred upon hours and wages, and incidentally whether working conditions and wages should be regulated by district settlements or on a national basis. These negotiations failed to reach an agreement. On the 30th April the subsidy came to an end. The whole of that day was spent in hectic conferences between Cabinet Ministers, owners, miners, and the Industrial Committee of the Trade Union Congress. In anticipation that all efforts to arrive at a settlement would be futile, the mine-owners had issued lock-out notices if the miners would not accept a longer working day and a reduction of wages.

3 Leo Amery, Conservative Cabinet Minister at the time: My Political Life

... A debate in June 1925 showed rising unemployment and general economic deterioration. In the coal industry the situation had become critical. Pits were closing down on every hand, and something like 300,000 miners were already out of work. Discussions between mine owners and miners led nowhere. The owners, not prepared to work their mines at a loss, could see no remedy except in reducing costs by lowering wages or returning to the eight hours' day. The miners, who had been led by the fantastic rise in coal prices at the end of the war and during the occupation of the Ruhr to regard the advances gained as a mere instalment of more to come, were indignant at the idea of being forced back upon the wage-slavery of the past. Determined not to yield an inch they looked more and more to the General Strike to get their way. An announcement on the part of the owners that they would only carry on from 1st August on a reduced scale of wages was answered on 31st July by a conference of a thousand trade union delegates which in fact promised the miners full support in standing out. If a general strike was to come Baldwin felt he would need more time to enable the public to understand the constitutional issue involved. Some workable compromise might possibly be found in the interval. Meanwhile the administrative machinery for dealing with such an emergency might be still further improved. So he hurriedly offered a subsidy to enable existing wages to be maintained, while the whole problem was being inquired into by a Commission under Sir Herbert Samuel's chairmanship.

The Commission reported in March 1926. It definitely recommended that the subsidy should stop after 30th April. It was not prepared to recommend longer hours, but recognized that there would have to be some reduction of wages. It rejected nationalization of the industry, but recommended the State purchase of royalties. For the rest it made a variety of suggestions none of which, though useful in themselves, could have affected the immediate situation. The Cabinet offered to carry out the whole Report if both sides accepted it as a settlement.

4 *Declaration of the Special Industrial Committee of the TUC,* Daily Herald *31 July 1925*
Never in the history of the modern working-class movement has the imagination of the workers been more roused and their resistance more stiffened than by the impending attack upon working-class standards threatened in several of the principal industries of this country to-day.

It is generally felt that if the miners are defeated in the present struggle, successive attacks will be launched in other industries. The textile industry is now in the throes of such a struggle.

The Committee is thoroughly satisfied that there can be no doubt of the moral support of the whole movement being undividedly behind the miners.

5 *E. Shinwell, a Labour MP at the time:* I've Lived Through It All *(1973)*
On 30 April 1926 the delegates learned of the mine owners' offer of the minumum wage, with its thirteen per cent cut, and an eight-hour day to earn it. The terms were worse than those suggested by the Samuel Commission. Even the placatory Thomas regarded the offer as intolerable. The trade unions agreed with him. The ballot for a national stoppage to begin at midnight on 3 May was approved by 3·6 million for and 50,000 against.

6 *Shinwell on negotiations on the night of 1 May 1926*
On the Saturday night the TUC General Council made an attempt to stave off the inevitable. Thomas, Swales, and Pugh of the TUC met Baldwin, Birkenhead and Steel-Maitland. Walter Citrine, general secretary of the TUC and a close friend of mine, was one of the vote takers. He subsequently told me that the discussions were amicable and constructive. When the meeting broke up it seemed that the strike would be avoided, or at least postponed. The TUC would withdraw the strike notices; the mine owners would cancel the lock-out orders, and the Government would continue the subsidy for an additional fourteen days.

7 *Philip Snowden, on events on the evening of Sunday 2 May:* An Autobiography *(1934)*
At this meeting with the Prime Minister, Lord

Birkenhead suggested a formula which the Trade Union Council might be able to accept as a basis for negotiations. This formula read:

> 'We, the Trade Union Council, would urge the miners to authorise us to enter upon discussion with the understanding that they and we accept the Report as a basis of settlement, and we approach it with the knowledge that it may involve some reduction in wages.'

The Trade Union Council had no powers to accept this formula in the name of the miners, but they left Downing Street to consult the miners' leaders. Mr. Thomas sent up word to Mr. Mac-Donald and myself that he felt that they were within an ace of a final settlement. . . .

It is impossible to believe that the action of the employees of the *Daily Mail* had been the reason for the Government breaking off negotiations. Mr. Baldwin had been overruled by the majority of his Cabinet. He, himself, would have been willing to continue the negotiations, but he had the majority of his Cabinet against him, who threatened that if he yielded to the Trade Union Council they would adopt direct action and go on strike.

8 *Leo Amery:* The Leo Amery Diaries 1896–1929 *(1980)*
. . . While we were discussing the news arrived that the *Daily Mail* had been suppressed altogether by the printers because they did not like its leading article. We had already had information that in the *Sunday Express* and other papers articles had been considerably censored or dropped out. This turned the scale and made it clear that the only issue that really mattered for the Government and with the public now was the issue of the general strike. The Cabinet decision which was adopted in the afternoon was toned up a little further so as to make it quite clear that there could be no discussion until the general strike had been withdrawn and it was then sent in to the TUC and miners who I gather went home shortly afterwards. Whether the miners were or were not prepared to look at Thomas's formula before they got our decision I do not know. Baldwin certainly did not think they would, mild though it was. We dispersed about 12.30.

9 *Letter from Baldwin, the Prime Minister, to the TUC, 3 May*

But since the discussions which have taken place between Ministers and members of the Trade Union Committee it has come to the knowledge of the Government not only that specific instructions have been sent (under the authority of the Executives of the Trade Unions represented at the Conference convened by the General Council of the Trade Union Congress) directing their members in several of the most vital industries and services of the country to carry out a general strike on Tuesday next, but that overt acts have already taken place, including gross interference with the freedom of the Press. Such action involves a challenge to the constitutional rights and freedom of the nation.

His Majesty's Government, therefore, before it can continue negotiations must require from the Trade Union Committee both the repudiation of the actions referred to that have already taken place, and an immediate and unconditional withdrawal of the instructions for a general strike.

10 *Letter from TUC to Baldwin in reply to the above, 3 May*

The first reason given is, that specific instructions have been sent under the authority of Trade Unions represented at the conference convened by the General Council of the Trades Union Congress directing their members in several industries and services to cease work. We are directed to remind you that it is nothing unusual for workmen to cease work in defence of their interests as wage earners, and the specific reason for the decision in this case is to secure for the mineworkers the same right from the employers as is insisted upon by employers from workers – namely, that negotiations shall be conducted free from the atmosphere of strike or lock-out. This is a principle which Governments have held to be cardinal in the conduct of negotiations.

With regard to the second reason, that overt acts had already taken place, including gross interference with the freedom of the Press, it is regretted that no specific information is contained in your letter. The General Council had no knowledge of any such independent and unauthorised action.

11 *The* Daily Herald, *4 May 1926*

The miners are locked out to enforce reductions of wages and an increase in hours. The Government stands behind the mineowners. It has rebuffed the Trade Union Movement's every effort to pave the way to an honourable peace.

The renewed conversations begun on Saturday were ended abruptly in the early hours of yesterday morning, with an ultimatum from the Cabinet. Despite this, the whole Labour Movement, including the miners' leaders, continued its efforts yesterday.

But unless a last minute change of front by the

General Strike, 1926: food convoy being escorted from the docks by armoured cars and troops

Government takes place during the night the country will today be forced, owing to the action of the Government, into an industrial struggle bigger than this country has yet seen.

In the Commons Mr Baldwin showed no sign of any receding from his attitude that negotiations could not be entered into if the General Strike order stood and unless reductions were accepted before negotiations opened.

12 Daily Mail *leader that the printers refused to print for the May 3 editions*
A General Strike is not an industrial dispute. It is a revolutionary movement intended to inflict suffering upon the great mass of innocent persons in the community and thereby to put forcible constraint upon the Government. It is a movement which can only succeed by destroying the Government and subverting the rights and liberties of the people.

13 *The* British Worker, *8 May 1926*
There is as far as the Trade Union Movement is concerned, no 'attack on the community'. There is no 'challenge to the Constitution.' The workers have exercised their legal and long-established right of withholding their labour, in order to protect the miners against a degradation of their standard of life, which is a menace to the whole world of labour.

14 *Leo Amery:* The Leo Amery Diaries 1896–1929 *(1980)*
11 May 1926: . . . At the close of the meeting the Prime Minister received information that the TUC were holding a meeting with the miners and that it was quite possible that we might hear later in the evening that the strike was to be called off. Soon after dinner we were warned that there might be a Cabinet late in the evening and it was not until midnight that the messages calling it off reached us. I understand that the TUC had 4 hours with the miners trying to get them to agree to certain proposals of Samuel's which he made on his own and without any authorisation from the Government. These have since been published and seem to me eminently unsatisfactory and quite unacceptable from our point of view. However they seemed to have sufficed the TUC as a sufficient argument to enable them to get out of the difficult position in which they were placed by [Lord Chief Justice] Astbury's judgment that morning declaring the strike to be illegal and consequently making it impossible to pay out strike pay as well as exposing the leaders generally for action for damages . . .
12 May 1926: . . . found a crowd outside Downing Street and a reporter told us that the Strike was off unconditionally, the TUC leaders having come round to Downing Street to tell the PM. Apparently they did so against the miners and undoubtedly did it unconditionally though with every effort since to try and make out that it was linked up with Samuel's proposals.

15 *A. J. Cook, miners' leader:* The Nine Days *(1926)*
Only a few days of magnificent working-class effort has passed before they [the TUC negotiating committee] were once more trying to get peace at any price. They began to win over one after another of their colleagues on the General Council. Bit by bit the process of persuading the others went on until the situation of complete surrender had been reached, the situation with which we are now faced.

16 *Baldwin's statement to the House of Commons, 12 May 1926*
'The Trade Union Council came to see me this morning and told me that they had decided to call

The Baldwins at Ascot in 1926

off the General Strike forthwith. I said that it would be the immediate effort of myself and my colleagues to bring about a resumption of negotiations of the two parties in the mining industry with a view to secure the earliest possible settlement. I can only add this at the moment. The peace that I believe has come – the victory that has been won, is a victory of the common-sense of the best part of the whole of the United Kingdom, and it is of the utmost importance, at a moment like this, that the whole British people should not look backwards, but forwards – that we should resume our work in a spirit of co-operation, putting behind us all malice and all vindictiveness.'

17 *Baldwin in a speech, 13 May 1926*
The General Strike . . . has ended, as I made it clear in my speech a few nights ago that it must end, without conditions entered into by the Government. No Government confronted by such a menace, could enter into a conditional negotiation, the very undertaking of which would involve treachery to the accepted basis of our democratic Constitution.

18 *Reminiscence of Bill Carr, a Yorkshire miner at the time of the Strike, 1976*
By November, the majority of the miners were still standing firm, though a quarter of the work force, nearly a quarter of a million workers, had returned to work. The Government now offered what they thought were reasonable terms as conquerors: (*a*) Immediate resumption of work. (*b*) Longer hours to be discussed at district level. (*c*) Rates of pay '*temporarily*' at pre-strike level (but conditional on acceptance of longer hours). (*d*) No guarantee against victimisation, etc.

Daily Herald *1925*

It was not surprising, after these humiliating terms were referred by the miners' executive to the districts, that they were rejected. We knew, though, that the end was near. On November 29, it was all over. The lockout had lasted seven months, and things would never be the same again. The bitter hatred of the miners against the Tories was deep indeed, and has continued until today. This is reflected in the almost obsessional desire in every miner's family to vote Labour in every mining village. Our lads know of the tortures inflicted on their innocent families and it will never be forgotten.

The blacklist at our pit was operated ruthlessly. No mercy was shown, by the coal-owner – or even expected by the miner.

HISTORIANS' VIEWS & OPINIONS

THE VERDICT ON STANLEY BALDWIN

In the 'Outlining the Events' section a number of extracts contained the opinions of historians about Baldwin and Conservative government achievements in the years 1922–37. In this section a single, lengthier passage is included from the concluding chapter of the most authoritative biography of Baldwin by K. Middlemas and J. Barnes. This extract provides the basis for you to make a further evaluation of the Conservative record in this period of Britain's history.

Activity

a Read through the passage and then draw up a list of all the points made by the authors which are favourable to Baldwin and those which are less favourable. Move into small groups and compare each others' lists to see if you have identified similar points. Discuss any problems you have in understanding what Middlemas and Barnes are saying and see if you can resolve these problems amongst yourselves.

b Working individually, assemble as many other views on Baldwin's political record as you can find. Go back over the assessments in the previous 'Outlining the Events' section, find out what the author of your textbook thinks, go to the library and discover what other authors have concluded about Baldwin and find out what your teacher thinks. Enter these views in your 'favourable' and 'unfavourable' lists with the names of the relevant authors.

c Now spend some time thinking about what your own view of Baldwin is and how this might differ, or not, with the opinions you have been examining. Think carefully about what evidence you have to support your point of view. Make some notes about what you think.

Class Debate

The motion is: 'In times of great difficulty, Stanley Baldwin's leadership of Britain and the Conservative Party was a triumph.'

K. Middlemas and J. Barnes: Baldwin *(1969)*
The mark he made in Britain in the twentieth century is like the footprint of a colossal dinosaur, so wide that commentators, seeking traces of the man, scurry about inside it and for want of evidence set him down as unimportant, a pawn in the hands of his more powerful subordinates.

... Baldwin has usually been given credit for certain things: for his handling of the General Strike and the Abdication and for his vision of harmonious industrial relations. With a wider documentation, a great deal more can be added. His part in foreign policy led directly to the settlement of reparations and of Europe in 1924, and at Locarno in 1925. From a position of subordinate power he, more than anyone, instigated the programme of rearmament and the policy of deterrence which then, as Prime Minister, he tried to enforce in the two troubled years of 1935–7. Deterrence failed, partly through lack of time but chiefly because, in peacetime conditions, the British economy could not sustain the effort it required. Deterrence required a rational response from Germany which was not forthcoming, and it was tacitly abandoned in the spring of 1937, when Baldwin handed over strategic planning to Neville Chamberlain.

... Of course, he made mistakes. They were, however, different mistakes from those of Chamberlain whose individual decisions often made excellent sense, taken separately, but whose cumulative effect diminished his authority against opponents who never accepted rational defeat and for whom no argument was ever closed. Baldwin failed to solve the underlying problems of Britain's relative economic and strategic decline. No political leader before or since has succeeded. It may be that, in a situation where after 1918 the problems were new, in kind and degree, his Governments were composed of men whose experience was evolved before 1914 and whose methods and ideas were essentially nineteenth century. Perhaps other responses, authoritarian demands for 'efficiency', for the rule of businessmen or the clean sweep which Churchill demanded in the 1930s might have succeeded. It must remain doubtful; and comparative European experience gives such judgements little long-term support. Baldwin's years of political leadership were not unlike those of his business career: he made the machinery work, preferring a little inefficiency to a greater alienation of faith from any form of democratic government, administering with humanity and innovating with caution and in peace. The National Government might easily have been Britain's authoritarian response to the experience of the great depression. It was not so. Baldwin was aware of the balance between efficiency and social justice, between the theory of rule and the spirit of responsible co-operation and he must be judged not so much for his technical achievements as for the part he took in the evolution of democracy in Britain.

... The manner in which a leader acts is no less important than what he does. The democratic spirit was one which Baldwin made his own over a period of twenty years so that, in a sense, all his philosophic speeches were one speech, all his themes one theme. His duties were threefold: to conceive the direction, if not the details, of his government; to keep public interest alive, because without interest there can be no participation; and to act as a catalyst upon opinion.

He was a skilled broker of ideas and a brilliant publicist, for his party and the general public. His claim to express the mind of the British people may have seemed arrogant (King Edward VIII put the feeling into words when he said that the Prime Minister spoke like a Gallup poll) but, as Hegel wrote, 'the great man of the age is the one who can put into words the will of his age, tell his age what its will is, and accomplish it' ...

B ACK TO THE PRESENT

The Conservative Party has been the dominant political force in Britain in the twentieth century. Between 1900 and 1990 the Tories have been in power or have been the dominant party in coalition governments for about 60 years. The paradox of this is that the Conservative Party's main purpose is to conserve existing institutions – to resist dramatic changes – yet twentieth-century Britain has witnessed some of the greatest changes in its history. These changes have included the establishment of universal suffrage, the development of new technologies and industries transforming the quality of people's lives, the rise of strong trades unions and a 'socialist' Labour Party and a major increase in the role of the state – in health, education, housing and management of the economy. Here, then, are some questions for discussion centred on this issue of the paradoxical success of the Conservative Party this century.

1 What do you think is the secret of the Conservative Party's success this century and is this success inevitable?
2 What similarities and differences can you detect in the principles and policies of the Conservatives in the 1920s and 1930s compared with their principles and policies in the 1980s and 1990s?
3 What kinds of change do you think would need to take place in Britain and in the non-Conservative political parties in order to limit the success of the Conservative Party?
4 Why has the Labour Party, seemingly the major alternative to the Tories, failed to become the dominant political force in Britain?

5 THE RISE AND FALL OF THE LABOUR PARTY

1900–31

INTRODUCTION

The rise of the Labour Party between 1914 and 1929 represented a major departure from the pattern of nineteenth-century politics. Before 1914 the franchise was possessed by only a minority of adults (one in three since the 1884 Reform Act) and politics were dominated by the Conservative and Liberal parties – many of whose leaders were members of a governing élite who believed they had a natural and inevitable right to rule the country. The Conservative and Liberal parties represented the interests of the middle and upper classes, and it was assumed that these interests were identical with those of the working classes who made up the vast majority of British people. In the absence of any major challenge to the rule of these parties and the classes they represented, this was not an unfair assumption. Indeed, both parties received often enthusiastic backing from the skilled working classes, most of whose male members had the vote. At certain moments the non-voting working classes also showed their keen support for the governing élite – Gladstone's 'Mid-lothian' campaign in 1879, British victories in the Boer War in 1900 and the call to arms when Britain entered the war against Germany in August 1914 are notable examples.

The 20 years or so up to the First World War, however, witnessed the gradual awakening of the working classes who began to develop independent and organised responses to the abiding problem of poverty, the lack of economic freedom and representation, the absence of political rights and, in general, the awareness that the interests of the property-owning classes were not the same as those of the working classes. The numbers of workers in trade unions increased significantly and 'new' unions amongst unskilled workers achieved some success in the 1880s and the 1890s. Socialist ideas and organisations took root in certain sections of the working classes and indeed, in the 1906 Election a Labour Party with 29 MPs took its place in the House of Commons.

A WAITING GAME.

LABOUR PARTY (to CAPITALIST). "THAT'S ALL RIGHT, GUV'NOR. I WON'T LET HIM BITE YOU. (Aside, to dog.) WAIT TILL YOU'VE GROWN A BIT, MY BEAUTY, AND YOU'LL GET A BIGGER MOUTHFUL."

Punch *29 January 1908*

Despite the emergence of these radical forces in society, the dominance of the Liberal and Conservative parties did not seem under any great threat up to 1914. The prospect of a Labour government in power on the basis of a socialist programme, whilst instilling fear in the hearts of some members of the ruling classes, was seen by most as a distinctly remote possibility. Nevertheless, by the 1930s the Labour Party had established itself as the major rival to the Conservatives in a two-party political system, with the Liberal Party reduced to a small faction of divided MPs in the House of Commons. The Labour Party had also experienced two periods in government with Ramsay MacDonald as Prime Minister on both occasions. In this theme you will be examining the rise to power of the Labour Party and the ideas and policies it advocated. In the Special Topic you will be investigating the second Labour government of 1929–31 and its downfall.

K EY QUESTIONS

I What were the main events and factors explaining the emergence of the Labour Party by the 1930s?

2 To what extent was the Labour Party a socialist organisation?

3 What did the Labour Party achieve in its two spells of government in the inter-war period?

4 What was the economic and political crisis of 1931 and why did it bring the second Labour government down?

5 What contribution did Ramsay MacDonald make to the Labour Party up to 1931?

C ONTEMPORARY VIEWS & OPINIONS I

PHILIP SNOWDEN AND THE IDEA OF SOCIALISM

Before looking at the actual events of the coming to power of the Labour Party, it is important to establish a basic grasp of what the doctrine of socialism is all about. Evaluations of the rise of the Labour Party between 1900 and 1929 hinge to some extent on how the relationship between the Party and the ideas of socialism is viewed. The following extracts from a speech by Philip Snowden in 1905 provide a review of some of the general arguments for and against socialism (although the balance of the argument is clearly in favour of socialism). The speech also gives a sense of the passion which underlay the socialist commitment at the time. The following exercises are designed to improve your understanding of the concept of 'socialism' and to promote discussion and debate.

Activity

a Read through the speech carefully, and comment on the devices and techniques used by Snowden to justify his belief in socialism.

b Next, make a list of the hypothetical arguments Snowden puts forward in support of capitalism and individualism and against socialism. Do the same for the arguments he uses in favour of socialism. Now write down in two or three sentences the best definition of socialism you can think of, using the ideas in the Snowden speech.

c Get together with someone else in the class and examine and discuss each other's analyses of the speech and definitions of socialism. Have both of you come up with similar points and ideas? What do both of you think about the socialist views of Snowden?

d As a class you should now review the work you have done so far. Perhaps as a class and with the assistance of your teacher you could try to reach a consensus on a suitable definition of socialism.

Discussion

Here are a range of interrelated questions to help stimulate discussion:

- What do you think of Snowden's ideas?
- Was (is) his depiction of capitalism and individualism fair?
- Are Snowden's socialist views appropriate to society today?

Philip Snowden, leading Labour politician, discussing socialism in a speech in 1905

Remove the incentive of gain, and we are told the motive force of all progress would be destroyed. Socialism would reduce all to one dead level of mediocrity. The individual would lose his identity in a cast iron State. Men would be converted into mere machines, life would be an intolerable servitude, the nation would be converted into one huge prisonhouse. The great principle of Socialism, these objectors remind us, is Equality; and to ensure a condition of perfect equality would be the work and function of the State. Aye, the State – a monster more terrible in its strength and more tyrannical in its despotism than ever the genius of Frankenstein created. To ensure this condition of perfect equality, the State will allot to each individual his appointed task, and the whip of the State taskmaster will enforce its full discharge. Intellectual equality would be secured by depriving superior ability of all encouragement to excel, the mental condition of the lowest would be the standard to which all would be degraded to maintain a condition of perfect equality. The State would decide and direct the minutest details of each individual life. The work, the place of abode, the dress, the food, the home, the amusement, the recreation – all would be directed by the State, leaving the individual no freedom but to obey. For the certainty of being fed and clothed, we are to sacrifice the glorious privilege of individual liberty and the blessings of a civilisation won for us by the efforts of gifted free individuals in all past ages. But in the end, it is further predicted, this dread mass of equality would sink into a condition of squalid animalism spurred on to effort only by the whip of the State taskmaster. Socialism, which promised liberty, equality, and plenty, will end in a cataclysm, and want.

... This picture of the Individual under Socialism, drawn by our opponents, is an illustration of the difficulty of getting away from the familiar ideas, for it is a very faithful representation of the condition of the individual of to-day under a system of boasted individualism. What to-day, under our much vaunted individual freedom, is the type of the developed individual? If you would see the works of Competition, and the play of the Incentive of Gain, look around! You will find their monuments everywhere. Surely but it must be in grim irony we are told that Socialism will destroy individual liberty and close the avenues for intellectual development. Let those who fear that Socialism will destroy individual liberty and hinder her intellectual development go with their talk to the machine workers of our great northern towns, who are chained for eleven hours a day to a monotonous toil with the eye of the overseer and the fear of dismissal spurring them on to an exertion which leaves them at the end of their day's work physical wrecks, with no ambition but to restore their wasted energies at the nearest public house. Let them go with their talk. Let them go with their talk of the blessings of civilisation to the pottery and chemical workers, whose systems are poisoned, whose sight is destroyed, where through the bodies of the parents being saturated with poison, half the children are born dead ... – tell them to hold fast to their share of the blessings of our glorious civilisation ... – talk to them of individual liberty and warn them of the tyranny of the coming Socialism.... Why not talk of individual freedom and equality of opportunity, under a system of cannabalistic competition like this, is like the mocking laughter of a raving maniac gloating over the torture of the victim it holds in its murderous grip.

There can be no individual liberty where land, the absolute essential to a man's existence, is the property of a few, and is used by this few to dictate to the many the terms on which they shall be permitted to live. There can be no individual liberty so long as machinery which has been made by the associated labour of all workers become the property of a class, and is used by that class to keep themselves in idleness and to pay the workers wages by wealth taken from them. Under such a system, where the common needs of life are the object of a competitive struggle in which all goes to the victors, leaving nothing to the vanquished; in which the sole object of life is to secure a monopoly of what all need so that by this monopoly one may get his fellows into his power to use them for his own selfish ends – under such a system there can be no individuality. . . .

. . . Look where we will in our life to-day and we find everywhere this lack of individuality, a slavery to fashion, to conventional ideas. . . .

Our ideal of individual liberty is freedom to develop those qualities which will enable a man to get rich. It is true that Socialism will destroy such individual liberty as that – the liberty of brute force and cunning wit to crush the weak and rob the innocent.

Socialism, by making land and machinery the common property of all, and using these instru-

ments to supply material needs, will completely change the business and object of life. Socialism will change human nature. The opportunity makes the man. Socialism will take away the desire for accumulating riches . . . under Socialism, the possession of riches will cease to be a ruling passion, for honest labour will be a guarantee against want, and riches will no longer be the passport to social position. Under such condition the possession of riches will be a superfluous burden which no sane man will wish to bear. . . .

When the acquiring of riches has ceased to be the object of life; when men's minds are free from the carking care of providing for the morrow, when the perpetual fear of poverty is removed; then men will seek for fresh avenues for the satisfaction of their individual desires. When men have leisure, and they are not enervated by exhausting toil, or demoralised by superfluous riches, they cannot help themselves from following their natural instincts. Man, under natural, that is under favourable, material conditions, is an intellectual being, and his intellectual aspirations will manifest themselves when his material needs are satisfied. . . .

OUTLINING THE EVENTS

THE EMERGENCE OF THE LABOUR PARTY 1900–31

The theme begins with activities concerned with establishing the narrative of the rise and temporary fall of the Labour Party in the period 1900–31. The activities are based on a miscellany of extracts taken from historical dictionaries and various kinds of statistics. The overview on events you should gain from the exercise will act as springboard for you to develop a deeper knowledge of the facts and arguments of the theme.

Activity

a Use the information to put together a chronology which encapsulates the main events in the development of the Labour Party in the period 1900–31. Divide up your chronology under different headings to indicate distinct phases in the emergence and the coming to power of the Labour Party. The investigation for this piece of work could be done in pairs, although everyone should finish up with their own chronology.

b Use your chronology and the extracts to make a list of as many reasons as you can find which explain in some way the rise of the Labour Party in this period. Discuss in groups and/or as a class the explanations you have identified. As the discussion progresses, note down any reasons you have overlooked.

Further Reading and Research

Now carry out some further reading and note-making on the history of the Labour Party, using textbooks, handouts and information from your teacher. The work you have done so far will provide a guide for your research. Set out below are some of the questions which you should be able to answer fairly fully as a result of your investigations. The questions relate to the period 1914–29.

- Why did the Labour Party emerge as a strong and unified party in 1918 – particularly in contrast to the Liberal Party?
- How did the Labour Party come to form its first government, albeit a minority one, in 1924?
- What were the aims and achievements of Mac-Donald's administration, and why had it fallen by October 1924?
- Why was the Labour Party able to return to power in 1929?
- What was the difference between 'direct action' and 'constitutionalist' or 'parliamentarist' tactics in securing radical change?

Discussion

Hold a discussion around the following two issues: 'Was the rise of the Labour party inevitable?' and 'How great was Labour's achievement by 1929?'

---

1 The Illustrated Dictionary of British History *ed. A. Marwick (1980)*

Labour Party By resolution of the 1899 trades union congress the Labour Representation Committee was formed, linking together unions, the Independent Labour Party and the socialist societies in a body whose one fundamental objective was to get labour men into parliament. In 1901, 3 LRC MPs were elected. Ramsay MacDonald, secretary of the LRC, in 1903 negotiated a secret pact with the Liberal whips to give the LRC's candidates a straight run against the Tories. As a result 29 candidates were elected in 1906, and in

parliament decided to call themselves the Labour party. One other trade union MP (elected as a Liberal) joined them, bringing the 1st parliamentary Labour party total to 30.

In 1909 the party was strengthened by the adherence of the Miners' Federation of Great Britain, hitherto a stronghold of 'Lib-Lab' politics; but it made no further electoral progress until after World War I. The extended franchise of 1918, growing trade union membership, the greater wartime role of the state, and the involvement of Labour politicians in government, prepared Labour to take advantage of the wartime decline of the Liberals, and in 1918 Sidney Webb and Henderson created a new constitution which provided for individual membership but retained the ILP, as an autonomous party, within a federal Labour structure. Although Labour gained only 57 seats in 1918, it increased this to 142 in 1922, while the Liberals remained divided. MacDonald its leader since 1922, was permitted by the other parties to form a minority government after the 1923 election. Although unremarkable save for John Wheatley's Housing Act and some conciliatory gestures in foreign policy, it proved decisive in making Labour the natural alternative to the Conservatives. However, the immaturity of its political ideology – a combination of orthodox Liberal attitudes in finance and foreign affairs with a moralistic commitment to a vague 'socialism' – proved disastrous when a further minority Labour government (1929–31) had to cope with the onset of world depression. Divided in its attitude to cuts in welfare benefits, it lost its most important leaders – MacDonald, Snowden and J. H. Thomas (1874–1949) – to the National Government, and was crushed in the election, its MPs falling in numbers from 288 to 52, of whom five disaffiliated with the ILP in 1932.

2 The Illustrated Dictionary of British History *ed. A. Marwick (1980)*

Taff Vale judgment 1901. A legal decision making the Amalgamated Society of Railway Servants liable for costs incurred as a result of a dispute with the Taff Vale Railway Company, south Wales. This gave a great impetus to the nascent Labour Party. In response to union agitation the Liberals passed the 1906 Trades Disputes Act, freeing unions from such liability.

3 *General Election results*

Date	Seats Contested	Members Returned	Total Votes Polled
1900	15	2	63,304
1906	50	29	323,195
1910 (Jan.)	78	40	505,657
1910 (Dec.)	56	42	371,772
1918	361	57	2,244,945
1922	411	142	4,241,383
1923	422	191	4,438,508
1924	512	151	5,489,077
1929	571	288	8,389,512
1931	491	46	6,362,561
1935	552	154	8,325,491

Adapted from H. Pelling: A Short History of the Labour Party *(1982)*

4 *D. Butler and A. Sloman:* British Political Facts 1900–1979 *(1980)*

The Labour Party – Organisation and Constitutions

The Labour Representation Committee was formed on 27 Feb 1900 to promote a distinct Labour group in Parliament, representing the affiliated trade unions and socialist societies. After the General Election of 1906 the L.R.C. group of M.P.s decided to assume the title of 'Labour Party' and elected their first officers and whips. Policy was determined by the Labour Party through the annual conference and its executive authority, the National Executive Committee. There was no official party leader, but an annually elected chairman of the parliamentary party. There were scarcely any official Labour Party constituency organisations (except for those provided by local trades councils, groups of miners' lodges, and local branches of the I.L.P.). In 1914 there were only two constituency associations with individual members, Woolwich and Barnard Castle, which Will Crooks and Arthur Henderson had built up on their own.

The Reorganisation of the Labour Party, 1918

The reorganisation of the Labour Party was projected by Arthur Henderson in collaboration with Sidney Webb. Their main aims were to provide local Labour Parties in every constituency or group of constituencies. These local Labour Parties were to be based fundamentally on individual subscribing membership, though representation was provided for trades councils, trade union branches, and socialist societies. The members of the N.E.C. were to be elected by the annual conference as a whole (though eleven were to be elected from candidates nominated by the trade unions and socialist societies as a single group, five were to represent the Local Labour Parties, and four were to be women). The scheme also involved an increase in affiliation fees.

The original plan was amended, so that the N.E.C. was increased to a membership of 23 (adding two to the number specified for affiliated organisations). It was agreed that the election programme should be produced by the N.E.C. and P.L.P. jointly – subject to the aims of the Party and the decisions of the annual conferences. The object of the pre-war Party had been to 'organise and maintain in Parliament and in the country a political Labour Party'. In 1918 this was changed to a new formula: 'to secure for the producers by hand and by brain the full fruits of their industry, and the most equitable distribution thereof that may be possible, upon the basis of the common ownership of the means of production and the best obtainable system of popular administration and control of each industry and service'.

5 Dictionary of British History *ed. J.P. Kenyon (1988)*

Independent Labour Party (ILP). A socialist organization founded in 1893 under the leadership of Keir Hardie. The ILP helped to establish the Labour Representation Committee (1900), which became the Labour Party in 1906. After individuals became eligible to join the Labour Party directly rather than through the ILP (1918), ILP influence waned. Disaffiliated from the Labour Party following policy disagreements (1932), it was represented in parliament by a steadily declining number of MPs, the last losing his seat in 1959.

The first Labour Government in Britain, 1924
Left to right: J. H. Thomas, Colonial Secretary;
Ramsay MacDonald, Prime Minister; Arthur Hen-
derson, Home Secretary

6 A Dictionary of Modern History *ed. A.W.*
Palmer (1975)

MacDonald, J. Ramsay (1866–1937). Born in
poverty in a small Scottish fishing village. He
joined the I.L.P. in 1894 and was a first-rate
organizer, although fired by ambition for social
success. He became an M.P. in 1906 and was
chairman of the I.L.P. 1906–9, but he had already
helped to found the Labour Representation Committee, and from 1911 to 1914 he led the Parliamentary Labour Party, with considerable dex-
terity. He lost influence during the war and was
defeated in the 1918 election. In 1922 he was
successful at Aberavon; he was promptly re-elected
leader of the Parliamentary Labour Party (largely
through Scottish support), and thus became Leader
of the Opposition, since Labour had 25 more seats
than the Liberals. After the indecisive 1923 election, he agreed to head a Labour Minority Government (January 1924), and was his own Foreign
Secretary. The election of November 1924 (held
under the shadow of the 'Zinoviev Letter') led to
MacDonald's defeat, but he was again Prime
Minister in 1929. The worsening financial situation
precipitated a split in his Government in August
1931, and he formed a coalition (the National
Government), which the majority of the Labour
Party refused to support. He led the coalition for
four years but was a mere figurehead for a predominantly Conservative administration. He re-

signed in June 1935 and was succeeded by Baldwin.

7 *Labour Party membership*

Date	Indi-vidual Member-ship	T.U. Member-ship	Co-operative Societies Member-ship	Socialist Societies etc. Member-ship	Total
1900–1	Nil	353,070	Nil	22,861	375,931
1901–2	Nil	455,450	Nil	13,861	469,311
1902–3	Nil	847,315	Nil	13,835	861,150
1903–4	Nil	956,025	Nil	13,775	969,800
1904–5	Nil	855,270	Nil	14,730	900,000
1905–6	Nil	904,496	Nil	16,784	921,280
1906–7	Nil	975,182	2,271	20,885	998,338
1907	Nil	1,049,673	472	22,267	1,072,413
1908	Nil	1,127,035	565	27,465	1,158,565
1909	Nil	1,450,648	678	30,982	1,486,308
1910	Nil	1,394,403	760	31,377	1,430,539
1911	Nil	1,501,783	911	31,404	1,539,092
1012	Nil	1,858,178	1,073	31,237	1,895,498
1913	Nil	Not com-piled‡	1,328	33,304	Not compiled
1914	Nil	1,572,391	1,526	33,230	1,612,147
1915	Nil	2,053,735	1,792	32,828	2,093,365
1916	Nil	2,170,782	1,792	42,190	2,219,764
1917	Nil	2,415,383	2,608	47,140	2,465,131
1918	Not compiled	2,960,409	Nil	52,720	3,013,129
1919	,,	3,464,020	Nil	47,270	3,511,290
1920	,,	4,317,537	Nil	42,270	4,359,807
1921	,,	3,973,558	Nil	36,803	4,010,361
1922	,,	3,279,276	Nil	31,760	3,311,036
1923	,,	3,120,149	Nil	35,762	3,155,911
1924	,,	3,158,002	Nil	36,397	3,194,399
1925	,,	3,337,635	Nil	36,235	3,373,870
1926	,,	3,352,347	Nil	35,939	3,388,286
1927	,,	3,238,939	20,000	34,676	3,293,615
1928	214,970	2,025,139	20,000	32,060	2,292,169
1929	227,897	2,044,279	32,000	26,669	2,330,845
1930	277,211	2,011,484	32,000	26,213	2,346,908
1931	297,003	2,024,216	32,000	4,847	2,358,066
1932	371,607	1,960,269	32,040	7,871	2,371,787
1933	366,013	1,899,007	32,040	7,970	2,305,030
1934	381,259	1,857,524	22,040	7,667	2,278,490
1935	419,311	1,912,924	36,000	9,280	2,377,515
1936	430,694	1,968,538 538	36,000	9,125	2,444,357

Adapted from H. Pelling: A Short History of the Labour Party
(1982)

8 *The Electorate 1900–37*

Year	Population	Population over 21	Electorate	Electorate as % of Adult Population Male	Total
1900	41,155,000	22,675,000	6,730,935	58	27
1910	44,915,000	26,134,000	7,694,741	58	28
1919	44,599,000	27,364,000	21,755,583	—	78
1929	46,679,000	31,711,000	28,850,870	—	90
1939	47,762,000	32,855,000	32,403,559	—	97

Adapted from Butler and Sloman: British Political Facts 1900–1979
(1980)

9 The Illustrated Dictionary of British History *ed. A. Marwick (1980)*

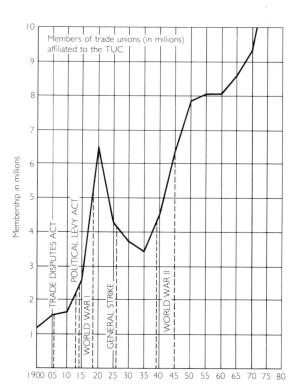

Members of trade unions (in millions) affiliated to the TUC

10 *J. Stevenson: British Society 1914–45 (1984)*
The Survival of Poverty
While the social investigations carried out between the wars demonstrated that there had been significant advances in average living standards and levels of material comfort, even using the most stringent standards, they also revealed that a considerable proportion of the population remained in poverty, with its attendant problems of poor housing and ill-health.

11 *Percentage of total wealth owned by top groups*

Wealth Group	1911–13	1924–30	1936
Top 1%	65·5	59·5	56·0
Top 5%	86·0	82·5	81·0
Top 10%	90·0	89·5	88·0
Top 20%	—	96·0	94·0
Top 25%	—	—	—

Adapted from Butler and Sloman: British Political Facts 1900–1979 (1980)

12 *Unemployment*

Year	Percentage Rate
1918	0·8
1919	2·1
1920	2·0
1921	12·9
1922	14·3
1923	11·7
1924	10·3
1925	11·3
1926	12·5
1927	9·7
1928	10·8
1929	10·4
1930	16·0
1931	21·3
1932	22·1

Adapted from Trends in British Society Since 1900 *ed. A. H. Halsey*

13 *Number of days lost through strikes*

1914	9,878
1915	2,953
1916	2,446
1917	5,647
1918	5,875
1919	34,969
1920	26,568
1921	85,872
1922	19,850
1923	10,672
1924	8,424
1925	7,952
1926	162,233
1927	1,174
1928	1,388
1929	8,287

Adapted from J. Stevenson: British Society 1914–45 (1984)

14 The Illustrated Dictionary of British History *ed. A. Marwick (1980)*
General Strike 1926. The strike was called by the trades union congress (4 May) in support of the

miners, after the breakdown of wage negotiations. The Baldwin government was well-prepared: when the 'first line' industries – transport, building, mining and printing – struck it made effective use of road transport, the press (when it appeared) and broadcasting, and the moderates on the TUC general council capitulated after 9 days. The miners stayed out on strike for the rest of the year. The government took its revenge by passing the Trades Disputes Act (1927), outlawing general strikes and making the political levy that trade unionists paid to the Labour party a case of 'contracting in' rather than 'contracting out'.

15 *R. Moore:* The Emergence of the Labour Party *1880–1924 (1978)*

Henderson, Arthur

1863–1935. Born in Scotland but family moved to north-east England when nine. Apprenticed as an iron-moulder. Active in trade union and local government affairs on Tyneside. Liberal agent for Sir Joseph Pease at Barnard Castle (1895–1903)

then left the Liberals and won the seat for Labour. At various times from then on he held the positions of chief whip, parliamentary chairman, treasurer and secretary. Distinguished ministerial career took him into Lloyd George's war cabinet and he was later home secretary (1924) and foreign secretary (1929–31).

Snowden, Philip

1864–1937. Born near Keighley. Father a weaver and a strong Wesleyan. Avoided going into the mill by becoming a pupil teacher. Later was a clerk before securing entry into the civil service as an excise man. After being crippled as the result of a cycling accident in 1891, he spent more time in serious study and reading which led to his conversion to socialism. Very active 1895–1905 in propaganda work for the ILP. MP 1906–18, 1922–31. Soon made a reputation as the party's financial expert and was chancellor of the exchequer in both MacDonald's Labour governments. Created Viscount Snowden in 1931.

C ONTEMPORARY VIEWS & OPINIONS II

THE LABOUR PARTY AND SOCIALISM IN THE 1920s

This section is designed to promote further thought and discussion on the socialist beliefs of the Labour Party in the period 1918–29 and the strategies used by the Party to implement those beliefs. The previous 'Contemporary Views and Opinions' section based on Snowden's speech of 1905 will be relevant. The tasks can be the basis for written work or for discussion carried out individually or in small groups.

Activity

a Read through the extracts and summarise the evidence which demonstrates the Labour Party's commitment to socialism.

b What appear to be the criticisms made by the ILP from within the Labour Party and by the Communist

Party from without about the socialism of the Labour Party in the 1920s? In what ways do Sidney Webb's comments reinforce these criticisms?

c What were the main tactics by which the Labour Party hoped to achieve socialism? Why do you think the Labour Party refused to endorse the affiliation of the Communist Party in 1924? What is the supporting evidence for the view you take?

d To what extent do you think the various criticisms of the Labour Party were justified – especially in relation to the record of the 1924 government?

Further Reading and Research

The questions above are concerned as much with tactics as with the nature of the Labour Party's 'socialist' policies. Find out something more about the actual policy proposals of the Labour Party in the 1920s and 1930s. To what extent do you think these proposals would have achieved the kind of socialist society outlined by Snowden in his speech in 1905? What do you think the Communist Party would have thought about some of these policies?

---

1 *'Labour and the New Social Order' – Labour Party statement of policy, 1918*
... The war, which has scared the old Political Parties right out of their dogmas, has taught every statesman and every government official, to his enduring surprise, how very much more can be done along the lines that we have laid down [at Labour Party Conferences] than he had ever thought possible. What we now promulgate as our policy, whether for opposition or in office, is not merely this or that specific reform but a deliberately thought-out systematic, and comprehensive plan for that immediate social rebuilding which any Ministry ... will be driven to undertake. The Four Pillars of the House that we propose to erect, resting upon the common foundation of the Democratic control of society in all its activities, may be termed, respectively:
(a) The Universal Enforcement of the National Minimum [Standard of Life];
(b) The Democratic Control of Industry;
(c) The Revolution in National Finance;
(d) The Surplus Wealth for the Common Good.

2 *The Labour Party Constitution of 1918, clause IV*
To secure for the producers by hand or by brain the full fruits of their industry, and the most equitable distribution thereof that may be possible, upon the basis of the common ownership of the means of production and the best obtainable system of popular administration and control of each industry or service;

3 *Statement endorsed by the Labour Party Conference, 1924*
The affiliation of the Communist Party has been consistently refused on the ground that neither its objects nor methods are in harmony with those of the Labour Party.
The Labour Party seeks to achieve the Socialist Commonwealth by means of parliamentary democracy.
The Communist Party seeks to achieve the 'Dictatorship of the Proletariat' by armed revolution.

4 *Herbert Morrison in the President's Address at the Annual Conference of the Labour Party, October 1929*
The Conference to-day meets in high spirits; the Party and the Labour Government are doing well. Success is not spoiling us. We refuse to water-down our final objectives. Let it be understood by everybody that the purpose of the Labour Party is as much as ever to secure the conquest of our country for the people of our country, the conquest of the world for the workers of the world. We go forward to make material wealth the servant of mankind and not the master of mankind.

We aim at a new society – the Socialist Commonwealth – and we aim at this society not merely that we may secure material betterment in the lot of the people: indeed, we seek this material improvement, not as an end in itself, but as a stepping-stone to the mental and spiritual regeneration of mankind.

5 *Willie Gallacher, from a speech at the Sixth Communist Party of Great Britain Conference, 1924*
Any Labour Government earnestly desirous of serving the workers must be ready at any moment of crisis to scrap procedure and openly identify itself with the workers, throwing itself energetically into the struggle as a part of the Labour Movement organised to combat capitalism. No one can accuse the present Labour Government of having the slightest tendency in this direction. It has been rightly called Conservative, for it would be difficult to find another government in this time of capitalist decay so keenly anxious to conserve the whole outworn fabric of Parliament and Parliamentary procedure. Such a government is extremely useful to the bourgeoisie, especially now when the general collapse of capitalism has thrown up so many conflicting elements in *their* own ranks, and they are taking full advantage of it. They are deliberately using it to disrupt the Labour Movement.

Comrades, I say to you with all earnestness, if the Labour Movement is saved from disruption, it is the Communist Party that will save it.

Already the Labour Government has thrown over all its original pretentions. It started off by assuring the movement that it only contemplated taking office for a short period for the purpose of preparing a definite Labour programme, and then going to the country and fighting both of the other parties. This met with general approval. But no sooner were they in office than they commenced playing up for an extended period of administration and for that purpose cynically scrapped anything and everything that could have distinguished a Labour Government from an ordinary capitalist administration.

6 *James Maxton, Labour MP and leading ILP spokesman, from a speech at the Labour Party Conference, 1927*

He wanted a programme that would be based on the assumption that they could get a majority for Socialism at the next General Election – a clear majority with a Socialist issue undiluted to meet people here, or approach people there, or interest people in some other place. He believed they could get such a majority at the next Election, and he wanted a programme that would be so devised that the Labour Cabinet coming into office would believe and intend to carry out in the term of their office two things: one, that their operations should carry them, before their term of office was concluded, right into the very heart of the citadels of Capitalism, and that they would have control by the end of that period of office of all the nerve-centres of industry and commerce throughout the country. That he wanted in a programme which he would be asked to support loyally; and that he would support loyally. Further, he wanted the programme to provide that while the Cabinet was taking over the Capitalist system and converting it into a Socialist system, every man, woman and child in this country, old or young, strong or feeble, employed or unemployed, should be assured of a standard of life that none of them need blush for shame about.

7 *Ramsay MacDonald, Leader of the Labour Party, replying to Maxton at the Labour Party Conference, 1927*

The principle in the background of their programme was "Socialism." Let them make no mis-

take about that. It was not in the background as a sort of nice palliative, but it was in the background as the completion of what was going on and being worked out on the great stage of the House of Commons and of Parliament in general. Socialism alone supplied the meaning of what they were doing for their miner friends, what they were doing for the unemployed, what they were doing for the widows and orphans. Their work would be absolutely meaningless unless they were Socialists and working it all into the great Socialist programme. Selecting what this item, that item, and the other item should be was the work of a Government that had Socialism constantly before its eyes. He repudiated these cheap sneers as to whether they were going to get Socialism in a thousand years. It was constantly and always in their minds.

8 *G.D.H. Cole:* The History of the Labour Party from 1914 *(1948)*

As against this the ILP and its sympathisers wanted to commit the Labour Party as decisively as possible to Socialism, not merely as an ideal, but as a practical immediate objective, and further to commit it to their particular notion of the way to achieve 'Socialism in Our Time.' Maxton, in his speech, prophesied that the next General Election would make Labour the largest party, but would fail to give it a clear majority. He wanted to make sure that, if a second minority Government took office, it would produce a challenging policy on which it could court defeat in Parliament in order to make a further appeal to the electors. This was, of course, exactly what MacDonald did not wish to have forced on him. when Maxton complained that *Labour and the Nation* gave the Socialist MPs and propagandists no guidance at all upon the immedi-

'*I have a little shadow that goes in and out with me*' – Daily Express *22 September 1924*

ate policy of the Labour Party, the sponsors of the draft replied that this was not what it was meant for, and that its purpose was to enlighten public opinion concerning the Labour Party's 'conception of society' and in MacDonald's world, 'to draw the minds of the electors from mere patchwork and direct them to fine, creative, and constructive work.' The critics retorted that what MacDonald regarded as 'fine, creative and constructive' appeared to them to be no better than a cloud of words, through which nothing definite could be seen.

9 Beatrice Webb's Diaries 1924–1932 *ed. M. Cole (1952)*
MacDonald wants 8 million voters behind him and means to get them even if this entails shedding the ILP, the idealistically revolutionary section who pushed him into power. That ladder will be kicked down! MacDonald is in fact returning to his policy of 1910–14, as we always foresaw he would; but with a different facet. In those years he was willing to merge the Labour Party in the Liberal Party: to-day he realises that the Liberal Party is dead; so he is attracting, by his newly-won prestige and personal magnetism, the Conservative Collectivist element – but he insists that his collectivists shall dub themselves 'Labour' and accept him as their Leader. I do not accuse him of treachery: for he was never a Socialist, either revolutionary like Lansbury or administrative like the Webbs; he was always a believer in individualist political demo-cracy tempered in its expression by Utopian Social-ism. Where he has lacked integrity is in *posing* as a Socialist, and occasionally using revolutionary jargon.

10 *Herbert Asquith:* Memories and Reflections *(December 1923)*
You would be amused if you saw the contents of my daily post-bag: appeals, threats, prayers from all parts, and from all sorts and conditions of men, women and lunatics, to step in and save the coun-try from the horrors of Socialism and Confisca-tion. . . .

S PECIAL TOPIC

THE SECOND LABOUR GOVERNMENT AND THE CRISIS OF 1931

The 20 secondary source extracts here provide a range of evidence and opinion relating to the second Labour government 1929–31 and its downfall in August 1931. The activities are devised to help you to establish an outline knowledge of the topic and to gain an insight into different historians' interpretations of the govern-ment – in particular MacDonald's 'betrayal'. As usual, the extracts and activities are best used in association with your textbooks and other relevant sources.

Activity I

Working individually, use the source extracts to con-struct six separate sets of notes under the headings:

'Foreign Policy' (extract 2), 'Domestic Policy' (extract 3), 'Unemployment and Economic Depression' (extracts 4–8), 'The Economic Crisis of 1931' (extracts 9–11), 'MacDonald and the Forming of a National Government in August 1931' (extracts 10–17) and 'The Continuing Crisis August–October 1931' (extracts 18–20). Supple-ment your six sections with information from other sources where necessary. Keep your notes brief and to the point.

Activity II

To help you advance your general understanding of the topic make sure you can answer the following ques-tions. This can be a verbal or written exercise, carried out individually or in pairs.

a What positions and responsibilities did the following hold in the Second Labour Government of June 1929:

MacDonald, Snowden, Henderson, Thomas and Mosley?

b What was the voting position of the Labour government in the House of Commons in June 1929? What aims did MacDonald have for his government?

c What was the Mosley Memorandum and why was it rejected? What criticisms and comments do the historians Pugh, Miliband and Skidelsky make about Labour's unemployment policy (or lack of one)? What is your view of their views?

d What was the relationship between the three different economic problems which Labour faced in 1931 – rising unemployment, the budget deficit and the run on gold? (This is a very hard question and you might need some help.)

e According to the extracts here at least, why did MacDonald form a 'National' government in August 1931? What other options did he have?

f What was the position of each of the following as regards making budget cuts, including cuts in unemployment benefit, in August 1931: Sir George May's Parliamentary Committee; MacDonald; Snowden; the Cabinet as a whole; the Opposition leaders; the TUC; the bankers?

Activity III

a Working individually and concentrating on extracts 12–16 write an appraisal of about 400–500 words of the different historians' views of MacDonald and his formation of a 'National' government in August 1931. Include in your appraisal an assessment of the views of the authors of the textbooks you are using. Also, bear in mind the ideas which emerged from the previous 'Contemporary Views and Opinions' sections.

b Now, exchange appraisals with another member of the class and make an assessment of each other's piece of work. What has been missed out or misunderstood in your partner's appraisal? Read the relevant extracts again if necessary. Hold a brief discussion with your partner to try to resolve differences and problems in each other's interpretations.

Discussion

At this point you have the opportunity of giving full vent to your own views and ideas about MacDonald and his so-called 'betrayal' of the labour movement in 1931.

The following questions could act as the focus for your discussion:

- Who was to blame for the downfall of the government in 1931?
- Was MacDonald a traitor to the Labour Party?

1 *1929 election results*

	Total Votes	M.P.s Elected	Candi-dates	Unopposed Returns	% Share of Total Vote
Conservative	8,656,473	260	590	4	38·2
Liberal	5,308,510	59	513	—	23·4
Labour	8,389,512	288	571	—	37·1
Communist	50,614	—	25	—	0·3
Others	243,266	8	31	3	1·0
Elec. 28,850,870 Turnout 76·1%	22,648,375	615	1,730	7	100·0

Adapted from D. Butler and A. Sloman: British Political Facts 1900–1979 *(1980)*

2 *R. Rhodes James:* The British Revolution *(1978)*
Although Henderson was Foreign Secretary in title, foreign affairs remained the obsession of the Prime Minister. He warmly supported Irwin's policies in India, pressed forward eagerly with international disarmament, and had his reward in the London Naval Conference of March 1930, in which Britain, America and Japan agreed to ratios which were certainly not to the advantage of the British. Henderson, for his part, worked successively for the resumptions of full diplomatic relations with the Soviet Union; the final withdrawal of Allied troops from the Rhineland; the acceptance of the principle of compulsory arbitration in international disputes; and a sharp reversal of policy in Egypt, starting with the removal of Lord Lloyd as High Commissioner and culminating in negotiations towards an Anglo-Egyptian Treaty. These initatives, in the context of 1929–30, can be fairly regarded as enlightened, progressive, and sensible. In this field at least, Labour had gone far to prove that it was responsible and fully fitted for government.

3 *G. Cole and R. Postgate:* The Common People 1746–1946 *(1949)*
If there had been no world crisis, the achievements of the second Labour Government might have

made in history a respectable, though by no means a brilliant, showing. In the course of 1929-31 they substantially reduced the hardships in unemployment insurance, by removing the provision which allowed applicants for benefit to be arbitrarily disqualified on the ground that they were 'not genuinely seeking work.' They extended the contributory pensions scheme (started in 1925 by the Conservatives) to about three hundred thousand persons previously excluded from it, passed an important Act for the improvement of mental hospitals, and set on foot a big housing and slum-clearance scheme under the Housing Act of 1930. They extended the Export Credits scheme to the Soviet Union, and made loans and grants more easily available both at home and by the Development Act and in the Colonies by the Colonial Development Act. They passed a Land Utilization Act for State demonstration farms and land settlement (but the clause providing for the State farms was struck out by the House of Lords), and the first Agricultural Marketing Act, setting up Marketing Boards for agricultural products. They instituted a system of public regulation of road transport under the Transport Act of 1930, and set on foot a scheme, subsequently enacted in a mutilated form by the National Government, for a London Passenger Transport Board.

4 *R. Miliband:* Parliamentary Socialism *(1972)*
At the time the Government took office, the number of insured workers unemployed in Britain was 1,164,000. There was at first much talk of vast schemes for the creation of work. This came to nothing. By July 1930, the unemployment figures had topped the two million mark. However, the very size of this stagnant pool of deprived humanity was a useful alibi to the Government. Britain, Ministers said, was engulfed in a world-wide 'economic blizzard', for which the Government was not responsible and which it could not reasonably be expected to control. Indeed, some of them said, the crisis was the most evident sign of the irrationality of capitalism. The crisis could only be resolved by a new, socialist order of society. But since the times, or the electorate, or the parliamentary situation, were not ripe for so fundamental a transformation, there was little that could im-

mediately be done.

It was an argument which was then deemed quite plausible by many people in the Labour movement. In fact, part of the argument, that which posited the virtual irremediability of crisis in a capitalist society, was an intrinsic element of left-wing thinking. Where the left differed from the Government was in its insistence that the latter should introduce socialist measures and, if defeated, go to the country on a socialist programme.

5 *Economic Depression 1929-33*

	Wholesale Prices (Board of Trade) 1929=100	Registered Unemployed (Ministry of Labour)		Index of Industrial Activity
		%	Numbers (000)	
1929	100	10·4	1,249	118·7
1930	87·5	16·1	1,975	107·4
1931	76·8	21·3	2,698	86·8
1932	74·9	22·1	2,813	81·1
1933	75·0	19·9	2,221	89·3

From S. Pollard: The Development of the British Economy 1914-50 *(1962)*

6 *R. Rhodes James:* The British Revolution *(1978)*
All the Government could do, and all that it did do, was to increase the unemployment benefits to the unemployed and abandon the principle of contributory relief. For this they were assailed by the Opposition for their extravagance and from the Labour back benches for their niggardliness. The Government retreated into a cloud of impressive-sounding Commissions and Committees. A Committee of Enquiry into Finance and Industry under Lord Macmillan was appointed in November 1929; in 1930 an Economic Advisory Council under MacDonald's chairmanship was set up. Later in 1930 a Liberal-Labour committee was established, followed by a Royal Commission. Most serious of all, Snowden virtually abdicated the Government's responsibility when he agreed to the appointment of a Committee on National Expenditure chaired by Sir George May in February 1931. Until the Committee reported the Government could only mark time. Meanwhile, what Churchill called 'the economic blizzard' grew even more fierce. The collapse of the Credit Anstalt in May caused further drainage of gold from London. Unemployment approached the figure of three million.

7 *M. Pugh:* The Making of Modern British Politics 1867–1939 *(1983)*

Only Mosley, a junior minister under Thomas, supplied the government with a coherent programme in February 1930 in a memorandum that envisaged deliberate expansion of purchasing power, restrictions upon imports, and public control of banking so as to finance industrial development. Although it seems that MacDonald had grown privately sceptical of Snowden's faith in balanced budgets and free trade, he did nothing to check the Cabinet's endorsements of the Treasury view: public works schemes would take a long time to bring into operation; they were inherently uneconomic, and since no idle reserves existed, they would only damage private industry by robbing it of investment. Mosley resigned, and Thomas escaped to the Colonial Office to be replaced by Vernon Hartshorn, upon whom the Prime Minister showered pathetic letters entreating him to do his job and put 'pressure on industries to put themselves in order'.

8 *R. Skidelsky:* Oswald Mosley *(1975)*

Mosley's memorandum was far from offering a comprehensive alternative to the Government's policy. Much of it seemed to be calling only for a comprehensive enquiry. To the modern reader it seems embarrassingly free of the weighty statistical matter that would have sharpened and supported its main thesis. Nevertheless, the point at issue with the Treasury emerges clearly enough. Mosley believed in state intervention. His proposals for reorganising government, setting up a state finance corporation, mounting a central public works programme, all reflect his view that the State must assume responsibility for economic welfare. The Treasury believed in the free market. All its arguments against Mosley's proposals were restatements of classic objections to state intervention in the economy. It would create inefficiency. It would impede the normal forces working for recovery, etc. Mosley knew all about these arguments. They were the arguments of Labour's *opponents*. He could hardly expect the Party to take them seriously since, in his view, it had arisen to challenge them. Had the free market been employing the community's resources profitably and wisely there would have been no slump, no unemployment, no need for government interference and no need for socialism. The Labour Party had arisen precisely because the system defended by the Treasury was breaking down.

9 *R. Rhodes James:* The British Revolution *(1978)*

By the early summer of 1931 the Labour Government was in serious trouble. Unemployment continued to rise with inexorable force, the value of British exports fell, Ministers became distraught and helpless, awaiting the solemn judgement of the May Committee. The party was confused and demoralised. By the time the May Committee reported at the end of July, withdrawals from London were running at nearly £2·5 million a day, and unemployment was over three million.

The Report of the May Committee was released after Parliament had risen for the summer recess. Its salient conclusions were that there would be a deficit of £120 millions by April 1932; that new taxation, to raise £24 millions, was required; and that immediate economies, totalling £96 millions, were needed, of which £66½ millions were to be achieved by the reduction of unemployment relief, including a twenty per cent reduction in benefit payments. By this time the situation was almost out of control; a run on sterling had already begun, and the May Report caused a panic among foreigners with short-term British investments.

10 *D. Marquand:* Coalitions in British Politics *ed. D. Butler (1978)*

In the most disastrous blunder of his [MacDonald's] life, he rejected Keynes's advice to devalue sterling, and fought with stubborn passion for cuts in spending on unemployment benefit large enough to balance the budget in the way that the Treasury and Bank of England thought essential to save the parity. But although this could reasonably be described as a coalition policy, there is no evidence that he wanted a coalition Government to carry it out. The Labour Government's death warrant was signed in the evening of 20 August, when a deputation from the TUC General Council made it clear that it would accept no cut in spending on the unemployed. On 21 August the Cabinet agreed to an economy programme of £56 million – £22 million less than the figure which had been unanimously agreed by the Cabinet economy committee three days before – but refused to make any cut in unemployment benefit. The Bank of England made it clear that this figure was too small to stop the drain of sterling; that evening, Neville Chamberlain and Sir Herbert Samuel, who were deputising for their respective party leaders, told MacDonald that if he wished to form a government with their co-operation, they would be prepared to serve under him. So far from accepting their offer MacDonald spent most of 22 and 23 August in a desperate attempt to persuade his colleagues to raise their bid by £20 millions – £12.5 millions of it to come from a cut in unemployment benefit of 10 per cent. He did not give up until the evening of 23 August, when it became clear that the Cabinet was split beyond repair. At lunchtime on 23 August, moreover, he explicitly decided not to form a National Government if the Labour Government should fall, on the grounds that if he did so he would 'face the whole antagonism of the Labour movt.'. Instead, he planned to leave office with his colleagues, and support the cuts he believed to be necessary from the Opposition benches below the gangway. He did not begin to waver until that evening, and did not change his mind until the following morning.

11 *A. J. P. Taylor:* English History 1914–45 *(1976)*
Not only must the budget be balanced. The bankers, and most other people, believed that it must be balanced mainly by reducing government expenditure – 'waste' as it was usually called, not by increasing taxation. They believed also that the gravest 'waste', crying out for reduction, was on unemployment relief, though the bankers, more generous than the May committee, were prepared to have their confidence restored by a 10 per cent cut instead of 20 per cent. Behind this financial opinion, there was an unconscious moral judgement: the unemployed, living on the dole, were felt to be somehow unemployed through their own fault. Some businessmen went further. Cutting unemployment relief would not only reduce government expenditure. It would also break 'the rigidities' and open the way for a general reduction of wages. Faced with a crisis, the responsible authorities fled back to antiquated prejudices and practices which they had been unwittingly abandoning in easier times. Renewed class war seemed to them the only way out.

The cabinet wrangled in vain from 20 to 24 August. Snowden was determined to enforce the cuts whatever his colleagues felt. MacDonald had no clear economic views. He supported the revenue tariff as well as the cuts. His aim was to lead the cabinet, or most of it, to an agreed programme, and then to carry this programme with the approval of the other parties. It looked at first as though he would get his way, as he had often done before. Resistance gradually hardened, particularly after 20 August, when the general council of the TUC, speaking through Bevin, firmly rejected the cuts in benefit and indeed the whole economy approach. Late on the evening of 23 August the cabinet finally failed to agree. Nine were determined to resign rather than accept the unemployment cuts. The other eleven were presumably ready to go along with MacDonald. Six of these had a middle-class or upper-class background; of the minority only one. Perhaps it was no accident that he had started his career under Lloyd George.

12 *A. Morgan:* J. R. MacDonald *(1987)*
MacDonald was a man who believed he was indispensable as Prime Minister. He saw himself as the saviour of the nation at that critical time, whereas, as Samuel had baldly stated to the King, he was the ruling class's ideal candidate for imposing a balanced budget at the expense of the working class. This was to be MacDonald's political function from 24 August 1931.

At 10.00 a.m., MacDonald, Baldwin and Samuel met the King. George V was determined that the leaders should issue a communiqué to end the political suspense. When MacDonald then said that he had the government's resignation in his pocket, the sovereign expressed the hope that his Prime Minister would remain in office. It was the decisive moment in the 1931 crisis and the point at which MacDonald failed to act on the expectations of all his cabinet colleagues. Baldwin and Samuel, by quickly agreeing to serve in an emergency government, made it difficult for MacDonald, if he was still so inclined, to resist.

13 *C.L. Mowat:* Britain Between The Wars 1918–1940 *(1955)*

Its failure lay months back in timid measures to deal with unemployment and a weakening trade balance, and in ignorance of the workings of finance. For this some of the blame lay on its leaders, MacDonald and Snowden; but much on the other ministers who in the past had offered no alternative proposals, and in the crisis accepted the pronouncements of MacDonald and Snowden, and resigned rather than insist on different measures.

Yet this does not absolve MacDonald for much of the responsibility for the failure, though to the public at large his translation to National leadership wiped off all old scores in the instant. Who makes a government, its leader or its followers? MacDonald, as leader, was doubly responsible for the fate of his government. Before the crisis he moulded it; at the crisis he determined it. He was not open in consulting with his colleagues; on the contrary, he seems to have avoided all of them save Snowden during the crisis. Instead, he compromised them by his meetings with the Opposition leaders, and by the misleading reports of Cabinet discussions which he gave them. He then delivered an ultimatum to the members of the Cabinet, for which he and not the Opposition leaders was responsible, and offered them no alternative but resignations which he seemed only too ready to accept. And if they had not agreed to resign, he could have brought about the same result, and was clearly ready to do so, by his own resignation. A Prime Minister's right to resign is absolute, and involves (save when it occurs through illness on his part) the fall of his government.

14 *D. Coates:* The Labour Party and the Struggle for Socialism *(1975)*

The events of August 1931, when MacDonald agreed to lead a National Government (of predominantly Conservative Ministers) that was willing to reduce unemployment benefit and defend the Gold Standard in the face of opposition from a Labour Party driven from office, provided the Party in the 1930s with yet another myth, that of the 'great betrayal'. Yet in a sense, MacDonald's willingness to reduce unemployment benefit and to introduce widespread wage cuts was a logical con-

sequence of the type of politics that the whole Labour Party had played through the 1920s: namely that of a search for accommodation with the private concentrations of industrial and financial power, whose co-operation and commercial viability were essential if Labour was to achieve its promise of a full utilisation of the nation's resources (including labour) in an economy that was still predominantly in private hands. Hence it is significant that the Labour Cabinet in August 1931 were slow to dispute with MacDonald the *need* for the cuts.

15 *H. Pelling:* A Short History of the Labour Party *(1982)*

For nine years MacDonald had dominated the Labour Party, and for nine years he had held an authority which no single individual had ever possessed over its members before. He had received great loyalty from the parliamentary party, and not least from the trade unionists. But the final demands of the 1931 crisis were too great a strain on that loyalty.

The rights and wrongs of the conflict between MacDonald and his party have been debated bitterly ever since. Was MacDonald a 'traitor' to his party or was he the 'saviour' of his country? We can probably allow him at least an honesty of purpose. He knew very little about economics and had to rely upon Snowden, who was a broken reed. He had devoted the previous two years to external affairs and diplomacy and had simply not kept in touch, either with domestic affairs generally or

'*Then none was for the Party; then all were for the State*' *(Horatius)* – Daily Express *25 August 1931*

with the rank and file of the labour movement. Consequently, he exaggerated the gravity of the financial crisis and over-estimated his own influence inside the labour movement. He expected to carry about half the parliamentary party with him into his so-called 'National' government; but when his supporters were all counted, they amounted to only Snowden and Thomas, his colleagues in the new government, his son Malcolm, and four others.

16 *D. Marquand:* Ramsay MacDonald *(1977)*

The case against forming a national government was, in essence, the same as the case against cutting unemployment benefit. It was based on the premiss that a Labour politician's chief function is to represent the organized working class, and that a party leader's chief duty is to keep his followers together. That view – a modern version of the view which Disraeli once expounded in his phillipics against Peel – has a great deal to be said for it; and it was both intolerant and unimaginative of MacDonald to assume that his colleagues who held it differed from him for base reasons. But they were at least as intolerant towards him. For he did not hold their view, and never had. In spite of later charges to the contrary, he was deeply attached to the Labour party; and, as we shall see, he never recovered from the emotional wounds inflicted by his separation from it. But he had always believed that party loyalty could conflict with higher national or international loyalties, and that it should come second if it did. That was why he had gone against his party in 1914; as he saw it, 1931 was 1914 all over again. He has often been accused of betraying his party, but if he had acted differently he would have betrayed his whole approach to politics. He and his party both paid a heavy price for his decision, and there can be little doubt in retrospect that the price was not worth paying. But it was his economics that were at fault, not his motives – his tragedy, not that he deserted to the enemy, but that he fought with characteristic courage in a battle that turned out to be unnecessary: and that in doing so he came near to wrecking the achievements of a lifetime.

17 *MacDonald's First National Cabinet formed August 1931*

Prime Minister	J. Ramsay MacDonald (N. Lab)
Lord President	S. Baldwin (C)
Lord Chancellor	Lord Sankey (N. Lab)
Chancellor of the Exchequer	P. Snowden (N. Lab)
Foreign Secretary	Lord Reading (Lib)
Home Secretary	Sir H. Samuel (Lib)
Colonial Secretary	J. H. Thomas (N. Lab)
Dominions Secretary	J. H. Thomas (N. Lab)
Minister of Health	N. Chamberlain (C)
Secretary for India	Sir S. Hoare (C)
President of the Board of Trade	Sir P. Cunliffe-Lister (C)

From A. Morgan: J. R. MacDonald *(1987)*

18 *1931 election results*

	Total Votes	M.P.s Elected	Candidates	Un-opposed Returns	% Share of Total Vote
1931. Tues., 27 Oct					
Conservative	11,978,745	473	523	56	55·2
National Labour	341,370	13	20	—	1·6
Liberal National	809,302	35	41	—	3·7
Liberal	1,403,102	33	112	5	6·5
(National Government)	(14,532,519)	(554)	(696)	(61)	(67·0)
Independent Liberal	106,106	4	7	—	0·5
Labour	6,649,630	52	515	6	30·6
Communist	74,824	—	26	—	0·3
New Party	36,377	—	24	—	0·2
Others	256,917	5	24	—	1·2
Elec. 29,960,071 Turnout 76·3%	21,656,373	615	1,292	67	100·0

Adapted from D. Butler and A. Sloman: British Political Facts 1900–1979 *(1980)*

19 *R. Miliband:* Parliamentary Socialism *(1972)*

On the 21st of September, the 'National' Government took Britain off the gold standard. Even though credits amounting to £80 million had been obtained from New York and Paris on the 28th of August, the drain on the Bank of England's gold reserves had continued. By the middle of September the credits were almost exhausted. What had earlier been deemed the end of civilization, to be avoided by economy cuts and a 'National' Government, was now accepted as the inevitable command of common sense, and, as Mr Mowat notes, 'hardly a leaf stirred'.

Given the fact that Britain was in 1931 one of the richest countries in the world, and blessed with one of the richest ruling classes in the world, it is surely amazing that there were actually found rational men to argue that the saving of a few million pounds a year on the miserable pittance allowed to unemployed men and women and their children was the essential condition of British solvency; even less credible that two men, exalted by the Labour movement and owing what they were to the faithful support of millions of working men and women, should have been the main actors in this obscene charade.

20 *B. Barker:* Ramsay MacDonald's Political Writings *(1972)*
In fact, MacDonald stayed well beyond the needs of the moment, and clinched the myth that he had

betrayed the Movement by presiding, with Philip Snowden and J. H. Thomas, over a General Election in October 1931, which saw Labour reduced to an ignominious rump of 52, and himself the prisoner of an overwhelming Conservative majority. The Labour Party expelled them all as soon as the National Government was formed, and bitterness and disillusionment set in which was to last a generation. MacDonald continued as Prime Minister until 1935, steadily more incoherent, isolated and unhappy. He died at sea in 1937, after two years as Lord President of the Council.

H ISTORIANS' VIEWS & OPINIONS

THE ACHIEVEMENT OF RAMSAY MACDONALD

The theme closes with an examination of the career of one of the major figures in Labour politics up to 1931 – Ramsay MacDonald – about whom there is much debate amongst historians. The aim of this section is to help you appreciate the different interpretations of his contribution to the labour movement and to enable you to reach your own opinions about the role he played. This section also serves as a means of revising the whole theme. To carry out the activities below you should use not only the three views here, but also historians' views in previous sections, especially those relating to the 1931 crisis in the 'Special Topic'.

Activity I

The following questions and tasks can be the basis for discussion or written work:

a Read through the three extracts carefully.
b Explain in your own words the arguments used by John Strachey in extract 1. What do you think Strachey's political sympathies were? Why? Does the

fact that Strachey's book was written in 1936 affect its value as a source in any way?
c Summarise the much more recent views taken by the historians Moore and Morgan in the other two extracts. In what ways do these verdicts differ from that of Strachey? Why?
d From your knowledge of these three appraisals and from your understanding in general of the whole theme, what are the main pieces of factual evidence upon which an evaluation of MacDonald hinges?

Activity II

Working in pairs, make a list of points and arguments in MacDonald's favour with appropriate factual evidence and reference to the views of historians (again refer back to the historians' opinions in the 'Special Topic' where necessary). Then construct an equivalent list of points and arguments which are unfavourable to MacDonald. In constructing this 'balance sheet' try to be as fair and objective as possible (ultimately it will be impossible to repress your own views, although working with someone else might act as a restraint!). The contrasting arguments you finish up with will be useful for the debate below or a possible essay on the subject.

Class Debate

The motion is:

'For the most part, Ramsay MacDonald's leadership of the Labour Party was a disaster.'

1 *J. Strachey:* The Theory and Practice of Socialism *(1936)*

Mr. MacDonald, Mr. Snowden, Mr. Thomas and Mr. Henderson were all profoundly convinced that British capitalist imperialism had many decades, if not centuries, of expanding development before it. Such a future would provide both the opportunity and the necessity of co-operation with the capitalists by the working class movement. For if British imperialism had another whole epoch of triumphant expansion before it, then it was going to be too strong to be overthrown and strong enough to grant substantial concessions. This wholly erroneous view of the possible future of capitalism, based on sheer ignorance, quite as much as their more obvious personal weaknesses, such as their desire for office, wealth, the applause of the capitalist world, and the simpler forms of personal success, induced the leaders of the British Labour Party to pursue a policy of accommodation to capitalism . . .

The British Labour movement, still under its original leaders, suffered between 1929 and 1931, a series of severe defeats. Nor could any other result be expected. The movement was still dominated by the disastrously false view that it was living in a period of expanding, ascendant capitalism. It had not yet realized what disasters could be caused by leaders who did everything in their power to damp down and to stifle the struggle of their supporters against the consequences of an actually declining system. In a word there did not yet exist in the British Labour movement any adequate realization, on the one hand, of the necessity of abolishing capitalism, if any substantial benefits were to be secured, and, on the other, of the immensity of that task . . .

The culminating disaster of the anti-Marxist, and in effect pro-capitalist, type of policy, organization and leadership of the British Labour movement was reached in 1931 when the second Labour Government collapsed, its three principal members deserted to head the succeeding capitalist administration, and the Parliamentary Labour Party was reduced to the size at which it had stood a quarter of a century before . . .

Moreover, lacking any conviction that the possibilities of capitalism really are exhausted, and that the time of its abolition has come, such leaders always fear nothing so much as being given the opportunity to abolish capitalism. They fear power, and consciously or unconsciously try to avoid it, instead of trying, as every convinced Marxist must do, to acquire power for the working class by the most resolute and energetic action.

2 *R. Moore:* The Emergence of the Labour Party 1880–1924 *(1978)*

Nor must we forget that in MacDonald we are dealing with the most controversial figure in the whole history of the labour movement whose fall from grace in 1931 still regrettably conceals his previous services. Certainly it is true that there were many unattractive features of his character which made themselves apparent from time to time. He seems to have been something of an intriguer, as is shown by the manoeuvres which attended his elevation to the party leadership on both occasions. He had a confidence in his abilities and his fitness for the position which bordered on arrogance and which Shinwell put down in part to his ancestry: 'The vision of his greatness was also displayed before him by his grandmother, a woman as proud as only a clanswoman who could trace pure descent from the romantic warriors of Skye could be.' His particular brand of 'evolutionary' socialism was too nebulous for some people and led to surprisingly early doubts as to the sincerity of his commitment. Shinwell thought that while he had had a difficult life 'his privations were insufficient to turn him into a revolutionary' and he seems to suggest that he had been deeply affected by hobnobbing with the Fabians 'who gave him a few entrancing glimpses of the comfortable life of the middle classes and an occasional one of the wealthy.' Shinwell also agreed with Hyndman's charge that 'personal ambition has been his one motive throughout.' But all this does not alter the fact that he performed certain essential services for the party. Thus, while subtlety and a penchant for intrigue and backstairs deals may be morally reprehensible, it was these very qualities which enabled him to conclude his electoral pact with Herbert Gladstone in 1903, without which the Labour Party might never have got off the ground. Of equal importance was his leadership in the two periods 1911–14 and after 1922. Whatever the means by which he achieved the position the fact remains that he was the only man who was acceptable to all sections of the party and, more important, was recognised as such by the outside world. It is not straining the facts too much to insist that MacDonald's leadership was one of the crucial factors which explain Labour's comparatively rapid rise.

3 K.O. Morgan: Labour People (1987)

Ramsay MacDonald's career should undoubtedly be viewed as a whole. To see him just as a noble idealist who lapsed unaccountably from the faith in 1931 is totally superficial. His failures after 1929 only make sense if they are related to the triumphs of earlier years. The inspiration he gave the labour movement before, during, and after the first world war, was based essentially on the Edwardian premises of the Progressive Alliance. MacDonald then was the supreme British embodiment of social Darwinism in its most optimistic form. While his strategy after 1918 was directed towards wiping out the Liberals as foremost rivals on the left, his philosophy was still based on the imperatives of the peaceful and evolutionary change of society, and an almost Burkean respect of the past, not on the disruptive dialectic of class conflict. Socialism was relegated to an increasingly distant and obscure future. This gradualist approach amply succeeded. It played a vital part in making Labour not merely a movement of protest but an instrument of government. After Marquand's biography, MacDonald will surely always be seen as an out-standing and dominating democratic leader in the first three decades of this century, a spellbinding orator, a masterly parliamentary tactician, a superb party organizer, with that rare touch of Celtic magic to touch the souls as well as the minds of the mass electorate.

Even after 1929, these qualities of greatness did not wholly disappear. MacDonald towered over the more pedestrian virtues of Henderson, the dogmatic rigidities of Snowden, the timidity or ignorance of most of his colleagues, to emerge as one of the most dominating party leaders in our history . . .

And yet, the rehabilitation of Ramsay Mac-Donald, so nobly attempted in Marquand's massive biography, can never really be complete. In spite of everything, he remains doomed, perhaps damned, by his fatal miscalculation in August 1931. No doubt, his financial ideas were out of date by this time. No doubt, his relative ignorance of economics was shared by almost all his Labour colleagues in 1929–31. The point of devaluing sterling was simply not grasped at all. But there is a fundamental sense in which MacDonald's ideas were always out of date or at least out of place, for the leader of a predominantly working-class party, committed to sweeping social change, class equality, and the transfer of economic power into collective hands.

By the twenties he was isolated within the ILP, painful though the process undoubtedly was for him. The pattern was soon repeated within the Labour Party generally, even if his lonely eminence masked the fact for so long. It is in this context that August 1931 remains central to an interpretation of MacDonald's career and the fatal flaw that it contained. In a supreme crisis of the capitalist system, one long prophesied though not really anticipated on the British left, MacDonald felt instinctively alienated from the organized working class on which his party was based.

B ACK TO THE PRESENT

Arguments within the Labour Party about how to achieve socialism, and to what extent socialist principles should be sacrificed for the sake of power, have continued right up to the present day. When you compare the debates within the Labour Party in the 1920s with those, say, in the 1980s, it can be appreciated that the basic arguments have not changed all that much over 60 years. The left of the Labour Party argue that it should be offering the British people a genuine socialist alternative in accordance with Clause 4 of the 1918 constitution. Those on the right and centre of the Party argue that Labour must be realistic and support policies of social democracy which are more likely to appeal to the voters who have always been suspicious of outright socialism. Some on the right of the Labour Party would like to abandon Clause 4 altogether, believing that this idealistic commitment to socialism is out-dated.

Unfortunately it would seem that these arguments between different types of socialists can sometimes damage the image of the Labour Party in the eyes of the electorate. Here are some questions about socialism and society which are as relevant and important today (whether or not you are a Labour sympathiser) as they were in the early years of the Labour Party:

1 Is the Labour Party today a socialist party?
2 Is socialism relevant to British society today?
3 To what extent are some of the current problems in the Labour Party due to the way the Party was established in the first three decades of the century?
4 Is it possible for a completely new political party to rise to power and government in Britain in this day and age in the same way as the Labour Party emerged 60 years ago?
5 Does the Labour Party get a fair deal in the press?

6 BRITISH FOREIGN POLICY AND APPEASEMENT

1919-40

I NTRODUCTION

The vast loss of life in the First World War, the bloody, senseless nature of the warfare, the economic havoc wrought by the fighting and the lack of clear moral and political reasons for the conflict convinced the leaders of Britain and the other 'victorious' powers that there must never be another war like it again.

Britain in 1919 was still a great world power. With Germany defeated, France demoralised, with Soviet Russia in the midst of revolutionary dislocation and America choosing to retreat into isolationism, Britain's moral authority and political influence in the world was perhaps even greater than it had been before 1914. In theory, Britain had the power to shape a healthier and more harmonious Europe and to ensure that there would indeed never be another world war. Yet by 1945 all the good intentions of 1919 had been shattered and a second world war had been fought with the loss of 45 million lives. Also, it soon became clear after 1945 that Britain was no longer a major power in the world, and that Europe was no longer the epicentre of world affairs. Instead, international relations became dominated by the super-power conflict between communist Russia and capitalist America.

In this theme you will be examining the foreign policy of British governments between the wars and trying to understand why this policy had failed by 1945 in its major objectives of sustaining Britain's status as a great power and preventing European conflicts resulting in another world war. In particular, the theme is concerned with the diplomacy pursued by British governments in the 1930s when the fascist and militaristic regimes in Germany, Italy and Japan began to pursue aggressive expansionist policies – policies which even-

Chamberlain delivering his 'peace in our time' broadcast

tually led to the Second World War. This diplomacy has traditionally been referred to by the term 'appeasement'. Unfortunately this term has developed rather negative associations which are perhaps unhelpful to objective historical analysis. One of the aims of the theme is for you to decide whether these negative associations are justified. It is Neville Chamberlain, the

Conservative Prime Minister of Britain between 1937 and 1940, who is most closely connected with the policy. The Munich agreement between Chamberlain and Hitler in September 1938 is seen as the classic example of appeasement in action. The Munich agreement and the whole issue of Nazi aggression towards Czechoslovakia is the subject of the Special Topic within the theme.

K EY QUESTIONS

1 What were the principles and provisions of the Versailles settlement in 1919 and how fair was it?

2 What were the aims, achievements and key events of British foreign policy in the 1920s?

3 What were the main events in British foreign policy in the 1930s?

4 What is meant by the term 'appeasement' in describing British foreign policy in the 1930s and what were the reasons for it? How did this policy differ before and after 1937?

5 To what extent was appeasement justified in the 1930s?

SIMULATION

A PEACE SETTLEMENT FOR EUROPE 1919

Introduction

The aim of the simulation is to help you think about the difficult moral and political issues which faced the victorious nations at the Versailles Peace Conference in 1919. The simulation gives you the opportunity of working in groups to produce your own fair and lasting peace settlement for post-war Europe. You will thus have the chance to change the whole course of world history if you so desire!

The Situation

It is 1919 and the Great War is over: Germany and Austria-Hungary have been defeated by the combined powers of Britain, France, America and Italy. You are an international advisory committee assisting the governments of the major powers in developing satisfactory solutions to the great problems which Europe faces after the war. The wisdom of your advice could determine the success or failure of the Peace Conference at Versailles. The 'General Aims and Issues' and 'Specific Problems' sections provide you with the terms of reference for the discussions and decision-making in your committees.

Europe 1919

Map labels: FINLAND, ESTONIA, DENMARK, LATVIA, LITHUANIA, E. PRUSSIA, Schleswing-Holstein border region, Polish corridor, POLAND, HOLLAND, BELGIUM, GERMANY, Saar, Upper Silesia, CZECHOSLOVAKIA, FRANCE, AUSTRIA, HUNGARY, RUMANIA, YUGOSLAVIA, ITALY, BULGARIA, ALBANIA, GREECE

Disputed regions — Boundaries of old Austro-Hungarian Empire

General Aims and Issues

- The general aim of the Peace Conference is to produce a just and permanent settlement so that the world will never be involved in such a terrible war as the 1914–18 war again.
- Another aim is to implement the principle of national self-determination in Europe.
- On the basis of the principle of self-determination there is a commitment to finally dismantle the Austro-Hungarian and Ottoman Empires and replace them with new and *viable* nation-states such as Czechoslovakia, Poland and Yugoslavia. But what should be done about areas where there are mixed-race populations?
- It has already been agreed in advance that a League of Nations should be set up to promote international co-operation rather than competition and war in the world.
- One problem is to decide whether Germany was to blame for the First World War and how she should be treated as the main defeated power.
- Finally, how are all the above requirements to be fulfilled whilst at the same time satisfying the needs and interests of the major powers – particularly Britain and France?

Specific Problems

- What should be done about Germany? Should she be punished or treated leniently for her part in the Great War? Should she lose her colonies? Should her military strength be permanently reduced? Should Germany actually financially compensate the allies for the material losses sustained in the war?
- Who should control the following three territories, all of which contain mixed populations – the Saar, the Schleswig-Holstein border region, Upper Silesia? Bear in mind that all three of these areas contain valuable industrial resources.
- Should Poland be given access to the sea by means of a 'corridor' of territory containing mainly German people?
- Where should the boundaries of the new Czechoslovakia be established, given the different ethnic groups in the possible Czechoslovakian territories? Bear in mind that the areas with higher proportions of non-Czechs than Czechs contain valuable industrial resources and certain natural features giving military protection.

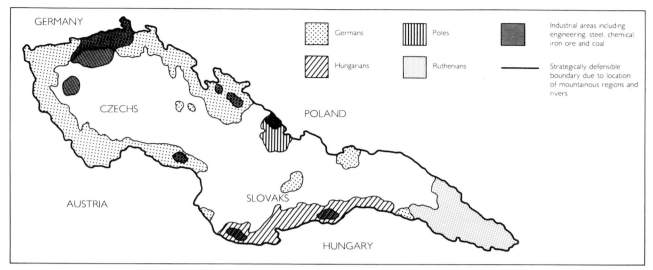

Creating Czechoslovakia 1919

- What powers should the new League of Nations have in order to keep peace in the world, particularly in relation to aggressor states?

It is essential to use the maps provided to help you understand these problems.

Procedures

1 The class should divide into several separate advisory committees, each of which should contain three or four people. Each committee should appoint a secretary and, if need be, someone to chair discussions.
2 The first thing your advisory committee should do is make sure each person understands the ideas in the 'General Aims and Issues' section, since these ought to form the basis for your decisions.
3 Each advisory committee should then go through each of the 'Specific Problems' outlined above and try to agree on proposals to deal with these problems.
4 After a period of time set by your teacher the class should come together as one committee and each of the groups should present its proposals. The class should then, through discussion and taking votes where appropriate, see if they can agree upon a common set of proposals.

Further Research and Discussion

Now study the actual Versailles Treaty provisions and those of other treaties. Discuss as a class the merits and defects of the peace settlement.

Using recommended materials investigate British foreign policies in the 1920s, particularly in relation to the following matters:

- The problem of German reparations payments
- The effectiveness of the League of Nations
- The Locarno Treaty 1925
- The question of disarmament
- The naval conferences of 1922 and 1930.

O UTLINING THE EVENTS

BRITISH FOREIGN POLICY IN THE 1930s

Before looking at the different explanations and arguments concerning British foreign policy in the 1930s we need to establish a basic factual knowledge of the important events. The collection of secondary source extracts in this section have been selected to provide a coverage of these events.

Activity I

a Working individually or in pairs construct a chronology of British foreign policy for this period. Include in your chronology a sentence or two of explanation for each event. Make sure you cross-check between extracts to ensure that the facts you note down are as accurate as they can be. Also, as you develop your chronology make a list of any obvious opinions and judgements that you have noticed in the passages, along with the name of the relevant historian.

b Now, as a class go over the different chronologies you have put together to see if everyone has arrived at the same version of events. Discuss some of the possible explanations and interpretations which are beginning to emerge from your investigations so far.

Further Reading and Research

The chronologies you have established should give you a general but inevitably superficial picture of the events leading up to the outbreak of war in 1939. At least that is a start. Now, to increase your historical understanding you need to carry out some further investigation. Your teacher will recommend books you can use to achieve this. Your chronology should help you in finding your way around the lengthier discussions in the books you use.

Activity II

The following questions and tasks are designed to test your understanding of British foreign policies in the 1930s.

a What were the main threats and problems which the National (Conservative) governments in the 1930s faced in international affairs?

b In the 1920s the general intention of British foreign policy, and indeed the ostensible policy of most European nations, was to prevent a major war ever happening again. This was to be achieved firstly by 'collective security' exercised mainly through the League of Nations and, secondly, by means of general disarmament – also associated with the aims of the League. How effective or ineffective were these policies in dealing with international problems in the 1930s? Illustrate your answer with specific examples.

3 Write down in one or two sentences a definition of appeasement. Make a list of all the examples of what you consider to be appeasement that you can find. Organise them in a rough order of significance. Compare and discuss the different lists you have drawn up. What would appear to be the difference between the policies of appeasement carried out before 1937 and those afterwards?

---

1 *N. Thompson:* The Anti-Appeasers *(1971)*
Scarcely had the National Government been formed than an international crisis was created by Japan's seizure of the nominally Chinese province of Manchuria on 18 September 1931. This event is often identified as the first step on the road to the Second World War: the Western Democracies, it is argued, by failing to stop Japan and to support the League of Nations in taking a firm line against the aggressor, created a precedent for Hitler and Mussolini and neglected the opportunity to build up the machinery for collective security that could be used against them.

2 *A.P. Adamthwaite:* The Making of the Second World War *(1977)*
There is no evidence to support the conspiracy theory. The myth that the Far Eastern crisis was the detonator of later crises has been effectively demolished. Inevitably the Manchurian affair was linked to later events but it did not 'cause' them.

Neither Mussolini's invasion of Abyssinia in 1935 nor Hitler's march into the Rhineland in 1936 can be related to Manchuria. That the League and collective security suffered a grievous blow is undeniable.

3 *Britain and the Abyssinian Crisis 1935*

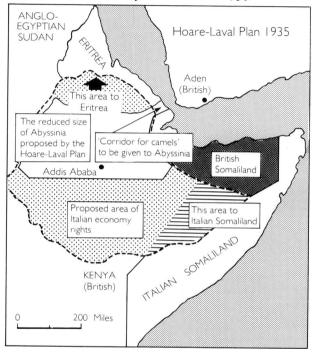

ANGLO-EGYPTIAN SUDAN

ERITREA

Hoare-Laval Plan 1935

Aden (British)

This area to Eritrea

The reduced size of Abyssinia proposed by the Hoare-Laval Plan

'Corridor for camels' to be given to Abyssinia

British Somaliland

Addis Ababa

Proposed area of Italian economy rights

This area to Italian Somaliland

KENYA (British)

ITALIAN SOMALILAND

0   200 Miles

4 *K.O. Morgan:* The Oxford Illustrated History of Britain *ed. K.O. Morgan (1984)*
When the opportunity for action came, public opinion was resistant. Hitler marched into the Rhineland in early 1936, in direct contravention of the Versailles settlement. But only a few voices, like the isolated and unpopular Winston Churchill, called for a military response from Great Britain. Earlier, the British public had generally endorsed, though with much embarrassment, the appeasement policy of the Foreign Office following the Italian invasion of Abyssinia. In effect, the Italians were allowed to occupy this ancient empire in the Horn of Africa with the minimum of British involvement, economic or military. Formal commitments were made to the League and to the spirit of collective security, but they added up to little enough. Sir Samuel Hoare, the Foreign Secretary, was offered up as a public sacrifice during the Abyssinian crisis, but it was clear that the appease-

ment of Mussolini's Italy was a collective government decision. Cabinet records now available confirm the point. In any event, Hoare re-entered the government a few months later with little controversy. Again, in Spain where a left-wing, democratically-elected Republican government was subjected to invasion by a right-wing Nationalist force led by General Franco, with later armed assistance from Italy and Germany, the British government adhered rigidly to 'non-intervention', even if this meant the eventual downfall of democracy in Spain. The advent of the powerful figure of Neville Chamberlain in October 1937, a confident man committed to an active, positive pursuit of a working accommodation with the Fascist dictators, as opposed to Baldwin's passive style of appeasement, confirmed a growing mood of non-involvement in Europe. Key figures in the civil service such as Sir Horace Wilson and Sir Nevile Henderson (ambassador to Berlin) pushed this policy forward.

The German advance in 1938, the seizure of Austria and the subsequent threat to Czechoslovakia, ostensibly on behalf of the Sudeten Germans in the western fringe of Bohemia, produced a national crisis of conscience. Chamberlain responded with managerial decisiveness. At Berchtesgaden, Bad Godesberg, and finally at Munich in September 1938, he came to terms with Hitler. In effect, he allowed the Germans to annex Sudetenland on the basis of any timetable they chose, without British or French armed retaliation.

5 *Dictionary of British History ed. J. P. Kenyon (1981)*
Chamberlain, Neville (1869–1940). Prime minister at the outbreak of World War II. Son of Joseph Chamberlain, he was a Conservative MP from 1918 to 1940. As minister of health (1923, 1924–29), he promoted council-house building and reformed poor-relief administration. Chancellor of the exchequer (1931–37) in the national government, he succeeded Baldwin as prime minister in May 1937 and rapidly developed personal direction of foreign policy, aimed at establishing peaceful relations with Hitler and Mussolini. This appeasement policy had wide public support, although provoking Eden's resignation and bitter opposition from,

notably, Winston Churchill. The Munich pact, ceding Czechoslovak territory to Germany, followed in Sept 1938. After Germany occupied the rest of Czechoslovakia (March 1939), however, Chamberlain's government 'guaranteed' Poland against German attack. Thus, when Germany invaded Poland Britain declared war (3 Sept). In May 1940, following allied disasters in Norway, many Conservatives rebelled against Chamberlain's leadership. He resigned, and Churchill became prime minister. Chamberlain joined Churchill's cabinet, but resigned, a dying man, in Oct 1940.

6 Dictionary of British History *ed. J. P. Kenyon (1981)*

Disarmament. A policy, adopted by Baldwin's Conservative government in 1925, to reduce the level of Britain's defences. Disarmament was desirable for reasons of economy, and it was defended on the grounds that, with the USA and France friendly and Germany defeated, massive armaments were no longer needed. Until the early 1930s, all three major political parties supported disarmament, and it was relinquished as a policy only in 1935, following the failure of the international disarmament conference held at Geneva (1932–34).

7 *A. Beattie:* British Prime Ministers in the Twentieth Century *ed. J. P. Mackintosh (1977)*

By 1933 a reappraisal of policy was taking place. The relative calm of the age of Locarno had been replaced by the rise of National Socialism and rearmament in Germany, by fear for British interests in the Far East aroused by the Japanese, and by bellicose language from Mussolini. Moreover, the Disarmament Conference which met in 1932, and on which many British hopes had been placed, broke upon the rocks of French unwillingness to disarm and German accusations of the failure of other nations to meet the disarmament promises allegedly made at Versailles. Mussolini's invasion of Abyssinia in 1935 confirmed British scepticism about the effectiveness of the League from the standpoint of military and economic sanctions, and reinforced existing doubts about the adequacy of British military strength. The Abyssinian crisis also threw light upon the confused and divided state of British public opinion with respect to both British

commitments abroad and the possibility of honourable appeasement.

8 *C. Cook and J. Stevenson:* The Longman Handbook of Modern British History 1714–1980 *(1983)*

1925   Locarno treaties, 15 October: France, Germany and Belgium agreed to the inviolability of the Franco-German and Belgo-German frontiers and the existence of the demilitarised zone of the Rhineland; this was guaranteed by Britain and Italy. Franco-Polish and Franco-Czech treaties of mutual guarantee were also signed . . .

1935   Anglo-German Naval Agreement 18 June, limiting the German Navy to 35 per cent of the British, with submarines at 45 per cent or equality in the event of danger from Russia . . .

1937   Anglo-Italian 'Gentleman's Agreement' to maintain the *status quo* in the Mediterranean, 2 January.

1938   Munich Agreement: agreement reached by Britain, France, Italy and Germany, by which territorial concessions were made to Germany, Poland, and Hungary at the expense of Czechoslovakia 29 September. The rump of Czechoslovakia was to be guaranteed against unprovoked aggression, but German control was extended to the rest of Czechoslovakia in March 1939.

9 *The Expansion of Nazi Germany 1935–9*

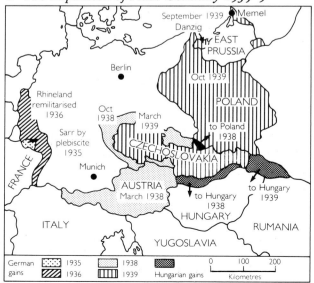

10 *A.J.P. Taylor:* English History 1914–1945 *(1965)*

The chiefs of staff increased their warnings, and now with a different emphasis. In 1932 they had asserted that Japan was the more immediate danger, though Germany would be ultimately the greater one. Their immediate concern therefore was with the navy. By the end of 1934 the chiefs of staff were coming to believe that Germany was the more immediate, as well as the greater, danger. For this and for other reasons, Baldwin pledged the government to maintain parity in the air, that is, an air force as large as Germany's. This had an unforeseen consequence. The navy and the air force had kept up their capital equipment better than the army even during the years of disarmament. Now the decision to maintain a great navy and to create a great air force put the army yet further down the list. The government, still anxious to maintain economy, virtually decided not to have an army at all. There was to be a 'limited liability' army, fit only for colonial defence. In this odd way, the practical effect of rearmament was actually to increase British isolation: not only the will, but the means, for British intervention on the Continent were lacking.

11 The Illustrated Dictionary of British History *ed. A. Marwick (1980)*

Non-intervention A policy adopted by Britain, France, Germany and Italy in the Spanish civil war (1936–9) and adhered to by the first two, despite gross violations by the others.

Anglo-Polish pact March 1939. Negotiated by Neville Chamberlain after the Germans broke the terms of the Munich agreement by occupying Prague, it offered an alliance to the Poles. With the German invasion of Poland (1 September 1939), adherence to it brought Britain into World War II.

12 *I. Colvin:* The Chamberlain Cabinet *(1971)*

The three broad issues upon which the Chamberlain Cabinet stands at the bar of history are that with a large Parliamentary majority it failed to rearm in time; that it surrendered over Czechoslovakia in 1938, when it need not so have done; and that it failed in 1939 to achieve an alliance with Russia, thus entering war with less effective allies than could have been found in 1938.

Hitler and Mussolini, May 1938

13 *R. Rhodes James:* The British Revolution *(1976)*

British foreign policy between 1933 and 1937 was unquestionably lacking in distinction or purpose. Simon's tenure of the Foreign Office (1933–5) was hapless, and Hoare's brief occupancy in 1935 was a fiasco. 'Everyone seemed to be over-excited', he subsequently complained. 'There appeared to be no generally accepted body of opinion on the main issues. Diametrically opposed views were pressed upon me, and sometimes with the intolerance of an *odium theologicum*.' Eden (1935–8) was far from being the vigilant foe of the dictators that he has been subsequently portrayed as. The central features of British policy in these years were to reach accommodations with Germany on specific issues – as demonstrated in the Anglo-German Treaty of 1935 – to avoid conflicts arising in Europe – as in the Rhineland crisis of March 1936 – and to attempt to retain the co-operation of Italy – as in the so-called British, French, and Italian 'Stresa Front' of 1935. The latter policy collapsed over Abyssinia in the storm that followed the revelation of the Hoare-Laval Pact, and the Stresa Front was accordingly a dead letter almost from the outset.

14 Dictionary of British History *ed. J. P. Kenyon (1981)*

Munich agreement (29 Sept 1938). A pact, signed in Munich by Britain, Germany, France, and Italy, that settled Germany's demands on Czechoslovakia. The agreement, imposed upon Czechoslovakia (which was unrepresented at Munich), was largely the work of Neville Chamberlain, pursuing a policy of appeasement. (France, unlike Britain, was allied to Czechoslovakia, but nevertheless acquiesced.) Czechoslovakia surrendered to Germany one-fifth of its territory and a quarter of its population (mostly from the Sudeten German-speaking border areas), great economic resources, and its defence fortifications. Further areas of Czechoslovakia were subsequently allocated to Hungary and Poland. The agreement was described by Chamberlain as 'peace with honour . . . peace for our time'. Six months later Germany invaded and occupied the rest of Czechoslovakia.

15 *K. Robbins:* Appeasement *(1988)*
The Anglo-Soviet discussions throughout the summer [1939] were slow and protracted. There were awkward sticking points, among them the status of the three independent Baltic republics and the dark suspicions in Warsaw concerning Soviet intentions. Possibly a greater sense of urgency might have brought success, but the effort came to a dramatic halt with the news of the Nazi-Soviet Pact in August. An enormous burden was lifted from Hitler.

CONTEMPORARY VIEWS & OPINIONS

EXPLANATIONS FOR APPEASEMENT 1931–38

Assembled here is a cross-section of primary evidence reflecting on the motives behind British foreign policies – policies which are often summarised under the heading of 'appeasement'. Bear in mind that this is only a particular selection of sources and may not be typical of informed opinion in Britain at the time.

Activity

a Study the extracts carefully and make a list of all the different reasons you can discover for the policy of accommodation with the dictators in the 1930s. Add to your list any additional reasons you can think of which do not seem to be expressed in these sources. Three of the extracts can be construed as 'anti-appeasement'. Which ones and why?

b Working in small groups compare each other's lists – make adjustments where necessary. Make sure that you understand each of the reasons you have noted down. Try and agree as a group, if possible, a collective opinion about British foreign policies at this time. Were they good, bad, realistic or understandable in the circumstances?

Discussion

Each group should present its opinions to the rest of the class. Then hold a general discussion around the following questions: Were British policies in Europe justifiable given the views expressed in these contemporary sources? Why? What alternative policies could have been pursued? Were these alternative policies realistic?

---

1 *Rumbold, British ambassador in Germany, to Sir John Simon, Foreign Secretary, 30 June 1933*
Unpleasant incidents and excesses are bound to occur during a revolution, but the deliberate ruthlessness and brutality which have been practised during the last five months seem both excessive and unnecessary. I have the impression that the persons directing the policy of the Hitler Government are not normal. Many of us, indeed, have a feeling that we are living in a country where fantastic hooligans and eccentrics have got the upper hand.

2 *Lord Rothermere in the* Daily Mail *discussing the return of colonies to Germany, 1934*
Though this proposal may not be so popular, I am convinced that it is wise. We cannot expect a nation of he-men like the Germans to sit forever with folded arms under the provocations and stupidities

of the Treaty of Versailles ... To deny this mighty nation, conspicuous for its organising ability and scientific achievements, a share in the work of developing backward regions of the world is preposterous.

3 'The Peace Ballot', some results, 1935

Question 2: *Are you in favour of an all-round reduction of armaments by international agreement?*

Total *Yes* answers:	10,058,026
Total *No* answers:	815,365
Percentage of *Yes* answers in relation to total *Yes* and *No* answers:	92·5
Percentage of *Yes* answers in relation to total *Yes*, *No* and *Doubtful* answers and *Abstentions*:	90·7

Question 5a *Do you consider that, if a nation insists on attacking another, the other nations should combine to compel it to stop by economic and non-military measures?*

Total *Yes* answers:	9,627,606
Total *No* answers:	607,165
Percentage of *Yes* answers in relation to total *Yes* and *No* answers:	94·1
Percentage of *Yes* answers in relation to total *Yes*, *No*, *Doubtful* and *Christian Pacifist* answers and *Abstentions*:	86·8

Question 5b *Do you consider that, if a nation insists on attacking another, the other nations should combine to compel it to stop by, if necessary, military measures?*

Total *Yes* answers:	6,506,777
Total *No* answers:	2,262,261
Percentage of *Yes* answers in relation to total *Yes* and *No* answers:	74·2
Percentage of *Yes* answers in relation to total *Yes*, *No*, *Doubtful* and *Christian Pacifist* answers and *Abstentions*:	58·6

4 The Sunday Times 31 March 1935

The underlying assumption of French policy in Eastern Europe is that the blessings are worthless in the West without some form of physical restraint on what Germany may do in the East, and that every local disagreement must be a world interest and every war a world war. It is a hard doctrine, especially for this country, which has no real interest in Eastern Europe, has no intention of taking an active part in defending a peace settlement in which she has ceased to believe and is, in addition, asked to compromise what might be some fair prospect of safety at home.

5 Stanley Baldwin, Prime Minister, in a speech 31 October 1935

We live under the shadow of the last War and its memories still sicken us. We remember what modern warfare is, with no glory in it but the heroism of man. We remember forcing ourselves to read the casualty lists. Have you thought what it has meant to the world in recent years to have had that swath of death cut through the loveliest and the best of our contemporaries, how public life has suffered because those who would have been ready to take over from our tired and disillusioned generation are not there?

6 H.A.L. Fisher: History of Europe (1936)

The Hitler revolution is a sufficient guarantee that Russian Communism will not spread westward. The solid German bourgeois holds the central fortress of Europe. But there may be secrets in Fascism or Hitlerism which the democracies of the West will desire, without abandoning their fundamental character, to adopt.

7 The American minister in Austria to the American Secretary of State, 9 March 1936

The fundamental fact which Europe has to face today is that the National Socialist regime in Germany is based on a program of ruthless force, which program has for its aim, first, the enslavement of the German population to a National Socialist social and political program, and then to use the force of these 67 million people for the extension of German political and economic sovereignty over south-Eastern Europe – thus putting it into a position to dominate Europe completely and to place France and England definitely in the position of secondary powers. ...

A determined stand by the powers now is almost certain not to lead to war, and it is the only thing which will bring to an end the series of *faits accomplis* which the German program provides for.

8 *The Honourable W. Astor MP in a speech to the House of Commons, March 1936*
The people of this country feel, I believe, that if there is a war now, it is possible that England may lose her influence for good, through many years to come, by having her economic and social system crippled if not destroyed . . .

9 Evening Standard *27 March 1936*
The 'Evening Standard' has long and consistently attacked the League of Nations and the principle of collective security as futile yet dangerous, and has been censured for so doing even though events have justified the attack.

But it is not enough to denounce the League and the collective system. If the League does not work, the British people must be presented with an alternative policy for the attainment of their ideal, which is to live at peace.

We have such a policy. It provides that Great Britain should adopt towards European affairs an attitude of detachment. She should be tied by neither pact, nor covenant, nor alliance to the destinies of Continental nations. She should be free.

10 *Chiefs of Staff report, April 1936*
If they [the French] think that they are strong

'*Off for the holidays*' – Evening Standard *31 July 1936*

enough at the present time to undertake hostilities against Germany, we may find ourselves committed to participation against Germany with forces which are not only inadequate to render effective support, but incapable of assuring our own security, with grave consequences to the people of this country.

11 *Harold Nicolson, writer and politician, in his diary after a meeting of Conservative backbench MPs, 16 July 1936*
The general impression left was that the majority of the National [Government] Party are at heart anti-League and anti-Russian, and that what they would really like would be a firm agreement with Germany and possibly Italy by which we could purchase peace at the expense of the smaller states.

12 *Baldwin in a speech, 12 November 1936*
You will remember the election at Fulham in the autumn of 1933, when a seat which the National Government held was lost by about 7,000 votes on no issue but the pacifist. My position as the leader of a great party was not altogether a comfortable one. I asked myself what chance was there – when that feeling that was given expression to in Fulham was common throughout the country – what chance was there within the next year or two of that feeling being so changed that the country would give a mandate for rearmament?

13 *Ernest Bevin, Labour MP, to the Executive Committee of his union March 1937*
From the day Hitler came to power, I have felt that the democratic countries would have to face war. I believe he was taken too cheap. We have been handicapped by the very sincere pacifists in our Party who believe that the danger can be met by resolution and prayers and by turning the other cheek. While I appreciate the sincerity, I cannot understand anybody who refuses to face the facts in relation to the happenings in China, in Abyssinia, in Spain, all virtually disarmed countries. I cannot see any way of stopping Hitler and the other dictators except by force.

14 *A German memo outlining the views of Halifax, Prime Minister Chamberlain's envoy, as expressed to Hitler, November 1937*
The view was held in England that it was perfectly

possible to clear out of the way the misunderstandings which existed at the present moment; the great services which the Chancellor had performed in the reconstruction of Germany were fully recognised, and, if the public opinion of England took up an attitude of criticism from time to time towards certain German problems, it might no doubt be in part because people in England were not fully informed of the motives and attendant circumstances of certain measures taken in Germany. Thus the Church of England followed with anxiety and disquiet the development of the Church question in Germany; and Labour Party circles were critical of certain action taken in Germany. In spite of these difficulties, he (Halifax) recognised that the Chancellor had not only performed great services in Germany but also, as he would no doubt feel, had been able, by preventing the entry of communism into his own country, to bar its passage further west.

15 *Chiefs of Staff report as summarised by Chamberlain, Prime Minister, 8 December 1937*
From the above Report it will be seen that our Naval, Military and Air Forces, in their present stage of development are still far from sufficient to meet our defensive commitments, which now extend from Western Europe through the Mediterranean to the Far East. . . . Without overlooking the assistance which we should hope to obtain from France, and possibly other allies, we cannot foresee the time when our defence forces will be strong enough to safeguard our territory, trade and vital interests against Germany, Italy and Japan simultaneously. We cannot, therefore, exaggerate the importance, from the point of view of Imperial defence, of any political or international action that can be taken to reduce the numbers of our potential enemies and to gain the support of potential allies.

16 *Sir E. Grigg: Britain Looks Back At Germany (1938)*
In this Country Conservatives prefer the German system to the Russian because it is nationalistic in spirit and does not seek to undermine the unity of other nations by dividing them on class lines against themselves.

17 *Tom Jones, confidante of leading politicians, in a letter 20 March 1938*
Well, the map of Europe has once more to be redrawn and the swastika splashed over Austria. I can't properly describe the moods through which we have passed in this country in the last ten days, days of a gravity unparalleled since the Great War. I need not repeat what you know already that for the last two years I have been in favour of trying to reach some amicable understanding with Hitler for the very reason that I believed him to be a fanatic to be humoured as far as possible and kept from breaking out and this for the most prudential reason: we could not take any offensive and our defensive preparations against sudden air attack were of the most meagre character. I don't think 'scoundrel' describes Hitler, it applies more accurately to some of those around him.

I do not regret Chamberlain's reversal of Eden's policy even if it proved too late. We have to convince the world that for peace we are prepared to go to absurd lengths. Our people will not fight unless they are satisfied that fair treatment of the potential enemy has been tried.

S PECIAL TOPIC

NEVILLE CHAMBERLAIN AND THE 'MUNICH' CRISIS 1938

Neville Chamberlain, Prime Minister of Britain 1937–40, is the man most closely associated with the policy of appeasement as a consciously pursued strategy. The Munich agreement with Hitler in September 1938 which authorised the transfer of the 'German' parts of Czechoslovakia to Germany was the centre-piece of this policy. At the time the agreement was greeted as a diplomatic triumph, saving Europe from war: in Chamberlain's immortal though not terribly original words it was 'peace for our time'. However, within a few months the Munich settlement had been ripped apart by Hitler as the Nazis continued their expansion into eastern Europe. On 3 September 1939 Britain finally found itself at war with the dictators in defence of the freedom of far-away Poland. Neville Chamberlain's policy of appeasement and thus his whole political reputation now seemed to be in ruins. The material in this Special Topic consists of various pieces of primary evidence, plus a brief chronology of the key events of 1938. This information has been selected to help you master both the details and the ideas of British policy concerning Europe and Czechoslovakia at this time, and to come to your own judgements about the wisdom of Chamberlain's course of action.

Activity I

a Study the chronology carefully in conjunction with other accounts of the European crisis over Czechoslovakia in 1938. Make sure you understand the course of events in 1938 leading up to the agreement at Munich in September. Also, take note of any of the factual differences between the events as described in the chronology and the narrative in the other accounts you are using. Do you think there is any significance in the differences?

b Write a paragraph summing up what the Czechoslovakian 'problem' was all about and how this problem was eventually resolved. Try to do this as factually as possible, concentrating on the main elements of the story – don't merely put the chronology here into words.

c In small groups or as a class, check that everyone shares a common understanding of the main events of the 'Munich Crisis'. In doing this try to hold back any judgements or interpretations you want to make at this stage – you need to get the facts fixed in your mind first.

Activity II

Study all the extracts carefully, paying particular attention to who the author of the source is and the date at which it was written. Working individually or in pairs use the ideas and the arguments in the contemporary sources to do the following:

a Summarise in two or three sentences the main ideas and aims of Chamberlain's policy of appeasement.
b Write a paragraph or a list of points *defending* Chamberlain's policy of appeasement with particular relation to the Munich agreement with Hitler.
c Write a paragraph or a list of points *attacking* Chamberlain's policy of appeasement and the Munich agreement with Hitler.

In carrying out the above you should make reference to the sources where necessary. You should also make use of your knowledge of foreign policy before 1937 where relevant.

Discussion

In small groups and/or as a class, review the different interpretations contained in the paragraphs/lists of points that you have written defending and attacking Chamberlain and his policies. What is your own view at this stage in the theme? To what extent has the benefit of hindsight influenced your interpretation?

Chronology

12 March   Germany invades Austria. It is clear that the question of self-determination for the Germans in the Sudetenland part of Czechoslovakia will be the next 'issue'.

20–21 May	Czechs mobilise versus possible German invasion. Britain and France issue a stern warning to Hitler. There is no invasion.
3 Aug.	Chamberlain sends Runciman to Czechoslovakia as his special mediator to produce a solution to the Sudetenland problem.
2 Sept.	Litvinov, Russian Foreign Secretary, proposes a joint French/British/Russian/Czech pact against Nazi aggression in Czechoslovakia – this comes to nothing.
4 Sept.	Benes, Czech President accepts the Runciman-sponsored idea of a federated Czechoslovakia with considerable autonomy for German, Czech and Slovak regions.
12 Sept.	Hitler's Nuremberg speech demands freedom for the Sudetenland to become part of Germany. Nazi plans for an invasion of Czechoslovakia on 1 October are well advanced by this time.
15 Sept.	Chamberlain meets Hitler at Berchtesgaden and accepts the principle of complete self-determination for the Sudetenland.
19 Sept.	Anglo-French proposals to Czechoslovakia for the *gradual* transfer of Sudetenland territories to Germany – by means of plebiscites, international supervision of the transfers and an international guarantee to the remainder of Czechoslovakia.
22 Sept.	Chamberlain meets Hitler at Godesberg. Hitler ups the stakes by demanding the *immediate* occupation of the Sudetenland by Nazi troops by 1 October.
26 Sept.	Britain makes it clear that she will support the French-Czechoslovakian alliance if Hitler persists with his plans for immediate take-over. Meanwhile, both Britain and France are preparing for war.
29 Sept.	Munich meeting of Hitler, Chamberlain and French and Italian representatives reaches agreement on the speedy transfer of the Sudetenland to Germany. War is thus avoided.
30 Sept.	Anglo-German 'friendship agreement' is reached between Chamberlain and Hitler.

1 *Chamberlain in his diary, 26 November 1937*

26 November 1937

... the German visit was from my point of view a great success, because it achieved its object, that of creating an atmosphere in which it is possible to discuss with Germany the practical questions involved in a European settlement.... Both Hitler and Goering said separately, and emphatically, that they had no desire or intention of making war, and I think we may take this as correct, at any rate for the present. Of course, they want to dominate Eastern Europe; they want as close a union with Austria as they can get without incorporating her in the Reich, and they want much the same things for the Sudetendeutsche as we did for the Uitlanders in the Transvaal ...

Now here, it seems to me, is a fair basis of discussion, though no doubt all these points bristle with difficulties. But I don't see why we shouldn't say to Germany, 'give us satisfactory assurances that you won't use force to deal with the Austrians and Czechoslovakians, and we will give you similar assurances that we won't use force to prevent the changes you want, if you can get them by peaceful means'.

2 *Chamberlain in a speech to the House of Commons, 21 February 1938*

Indeed, we were the last of the nations to rearm, but this process of general rearmament has been forced upon us all, because every country is afraid to disarm lest it should fall a victim to some armed neighbour. I recognise the force of that hard fact, but I have never ceased publicly to deplore what seems to me a senseless waste of money, for which everyone will have to pay dearly, if they are not paying for it already. I cannot believe that, with a little good will and determination, it is not possible to remove genuine grievances and to clear away suspicions which may be entirely unfounded.

For these reasons, then, my colleagues and I have been anxious to find some opportunity of entering upon conversations with the two European countries with which we have been at variance, namely, Germany and Italy, in order that we might find out whether there was any common ground on which we might build up a general scheme of appeasement in Europe.

3 *Chamberlain in his diary, 20 March 1938*
... with Franco winning in Spain by the aid of German guns and Italian planes, with a French government in which one cannot have the slightest confidence, and which I suspect to be in closish touch with our Opposition, with the Russians stealthily and cunningly pulling all the strings behind the scenes to get us involved in war with Germany (our Secret Service doesn't spend all its time looking out of the window), and finally with a Germany flushed with triumph, and all too conscious of her power, the prospect looked black indeed.

You have only to look at the map to see that nothing that France or we could do could possibly save Czechoslovakia from being overrun by the Germans, if they wanted to do it. The Austrian frontier is practically open; the great Skoda munitions works are within easy bombing distance of the German aerodromes, the railways all pass through German territory, Russia is 100 miles away. Therefore we could not help Czechoslovakia – she would simply be a pretext for going to war with Germany. That we could not think of unless we had a reasonable prospect of being able to beat her to her knees in a reasonable time, and of that I see no sign. I have therefore abandoned any idea of giving guarantees to Czechoslovakia, or the French in connection with her obligations to that country.

4 *Adolf Hitler: secret military directives, 20 May 1938*
1) *Political Assumptions:*
It is my unalterable decision to smash Czechoslovakia by military action in the near future. It is the business of the political leadership to await or bring about the suitable moment from a political and military point of view.

An unavoidable development of events within Czechoslovakia or other political events in Europe providing a suddenly favorable opportunity which may never recur, may cause me to take early action.

The proper choice and determined exploitation of a favorable moment is the surest guarantee of success. To this end preparations are to be made immediately.

5 *Memo from the Czech minister in London to the British government, 26 April 1938*
The Czechoslovak nationality policy has safeguarded extensive civil and political liberties for all the nationalities in the republic; it has given them an opportunity of freely putting into effect whatever political ideas they may hold, of building up and developing political movements and cultural associations, of publishing periodicals and newspapers, and also of bringing their influence to bear upon economic matters.

This nationality policy has given them an equitable share in the legislative bodies, and thus a full opportunity of asserting their national interests. Thus of the 450 members of the Czechoslovak Chamber of Deputies and the Senate:

106 (or 23 per cent) are Germans
18 (or 4 per cent) are Magyars
2 (or .5 per cent are Poles
9 (or 2 per cent) are Ruthenes

These percentages correspond almost precisely with the actual numerical strength of the respective nationalities in the State.

6 *Chiefs of Staff report: 'Appreciation of the Situation in the Event of War Against Germany', 14 September 1938*
It is our opinion that no pressure that Great Britain and France can bring to bear, either by sea, on land, or in the air, could prevent Germany from overrunning Bohemia and from inflicting a decisive defeat on Czechoslovakia. The restoration of Czechoslovakia's lost integrity could only be achieved by the defeat of Germany and as the outcome of a prolonged struggle, which from the outset must assume the character of an unlimited war.

The intervention of Italy and/or Japan on the side of Germany would create a situation which the Chiefs of Staff in the Mediterranean and Middle East Appreciation described in the following language:

'Moreover, war against Japan, Germany and Italy simultaneously in 1938 is a commitment which neither the present nor the projected strength of our defence forces is designed to meet, even if we were in alliance with France and Russia, and which would, therefore, place a dangerous strain on the resources of the Empire. . . .'

7 *Relative military strengths of the European powers 1938–9*

Land forces (strengths, expressed in divisions, are war strengths)

	January 1938	August 1939
Germany	81	120–30
Italy	73	73
France	63	86
Great Britain	2	4
USSR	125	125
Czechoslovakia	34	—
Poland	40	40

Air strengths (for Great Britain, France and Italy metropolitan strengths only are given)

	January 1938	August 1939
Germany	1,820	4,210
Italy	1,301	1,531
France	1,195	1,234
Great Britain	1,053	1,750
USSR	3,050	3,361
Czechoslovakia	600	—
Poland	500	500

8 *Letter from Lord Runciman to the Prime Minister, 21 September 1938*

. . . I have much sympathy, however, with the Sudeten case. It is a hard thing to be ruled by an alien race; and I have been left with the impression that Czechoslovak rule in the Sudeten areas for the last twenty years, though not actively oppressive and certainly not 'terroristic', has been marked by

'*Our new defence*' – Evening Standard 4 October 1938 (David Low)

STILL HOPE

Punch *21 September 1938*

tactlessness, lack of understanding, petty intolerance and discriminations, to a point where the resentment of the German population was inevitably moving in the direction of revolt. . . .

9 *C. R. Attlee, Leader of the Labour Party, in an article 'Stand Fast for Peace and Freedom' in the* Daily Herald, *23 September 1938*

A civilised people, the last outpost of democracy and freedom in Central Europe, is being betrayed and handed over to a ruthless and intolerant dictatorship.

Another ignominious surrender has been made to violence. Herr Hitler has been made the master of Europe and the danger of another world war has not been averted. . . .

This is called a peaceful settlement. It is nothing of the kind. The Czechs have been denied the right to discuss these terms. They are terms of surrender forced upon the Czechs by the Western democracies, which have themselves acted not from any considerations of justice, but under threat of war by Germany. . . .

10 *The Anglo-German 'Declaration of Friendship' agreed 30 September 1938*

We regard the agreement signed last night and the Anglo-German Naval Agreement as symbolic of the desire of our two peoples never to go to war with one another again.

We are resolved that the method of consultation shall be the method adopted to deal with any other questions that may concern our two countries, and we are determined to continue our efforts to remove possible sources of difference and thus to contribute to assure the peace of Europe.

11 *Chamberlain speaking to the House of Commons in the debate on the Munich agreement, 3 October 1938*

When the House met last Wednesday, we were all under the shadow of a great and imminent menace. War, in a form more stark and terrible than ever before, seemed to be staring us in the face. Before I sat down, a message had come which gave us new hope that peace might yet be saved, and today, only a few days after, we all meet in joy and thankfulness that the prayers of millions have been answered, and a cloud of anxiety has been lifted from our hearts . . .

Ever since I assumed my present office my main purpose has been to work for the pacification of Europe, for the removal of those suspicions and those animosities which have so long poisoned the air. The path which leads to appeasement is long and bristles with obstacles. The question of Czechoslovakia is the latest and perhaps the most dangerous. Now that we have got past it, I feel that it may be possible to make further progress along the road to sanity . . .

I believe there are many who will feel with me that such a declaration, signed by the German Chancellor and myself, is something more than a pious expression of opinion. In our relations with other countries everything depends upon there being sincerity and goodwill on both sides. I believe that there is sincerity and good will on both sides in this declaration. That is why to me its significance goes far beyond its actual words. If there is one lesson which we should learn from the events of these last weeks it is this, that lasting peace is not to be obtained by sitting still and waiting for it to come. It requires active, positive efforts to achieve it.

12 *Churchill speaking to the Commons in the same debate, 3 October 1938*

. . . I will therefore, begin by saying the most unpopular and most unwelcome thing. I will begin by saying what everybody would like to ignore or forget but which must nevertheless be stated, namely, that we have sustained a total and unmitigated defeat, and that France has suffered even more than we have. . . . The utmost my right hon. Friend the Prime Minister has been able to secure by all his immense exertions, by all the great efforts and mobilisation which took place in this country, and by all the anguish and strain through which we have passed in this country, the utmost he has been able to gain – (Hon. Members: 'Is peace.') I thought I might be allowed to make that point in its due place, and I propose to deal with it. The utmost he has been able to gain for Czechoslovakia and in the matters which were in dispute has been that the German dictator, instead of snatching his victuals from the table, has been content to have them served to him course by course. . . .

When I think of the fair hopes of a long peace which still lay before Europe at the beginning of 1933 when Herr Hitler first obtained power, and of all the opportunities of arresting the growth of the Nazi power which have been thrown away, when I think of the immense combinations and resources which have been neglected or squandered, I cannot believe that a parallel exists in the whole course of history. So far as this country is concerned the responsibility must rest with those who have the undisputed control of our political affairs. They neither prevented Germany from rearming, nor did they rearm ourselves in time. They quarrelled with Italy without saving Ethiopia. They exploited and discredited the vast institution of the League of Nations and they neglected to make alliances and combinations which might have repaired previous errors, and thus they left us in the hour of trial without adequate national defence or effective international security.

HISTORIANS' VIEWS & OPINIONS

VERDICTS ON APPEASEMENT

There has been a great deal of controversy amongst historians about Neville Chamberlain and the policy of appeasement. After the Second World War historians tended to condemn Chamberlain's attempt to buy off the fascist dictators as both naive and immoral. In the 1960s 'revisionist' historians, influenced by hitherto unreleased documents, attempted to demonstrate that appeasement was a legitimate policy in its aims of trying to prevent a major war and to gain time to allow Britain to strengthen its military position. Since then, with further research, a more complex range of arguments has been developed by historians. The four secondary source extracts in this concluding section of the theme provide contrasting interpretations of Chamberlain and appeasement. If you have carried out some of the activities in previous sections then some of the arguments and evidence deployed in the extracts will be familiar to you.

Activity

a Read the extracts carefully and decide which two defend or justify Chamberlain's appeasement policies in some way and which two are critical of them.

b Now, identify the distinct points the historians make to support their overall arguments. Make a note of these points in columns representing the contrasting positions taken by the pairs of authors. Indicate in your table which historians are responsible for which points.

c Look again at the textbook(s) you have been using to study this theme and discover what view the author takes of appeasement. Enter the points he/she makes into your table of views.

d Using the knowledge and ideas you have gained about appeasement so far, jot down any additional arguments which you think are relevant and which are not mentioned in the extracts. Which argument do you support? Why?

Debate

The motion is: 'Chamberlain's policy of appeasement and the Munich agreement were justifiable in the circumstances.'

---

1 *M. Gilbert and R. Gott:* The Appeasers *(1963)*
Those who supported appeasement after October, 1938, did so for two reasons. Munich "bought" a year of peace, in which to rearm. It brought "a united nation" into war, by showing Hitler's wickedness beyond doubt. Both these reasons were put forward by the Government, and accepted by many who could not check them. Both were false.

If a year had been gained in which Chamberlain could have strengthened Britain's defences and equipped the country for an offensive war, there should be evidence of growing strength, growing effort, and growing Cabinet unity. But while some members of the Government sought to use the "bought" year, others did not. Chamberlain and his closest advisers were unwilling to allow the Minister of War, Hore-Belisha, to introduce conscription. The Air Minister, Kingsley Wood, failed to achieve the needed air parity with Germany. Machines were not lacking. Will-power was. Germany, not Britain, gained militarily during the extra year. German forces were strengthened by Czech munitions, western forces weakened by the loss of the Czech Army and Air Force . . .

Chamberlain and his advisers did not go to Munich because they needed an extra year before they could fight. They did not use the year to arouse national enthusiasm for a just war. The aim of appeasement was to avoid war, not to enter war united. Appeasement was a looking forward to better times, not to worse. Even after the German occupation of Prague, Chamberlain and those closest to him hoped that better times would come, and that Anglo-German relations would improve. They gave the pledge to Poland, not with enthusiasm, but with embarrassment. They wanted to befriend Germany, not anger her.

2 *D. Dilks:* The Conservatives *ed. Lord Butler (1977)*
Though Chamberlain loathed the very idea of a

great war, which was generally anticipated to produce horrors still more dreadful than those of the First, he did not rule it out on any grounds of principle. Rather, he said that he would not contemplate such a guarantee 'unless we had a reasonable prospect of being able to beat her [Germany] to her knees in a reasonable time, and of that I see no sign.'

When the British and French ministers discussed the whole issue at the end of April, Chamberlain put the point in similar terms, adding that he thought a time would come 'when a gamble on the issue of peace and war might be contemplated with less anxiety than at present.' In other words, the buying of time remained a strong element in British foreign policy, as it had been for several years. This was the line which Eden had recommended to the Cabinet early in 1936; to reach agreements with Germany where they could honourably be reached, to be under no illusions that Germany would keep them when they ceased to suit her, and to accelerate British rearmament, the spending upon which was moving swiftly forward in 1938 and 1939 and which far exceeded any expenditure upon arms ever undertaken by Britain in peace time. This is not to say that the sole purpose of the policy pursued in 1938 was simply to obtain a breathing space. Chamberlain had some sympathy for German grievances, and was acutely sensible of Hitler's capacity to exploit them; he felt much doubt about the outcome of a war; he could hardly bear to think of the wanton destruction; but there is not a sign he felt any fondness for dictatorships or sneaking sympathy for fascism.

3 *A.P. Adamthwaite:* The Making of the Second World War *(1977)*
To recapitulate briefly the argument of this essay. Though the settlement that ended the First World War was a patched-up peace it was not foredoomed to failure. A solid Anglo-French alliance might have contained Germany. The reasons for the rapid breakdown of the European security system erected in 1919 are to be found in the explosive mixture of power politics and ideology that propelled Germany, in the general detestation of war and in the appreciation of economic, political and military weaknesses that weighed down

western statesmen. Essentially it was a failure to envisage alternative political and military strategies. But the failure was not inevitable. It has become almost axiomatic in assessments of British and French leaders to see them as realistic statesmen, oppressed by the knowledge of their countries' weaknesses and the strength of potential enemies. The uncritical premise of these assessments is that the policy pursued was the only practicable one at the time. In fact there were many variables, and ministerial appraisals were the product of prejudice and opinion . . .

The feebleness and timidity of British and French foreign policies in the late 1930s were symptomatic of the shortsighted selfishness of a ruling class set on self-preservation.

4 *J. Charmley in the* Independent, *1989*
Chamberlain's foreign policy was an attempt to see if co-existence was possible; that it turned out not to be is no reason for condemning out of hand the only policy which promised any hope of avoiding war.

Neville Chamberlain's reputation has been blasted by a few hasty words in the aftermath of Munich, but "peace in our time" was not an unworthy objective, and it was worth pursuing to the uttermost. Men of honour will cavil at trying to appease a dictator, while the more cynical will assert that as Hitler was bound to attack us, we were wrong to try to postpone the evil day. But most of the men of honour managed to appease Stalin after 1941, and turkeys are seldom well-advised in pressing for an early Christmas. Even Duff Cooper, who resigned from the Cabinet over the Munich agreement which consigned the Sudetenland to Germany, could not suggest any alternative policy that was viable; he simply could not stomach Munich. Chamberlain, who bore the responsibility for millions of lives, could not afford the luxury of a weak stomach. Hitler's demands were not, in themselves, unreasonable (although his methods of prosecuting them were), and Britain was hardly in any military position to veto them had they been so.

The eastern borders bequeathed to Germany by the Versailles system were such that only a defeated nation could be forced to accept. Just as the

French, once they began to recover their power after 1871, wanted Alsace-Lorraine back, so did a renascent Germany want the return of territory which historically belonged to her. The triumph of liberalisn and nationalism at Versailles made a rod for the backs of western statesmen facing Hitler; why should Austria not unite with Germany, why should Hitler not seek to protect ethnic Germans in Czechoslovakia and Poland? Moreover, liberals in the West believed neither in the moral validity of the Versailles and associated treaties, nor yet in the retention by their governments of the military force which would have been necessary to enforce their terms. This was Chamberlain's inheritance, along with a shaky economy, a strategically over-extended empire and a France suffering from terminal loss of nerve.

B ACK TO THE PRESENT

Since 1945 there hasn't been a world war. Many people would claim that this is to do with the deterrence effect created by the possession of infinitely destructive arsenals of nuclear weapons by the two rival power blocs in the world – the Warsaw Pact led by Soviet Russia, and the NATO alliance led by America. However, there have been many 'smaller' wars and conflicts which have resulted in a huge loss of life – the Korean War, the Vietnam War, the Iran–Iraq War and so on. The basic problem of how to prevent one nation violating the sovereignty, the freedoms and the lives of another nation still remains. Yet many politicians would agree, drawing on the apparent lessons of the 1930s, that appeasing aggressors – satisfying their demands – is not the best way to prevent future aggression in support of further demands, although this is easier said than done. Explaining Britain's military action to remove Argentinian troops from the British colony of the Falklands Islands which they had seized in 1982, the British Prime Minister Mrs Thatcher made it clear that force must be met with force and that she was not going to repeat the mistakes of the policy of appeasement pursued in the 1930s. For her, appeasement was a policy of weakness and surrender. Here are some questions for discussion linking the moral and political dilemmas in international affairs in the 1930s with similar moral and political dilemmas today:

1 In what circumstances should one country support another country which has been attacked by a third country?

2 What should, or can, 'free' nations do to help countries in which there are repressive or totalitarian governments?

3 Are there circumstances where a policy of appeasement is morally justified (as opposed to being justified by necessity)?

4 Is rivalry and competition between nations inevitable and, if your answer is 'yes', is war therefore always a possibility?

5 Do you think discussion and negotiation are the best ways of resolving international conflicts and problems?

7 CONSENSUS AND COLLECTIVISM: LABOUR IN POWER

1940–51

I NTRODUCTION

In 1945 Britain and her allies finally won the war against Nazi Germany. The triumphant Prime Minister of our country was Winston Churchill, the Conservative leader of a wartime Coalition government in which the Conservative Party, as a result of their 249 seat victory in the 1935 election, were the dominant partners. In July 1945, in the first election to be held since 1935, the Labour Party, under the leadership of Clement Attlee, won an overwhelming victory and Winston Churchill and the Conservative Party found themselves in the unfamiliar position of His Majesty's Opposition.

The third Labour government of the twentieth century proceeded to implement a radical series of reforms. These reforms seemed not only to help Britain recover from the dislocation created by war but also to create a new role for governments and the state in society – and therefore, in certain respects, a new kind of society. Many historians and commentators believe that the Attlee governments of 1945–51 established a 'consensus' in British politics in which Labour and Conservative governments pursued a similar approach to running the country in the 1950s and 1960s. This 'consensus' approach involved the maintenance of the Welfare State, the pursuit of the goal of full employ-

ment, state management of the economy and a foreign policy based on a close relationship with the United States both in and outside NATO. Historians and commentators now see this 'consensus' as breaking down in the 1970s and indeed being reversed by the Conservative governments of the 1980s. In these changed historical circumstances, many from the Right and the Left have sharply criticised the policies and ideas of the Labour governments between 1945 and 1951 and their continuation by subsequent governments.

In this final theme of the book you will be examining how the experience of war led to such a resounding victory for the Labour Party in the 1945 election. You will then have the opportunity to find out about the policies and plans which the post-war Labour governments introduced and assess their significance. This will include looking at the extent to which these policies naturally evolved from the changed outlook and commitments of the wartime Conservative-Labour Coalition government. Finally, there will be an opportunity to analyse some of the views of historians from all shades of the political spectrum on the nature of the Labour achievement and its legacy for post-war Britain.

K EY QUESTIONS

1 What were the reasons for the Labour Party's victory in the 1945 General Election?

2 What were the main plans and policies introduced by Labour governments of 1945–51? What were the ideological principles underlying them?

3 What part did the policies and initiatives of the Churchill Coalition government of 1940–45 play in the shaping of Labour policies after 1945?

4 How significant were Labour achievements 1945–51?

S PECIAL TOPIC

THE LABOUR VICTORY IN THE 1945 GENERAL ELECTION

In July 1945, immediately after the end of the war against Nazi Germany the Labour Party won a decisive victory in the General Election and for the first time in its history gained an overall majority in the House of Commons. This gave Labour the power to embark upon a radical programme of reforms. How radical this programme actually turned out to be and to what extent the reforms were distinctively 'Labour' or 'socialist' reforms are questions you will be able to look at later on. In this Special Topic your concern will be to work out for yourselves why Labour won such a clear victory in 1945, especially when many official commentators had confidently predicted a win for Churchill and the Conservative Party.

The extracts in this section are taken from a variety of contemporary sources – memoirs, speeches, pamphlets, reports and commentaries. They have been selected to provide a range of evidence on the reasons for the Labour Party victory in 1945. Also included are some relevant statistics.

Activity

a Examine the piece from the *Daily Express* (extract 1) and the statistics for the elections of 1935 and 1945 (extract 2). Why do you think many political commentators found the 1945 election result so surprising?

b Study all the extracts of contemporary views and try to identify as many reasons and explanations as you can which account in some way for Labour's extraordinary success in the election. Bear in mind who the authors of the sources were and what purposes their 'communications' served, since this might influence your interpreta-

tion of what they said. Draw up a list of all the reasons you can find. Place these reasons in what you consider to be their order of importance.

Discussion

Now as a class come together and compare each other's analyses of the General Election of 1945. Have you identified a similar range of explanations based on the evidence? Do you agree on which were the most and which were the least important factors? What gaps still exist in your account of the Labour victory? What more do you need to find out in order to reach what you feel might be a comprehensive explanation of events?

Further Reading and Research

At this point it is essential to discover more about the running of the war on the 'Home Front' and the various plans and policies which emerged between 1940 and 1945 concerned with 'reconstruction' after the war was over. Use textbooks and other works of history to uncover the important historical details – the brief chronology in this section should be a useful guide for certain aspects of your investigations. Alternatively, your teacher will provide you with the essential information and ideas.

Further Discussion

Now that you have examined the domestic policies of the wartime Coalition, how does your knowledge change or develop your understanding of why Labour won the 1945 election so convincingly? In what way might it be argued that the initiatives of the Conservative-Labour Coalition led by Churchill paved the way for a Labour victory?

1 *The* Daily Express, *6 July 1945*

Mr. Churchill's Government is almost certainly "in." On that there was general agreement among electoral experts of all parties when polling closed last night ...

Because there had been a big poll some experts were prophesying a three-figure majority for the Government. The most cautious estimate I heard, from a source not too well disposed towards the Government was "60 to 90."

2 *The 1935 and 1945 General Election results*

	Total Votes	M.P.s Elected	Candi- dates	Un- opposed Returns	% Share of Total Vote
1935. 14 Nov					
Conservative	11,810,158	432	585	26	53·7
Liberal	1,422,116	20	161	—	6·4
Labour	8,325,491	154	552	13	37·9
Independent Labour Party	139,577	4	17	—	0·7
Communist	27,117	1	2	—	0·1
Others	272,595	4	31	1	1·2
Elec. 31,379,050 Turnout 71·2%	21,997,054	615	1,348	40	100·0
1945. 5 Jul					
Conservative	9,988,306	213	624	1	39·8
Liberal	2,248,226	12	306	—	9·0
Labour	11,995,152	393	604	2	47·8
Communist	102,780	2	21	—	0·4
Common Wealth	110,634	1	23	—	0·4
Others	640,880	19	104	—	2·0
Elec. 33,240,391 Turnout 72·7%	25,085,978	640	1,682	3	100·0

Adapted from D. Butler and A. Sloman: British Political Facts *1900–1979 (1980)*

3 *E. Shinwell, member of the Labour Cabinet after 1945, in* The Labour Story *(1963)*

After the initial shock of Nazi successes in the Low Countries, reported almost hourly, there developed a sense of having an almost impossible job to do – and to achieve success – which was soon to encompass the whole nation. By Friday [May 1940], therefore, when a meeting of the Joint Executive took place, there was virtually unanimous agreement that Labour should serve under Churchill, who that morning had begun the task of forming a Government.

Attlee and other leaders were moved by a natural sense of patriotism, and they were impressed with the generosity of Churchill's offers to the Labour Party. Considering the size of the Labour Opposition in the Commons the chance of having two out of five offices in the War Cabinet was extremely good, especially as Attlee, in effect Deputy Prime Minister, and Greenwood, as Minister without Portfolio, could inevitably be the leading personalities in the Commons' day-to-day business.

Other Labour posts were those of A.V. Alexander at the Admiralty; Hugh Dalton, after a short period of suspense and insistence about his claims, became Minister of Economic Warfare; Sir William Jowitt, who had joined MacDonald in 1931, but had recanted, as Solicitor-General; Herbert Morrison, as Minister of Supply (later to be transferred to the Home Office and Ministry of Home Security); and finally, and significantly, Ernest Bevin, as Minister of Labour.

4 *The Labour Party election manifesto 'Let Us Face The Future' (1945)*

The interests have not been able to make the same profits out of this war as they did out of the last. The determined propaganda of the Labour Party, helped by other progressive forces, had its effect in 'taking the profit out of war'. The 100% Excess Profits Tax, the controls over industry and transport, the fair rationing of food and control of prices – without which the Labour Party would not have remained in the Government – these all helped to win the war. With these measures the country has come nearer to making 'fair shares' the national rule than ever before in its history.

But the war in the East is not yet over. There are grand pickings still to be had. A short boom period after the war, when savings, gratuities and post war credits are there to be spent, can make a profiteer's paradise. But Big Business knows that this will happen only if the people vote into power the party which promises to get rid of the controls and so let the profiteers and racketeers have that freedom for which they are pleading eloquently on every Tory platform and in every Tory newspaper.

They accuse the Labour Party of wishing to impose controls for the sake of control. That is not true, and they know it. What is true is that the anti-controllers and anti-planners desire to sweep away public controls, simply in order to give the profiteering interests and the privileged rich an entirely free hand to plunder the rest of the nation as shamelessly as they did in the nineteen-twenties.

5 *J.B. Priestley in a BBC broadcast, 'Postscripts' July 1940*
Now, the war, because it demands a huge collective effort, is compelling us to change not only our ordinary, social and economic habits, but also our habits of thought. We're actually changing over from the property view to the sense of community, which simply means that we realize we're all in the same boat. But, and this is the point, that boat can serve not only as our defence against Nazi aggression, but as an ark in which we can all finally land in a better world.

6 *The Beveridge Report on social welfare, 1942*
... Want could have been abolished before the present war by a redistribution of income within the wage-earning classes, without touching any of the wealthier classes. This is said not to suggest that redistribution of income should be confined to the wage-earning classes; still less is it said to suggest that men should be content with avoidance of want, with subsistence incomes. It is said simply as

'Under the counter' – Daily Mirror *June 1945*

the most convincing demonstration that abolition of want just before this war was easily within the economic resources of the community; want was a needless scandal due to not taking the trouble to prevent it.

7 *Letter from a Tory MP to the Tory Chief Whip, October 1942*
Throughout the country the Conservative Party has become a cheap joke: the press and the B.B.C. treat us with the contempt that we have earned and deserve.

You yourself are well aware of what the P.M. thinks of the Tory Rump: he may not say so himself, but R.C., B.B. [Randolph Churchill, Brendan Bracken] and his other satellites are not so careful of their tongues.

You must agree with the fact that as an effective body of opinion either in the House or in the Country, the Conservative Party have ceased to exist.

8 *Mass Observation report in the* New Statesman, *1943*
... but Mass Observation had made many studies of Churchill popularity, short-term and long. While he has outstandingly maintained his position as a popular war leader – in October, nine people in ten were favourable, a higher figure than in the same month last year – his position as a post-war figure is far from certain in the public mind. At some point in most of our political enquiries it emerges that most people do not expect he will be the primary post-war leader, while many do not expect that he will himself seek to be a post-war leader at all. His age, his already almost complete achievement, his supposed disinterest in home affairs, and his alleged lack of sympathy with working people over domestic issues, all add up in the public mind. In addition, there is to some extent an automatic process of peace which tends to underline the contrast by wanting to be rid of the primary figures from war-time. Thus, in answer to a straight question on whether or not Churchill could or should be post-war prime minister, the majority reject the proposition.

9 *A British Institute of Political Opinion poll quoted in the above report, 1943*

'If there was a General Election tomorrow, how would you vote?'

Would vote for	Percentage who said they would vote this way in:	
	June 1943	August 1943
Conservative	25	23
Labour	38	39
Liberal	9	9
Communist	3	3
Common Wealth	2	1

10 *Herbert Morrison, Labour Home Secretary, in a speech in 1946*
The Labour Party has itself been developing an instrument. That is to say, in the ten or fifteen years leading up to the war, things were not too happy, either in the Party, in the country, in Parliament or at Head Office. But I think in the months that led up to that recent election, there was a great change in the whole heart, mind and spirit of the Labour Party. There had been a considerable degree of modernisation, a considerable degree of political realism, a considerable degree of improvement in its publicity technique. So that the Labour Party rendered a much better account of itself at the recent General Election than it ever did before.

One of the great things it did was to accept or to determine that it would have an election programme that was realistic. It used up-to-date, clear-cut publicity methods, greatly improved organisation, and an honest, objective, bold, factual policy statement at the election. Hitherto the Party was tempted to put wishful thinking into its electoral programmes. This time it did not put anything in the programme which it did not think could be done.

11 *A pamphlet on housing, 1945*
As this war draws to a victorious conclusion, this desire [for a home] will be expressed in no uncertain terms by millions of people who have worked, fought and sacrificed in this war against Fascism. They will not be prepared to tolerate the slums, the overcrowding and inadequate housing to which they have been condemned in the past. They will demand modern, up-to-date houses and flats as part of the better life they are determined to have. Nor will they be content to wait 10 or 20 years. . . .

12 *Winston Churchill in an election broadcast, 4 June 1945*
But I will go farther. I declare to you, from the bottom of my heart, that no Socialist system can be established without a political police. Many of those who are advocating Socialism or voting Socialist to-day will be horrified at this idea. That is because they are short-sighted, that is because they do not see where their theories are leading them.

No Socialist Government conducting the entire life and industry of the country could afford to allow free, sharp, or violently-worded expressions of public discontent. They would have to fall back on some form of *Gestapo*, no doubt very humanely directed in the first instance.

13 *James Chuter Ede, leading Labour Party politician, in his diary 5 July 1945*
Tuesday 5 June The *Times* reproves Churchill for the tone of his speech last night. H. Morrison answers it point by point in the *Daily Herald*. I caught the 10.37 at Ewell West & on arrival at the House read the *Manchester Guardian* which was very satirical about the P.M.'s speech. At the Party Meeting we decided to let the Family Allowances Bill go through.1940 In the House the P.M. was given a boisterous welcome, Pritt declaring his speech had given us 50 seats.

14 *Clement Attlee, Leader of the Labour Party, in an election broadcast June 1945*
The Conservative Party remains as always a class Party. In twenty-three years in the House of Commons, I cannot recall more than half a dozen from the ranks of the wage earners. It represents today, as in the past, the forces of property and privilege. The Labour Party is, in fact, the one Party which most nearly reflects in its representation and composition all the main streams which flow into the great river of our national life.

Our appeal to you, therefore, is not narrow or sectional.

15 *Palme Dutt in an article in* Labour Monthly *August 1945*
This glorious political leap forward in Britain is the sequel of military victory in the people's war of the

United Nations against fascism. . . .

The 1945 leap forward is the counterpart of the sweep to the left throughout Europe, following victory over fascism, the alliance with the Soviet Union, the tremendous role of the Soviet Union and the resistance movements in the struggle, the triumph of the Left in the French municipal elections, and the formation of new democratic Governments with Communist representation in the majority of European countries.

16 *S. Haffner:* A Book of British Profiles *(1954)*
. . . As a statesman, Attlee's formative period undoubtedly began in 1935. His party had been crushed at the 1931 election after the MacDonald 'betrayal'; and Lansbury had proved quite ineffective as a parliamentary leader. So Attlee – one of the few Labour candidates to have survived the landslide – was told to act as leader until after the next election.

The Labour Party was in an almost hopeless mess – utterly defeated, and divided into quarrelling factions. Attlee, loyal, modest, impartial, clearheaded, capable of decision, and with the courage of his personal detachment, had precisely the qualities needed. In reuniting his broken party he added to those qualities a volume of experience in political management – so that he has quietly led the party ever since. It was at this time that the loyal Attlee learned to stomach disloyal colleagues . . .

17 *Clement Attlee:* As It Happened *(1954)*
I think, first of all, people wanted a positive new policy, and not an attempt to go back to the old. Secondly, there was by that time a good deal of feeling among many people against what was felt to be the one-man business Churchill was running. And there was a good deal of suspicion of the forces behind him – Beaverbrook in particular . . . And even those who would have liked Churchill weren't prepared to have him if it meant having the Tories too. They remembered Munich and they remembered pre-war unemployment. They didn't want the Tories again. . . .

Quite naturally, in war, when the public good must take precedence over private interests, the solutions had a strong socialist flavour.

18 *E. Watkins:* The Cautious Revolution *(1950)*
It is not difficult, after the event, to find smooth answers to the question of why the Labour party won in 1945 and why Mr. Churchill lost. There is no single easy answer. With a poll of some eleven million votes to the Conservatives' eight million, it would be plausible to say that it was the men and women in the forces who turned the scale. Indeed, there were then five million of them, all with votes.

One basic fact is that the Labour party had become a recognized, constitutional and orthodox political party, and the alternative to the Conservatives. From 1918 to 1929, it had fought with and defeated the Liberal party on the issue of which was the second party in the country. In 1931, it shed its top growth of men from a past period of time, and between 1931 and 1939 it had learned, in opposition, some of the lessons and rules of government. During the war, it had shared the risks and the glories (lesser) of triumph. Above all, at the start of 1945, it had seized its chance. It had said what so many were thinking, that Britain would not survive the peace with the kind of government it had possessed before the war.

19 *Harold Macmillan, leading Conservative at the time:* Tides of Fortune *(1969)*
Churchill was buoyed up by the enthusiastic reception which he had received in his 1000-mile electoral tour. Vast crowds, who had hardly seen him in person since the beginning of the war and had only heard his voice through those famous broadcasts by which they had been sustained in times of disaster and inspired in moments of success, turned out in flocks to see and applaud him. They wanted to thank him for what he had done for them; and in all that they were sincere. But this did not mean that they wanted to entrust him and his Tory colleagues with the conduct of their lives in the years that were to follow. They had been persuaded, civilians and servicemen alike, during the last years of war, that immediately the struggle was over there would follow a kind of automatic Utopia. The British people would move with hardly an effort into a Socialist or semi-Socialist State under their own leaders, which would bring about unexampled prosperity in a world of universal peace. Nor had they forgotten or been allowed to forget

26 July 1945: Clement Attlee and his wife Vi after Labour's victory in the General Election

the years before the war. Pamphlets and books attacking the 'guilty men of Munich' were published and circulated in vast numbers. It was not Churchill who lost the 1945 election; it was the ghost of Neville Chamberlain.

20 *Reginald Maudling, an up-and-coming Conservative in 1945 in his memoirs, 1978*
In the result we were heavily defeated. I suppose we should have expected this. Certainly when the Forces' vote, which on that occasion was counted early, came through, we could see the way things were going. There was a desire for change, a determination not to go back to the pre-war days. The Conservative Party had not much to offer at that time to those who wished to see change, and we relied heavily on the personality of Winston Churchill. There was no doubt about his popularity, or, indeed, the reverence, in which people held him, but as it turned out we overestimated the effect this would have on their voting. People distinguished between Churchill the War Leader, and the Conservative Party as a peacetime Government.

Chronology: Reconstruction 1940–45

Jan 1940	The Barlow Report recommends that the government should assume responsibility for the pattern of land use throughout the country.
Feb 1941	Reconstruction Committee established to develop plans for post-war Britain.
Sept 1942	The Uthwatt Committee recommends that the state should control the rights of development of land outside built-up areas.
Dec 1942	The Beveridge Report outlines plans for a Welfare State with a National Health Service, full employment and family allowances.
Feb 1943	Ministry of Town and Country Planning set up.
Feb 1943	Bevin at the Ministry of Labour introduces a Catering Wages Act to enable minimum wages to be established in the catering industry.
Feb 1944	White Paper outlining plans for a National Health Service is supported by the Coalition government.
May 1944	White Paper on employment policy advocates full employment as a primary aim of governments after the war.
Aug 1944	Butler Education Act rationalises the provision of secondary education for 5 to 15 year-olds.
May 1945	Family Allowances Act authorises allowances for second and subsequent children.

CONTEMPORARY VIEWS & OPINIONS

THE LABOUR PARTY MANIFESTO 1945

This section is designed to help you understand the significance of the ideas and the policies which the Labour Party was putting forward in the election campaign after the end of the war. It was these ideas and policies to which the electorate gave their support when they voted in a Labour government with a 146 seat majority in July 1945.

Activity

The following exercises can be used for written work and/or for discussion and should be carried out individually or in pairs:

a Read the manifesto carefully and then put together two sets of notes containing the following:

- The ways in which the proposals in this document differ from the ideas and policies of Conservative and Labour governments in the inter-war period.
- The ways in which these proposals differ from the ideas and plans developed by the Coalition government between 1940 and 1945.

To do this properly you will need to refer back to the work you have already done on inter-war politics as well as the work you may have just carried out in the 'Special Topic' section of the theme.

b Remind yourself about what the doctrine of socialism in its 'pure' sense involves – your teacher will help you here if necessary. Now make an assessment of the extent to which the proposals in the Labour manifesto represented a truly socialist programme concerned with transforming the capitalist nature of society.

Discussion

As a class, if you haven't already done so, discuss your observations and conclusions in relation to the activities above. The following questions will be useful to consider: How radical and different were the ideas and plans in the Labour manifesto? What criticisms could be made of the Labour manifesto? What kinds of problems could the Labour government voted into power in 1945 on the basis of this manifesto expect to face?

---

1 *The Labour Party election manifesto, 1945*
What the election will be about

Britain's coming Election will be the greatest test in our history of the judgment and common sense of our people.

The nation wants food, work and homes. It wants more than that – it wants good food in plenty, useful work for all, and comfortable, labour-saving homes that take full advantage of the resources of modern science and productive industry. It wants a high and rising standard of living, security for all against a rainy day, an educational system that will give every boy and girl a chance to develop the best that is in them . . .

Jobs for all

All parties pay lip service to the idea of jobs for all. All parties are ready to promise to achieve that end by keeping up the national purchasing power

The Labour Victors, August 1945: Bevin, Attlee and Morrison

and controlling changes in the national expenditure through Government action. Where agreement ceases is in the degree of control of private industry that is necessary to achieve the desired end.

In hard fact, the success of a full employment programme will certainly turn upon the firmness and success with which the Government fits into that programme the investment and development policies of private as well as public industry . . .

What will the Labour Party do?

First, the whole of the national resources, in land, material and labour must be fully employed. Production must be raised to the highest level and related to purchasing power.

Secondly, a high and constant purchasing power can be maintained through good wages, social services and insurance, and taxation which bears less heavily on the lower-income groups. But everybody knows that money and savings lose their value if prices rise, so rents and the prices of the necessities of life will be controlled.

Thirdly, planned investment in essential industries and on houses, schools, hospitals and civic centres will occupy a large field of capital expenditure. A National Investment Board will determine social priorities and promote better timing in private investment . . .

Industry in the service of the nation

By the test of war some industries have shown themselves capable of rising to new heights of efficiency and expansion. Others, including some of our older industries fundamental to our economic structure, have wholly or partly failed . . .

Each industry must have applied to it the test of national service. If it serves the nation, well and good; if it is inefficient and falls down on its job, the nation must see that things are put right . . .

The Labour Party is a Socialist Party, and proud of it. Its ultimate purpose at home is the establishment of the Socialist Commonwealth of Great Britain – free, democratic, efficient, progressive, public-spirited, its material resources organised in the service of the British people.

But Socialism cannot come overnight, as the product of a week-end revolution. The members of the Labour Party, like the British people, are practical-minded men and women.

There are basic industries ripe and over-ripe for public ownership and management in the direct service of the nation. There are many smaller businesses rendering good service which can be left to go on with their useful work . . .

In the light of these considerations, the Labour Party submits to the nation the following industrial programme:—

1. Public ownership of the fuel and power industries . . .
2. Public ownership of inland transport . . .
3. Public ownership of iron and steel . . .
4. Public supervision of monopolies and cartels . . .
5. A firm and clear-cut programme for the export trade . . .
6. The shaping of suitable economic and price controls to secure that first things shall come first in the transition from war to peace and that every citizen (including the demobilised Service men and women) shall get fair play . . .

Houses and the building programme . . .

Housing will be one of the greatest and one of the earliest tests of a Government's real determination to put the nation first. Labour's pledge is firm and direct – it will proceed with a housing programme with the maximum practical speed until every family in this island has a good standard of accommodation. That may well mean centralised purchasing and pooling of building materials and components by the State, together with price control. If that is necessary to get the houses as it was necessary to get the guns and planes, Labour is ready . . .

Health of the nation and its children

By good food and good homes, much avoidable ill-health can be prevented. In addition the best health services should be available for all. Money must no longer be the passport to the best treatment.

In the new National Health Service there should be health centres where the people may get the best that modern science can offer, more and better hospitals, and proper conditions for our doctors and nurses. More research is required into the causes of disease and the ways to prevent and cure it . . .

Social insurance against the rainy day

The Labour Party has played a leading part in the long campaign for proper social security for all

– social provision against rainy days, coupled with economic policies calculated to reduce rainy days to a minimum. Labour led the fight against the mean and shabby treatment which was the lot of millions while Conservative Governments were in power over long years. A Labour Government will press on rapidly with legislation extending social insurance over the necessary wide field to all . . .

A world of progress and peace

No domestic policy, however wisely framed and courageously applied, can succeed in a world still threatened by war. Economic strife and political and military insecurity are enemies of peace. We

cannot cut ourselves off from the rest of the world – and we ought not to try.

Now that victory has been won, at so great a cost of life and material destruction, we must make sure that Germany and Japan are deprived of all power to make war again. We must consolidate in peace the great war-time association of the British Commonwealth with the U.S.A. and the U.S.S.R. Let it not be forgotten that in the years leading up to the war the Tories were so scared of Russia that they missed the chance to establish a partnership which might well have prevented the war . . .

O UTLINING THE EVENTS

THE ACHIEVEMENTS OF LABOUR GOVERNMENTS 1945–51

The extracts in this section are taken from different history textbooks and more specialist works. They have been selected to provide you with summaries of the whole range of Labour policies and achievements in the period. As in previous themes, the activities based on these sources have been devised not only to help you establish a basic knowledge of the narrative of events, but also to help you begin to appreciate different interpretations of the Labour record. The extracts should be used in conjunction with the Labour manifesto given in the previous section.

Activity I

Examine the material in each of the four sections entitled 'Nationalisation', 'Social Policy', 'The Economy' and 'Foreign Policy'. For each of these areas construct a brief chronology of the main policies carried out by Labour governments and follow this with a short paragraph summarising the nature of their achievements as discussed by the historians. In each paragraph make explicit reference to any obvious judgements which the historians make. Obviously, given the nature

of the exercise, there will be much which you do not fully understand or are not very clear about at this provisional stage. But, don't panic!

Discussion

As a class go through the work you have just carried out and compare each others' accounts and understandings of the historians' extracts. At this stage your teacher may begin to fill you in with additional details and explanations.

Further Reading and Research

Using the work you have carried out above as a starting point and a guide, carry out further research into the Labour governments' achievements 1945–51. Make notes where necessary. Your teacher will advise you about this. In addition to researching in greater depth the areas of policy indicated in the activity above, find out why the Labour Party's majority was so greatly reduced in the 1950 General Election and why it lost the 1951 election.

Activity II

Have a look again at the Labour manifesto of 1945 in the previous 'Contemporary Views and Opinions' section and, working individually or in small groups, answer the question: 'To what extent did the policies of Labour administrations 1945–51 fulfil the pledges given in the manifesto of 1945?' This can be a written or a discussion exercise.

Discussion

The class as a whole should now review the work done in the above activity. You should then begin to discuss possible criticisms that could be made of the Labour record from both a right-wing and a left-wing point of view. You should also consider how you might defend the Labour record from these possible criticisms.

GENERAL INFORMATION

1 The Illustrated Dictionary of British History *ed. A. Marwick*

Attlee, Clement, earl 1883–1967. Attlee went to Oxford and became a socialist at Toynbee Hall. After a gallant war record he became Labour mayor of Stepney (1919) and MP for Limehouse (1922). He survived the 1931 Labour collapse and became leader of the party in 1935. Having played an instrumental part in ousting Neville Chamberlain (May 1940) he became deputy prime minister with responsibility for domestic policy in Churchill's coalition cabinet, where his tact and administrative grasp complemented Churchill's imagination and eloquence. The 1945 election returned him with a mandate to nationalize key industries and create the national health service. His period of office (1945–51) also saw the granting of independence to India (1947) and, on a more sombre note, attempts to cope with a rundown economy and a worsening international situation. His 2nd government (February 1950–October 1951) joined the USA in the Korean war, but party divisions and the loss of Cripps and Bevin led to an election which he lost, and he was succeeded by Gaitskell (1955).

2 *C. Cook and J. Stevenson:* The Longman Handbook of Modern British History 1714–1980 *(1983)*
Bevin, Ernest (1881–1951: Labour MP Central Wandsworth, 1940–50 and East Woolwich, 1950–1; chairman TUC General Council, 1937; minister of labour 1940–5; foreign secretary, 1945–51; lord privy seal, 1951. Rose through Dockers' Union to unite 50 unions into Trnasport and General Workers' Union in 1921, the largest union in world; prominent in TUC. General Council service, 1925–40; supported creation of NATO in April 1949; summoned Commonwealth Foreign Ministers' Conference, February 1950.

3 Dictionary of British History *ed. J.P. Kenyon (1988)*
Bevan, Aneurin (1897–1960). An MP from 1929 to 1960, who as health minister under Attlee (1945–51) established the National Health Service. Leader of the Labour Left and a noted orator, he resigned from office in 1951 in protest against cuts in spending on social services. He ultimately cooperated with Gaitskell, after being defeated by him in the contest for the party leadership (1955).

4 *The 1950 and 1951 General Election results*

	Total Votes	M.P.s Elected	Candidates	Unopposed Returns	% Share of Total Vote
1950. 23 Feb					
Conservative	12,502,567	298	620	2	43·5
Liberal	2,621,548	9	475	—	9·1
Labour	13,266,592	315	617	—	46·1
Communist	91,746	—	100	—	0·3
Others	290,218	3	56	—	1·0
Elec. 33,269,770 Turnout 84·0%	28,772,671	625	1,868	2	100·0
1951. 25 Oct					
Conservative	13,717,538	321	617	4	48·0
Liberal	730,556	6	109	—	2·5
Labour	13,948,605	295	617	—	48·8
Communist	21,640	—	10	—	0·1
Others	177,329	3	23	—	0·6
Elec. 34,645,573 Turnout 82·5%	28,595,668	625	1,376	4	100·0

Adapted from D. Butler and A. Sloman: British Political Facts 1900–1979 *(1980)*

NATIONALISATION

5 *P. Addison:* The Road to 1945 *(1977)*
The nationalization programme embraced the Bank of England (May 1946), the coal mines (January 1947), electricity (April 1948), gas (May 1948) and the railways (May 1948). To these measures the Conservatives put up only a token opposition. In each case the argument for state control was as much accepted by businessmen as by Labour politicians, and the industries concerned were either public utilities or ailing concerns of

THE UNIVERSAL UNCLES

Punch *25 December 1946*

little value to their owners and no interest to other capitalists. Because of the conference resolution passed against the wishes of the National Executive in 1944, Labour were committed to the nationalization of iron and steel, one of the most glittering prizes in the private sector. In vain did Morrison, encouraged by Attlee, try to evade the commitment by devising a system of control which fell short of public ownership. The industry was nationalized in February 1951.

6 *R. Eatwell:* The 1945–1951 Labour Government *(1979)*

The nationalisation programme took up considerable Parliamentary time; the iron and steel bill was an especially controversial one. By 1951 ten per cent of the workforce were in the nationalised industries. However, the industries nationalised were either derelict, or public service industries; even iron and steel was a dubious asset commercially. This meant that nationalisation was quickly identified with loss-making and inefficiency; social arguments in favour of maintaining loss-making

plant, of keeping prices down, tended to be obscured. Moreover, the public corporation form of nationalisation took no account of the various arguments for common ownership in terms of workers' control.

7 *P. Hennessey: 'The Attlee Governments, 1945–51' in* Ruling Performance *ed. P. Hennessey and A. Seldon (1987)*

On the industrial front, nationalization advanced apace in 1945–6 with Morrison the key figure as chairman of the Cabinet's Socialization of Industry Committee and, as Leader of the House of Commons, the minister responsible for piloting the hefty tranche of legislation through Parliament. In the protracted parliamentary session of 1945–6 no fewer than seventy-five measures passed through the legislative process. By autumn 1946 four nationalization statues were in place – covering the Bank of England, civil aviation, cable and wireless, and, most emotive of all for the Labour movement, coal. The nationalization of railways, electricity and long-distance transport followed in 1947. None of the measures caused any real controversy. The model, much derided in later years from left and right, was Morrison's beloved London Passenger Transport Board of 1934, created in his London County Council days along lines adumbrated earlier in his first book, *Socialisation and Transport.* Whitehall departments would sponsor public corporations. Ministers would appoint efficient expert people to boards which would run the industries at arm's length from Whitehall, Westminster and, it should be added, the workforce.

SOCIAL POLICY

8 *P. Calvocaressi:* The British Experience 1945–1975 *(1979)*

The National Health Act became law before the end of 1946. It decreed free medical and dental services for all. It established local health centres and invited doctors, dentists and pharmacists to join them. The remuneration of GPs was to consist of a basic salary augmented by capitation fees inside the service and private practice outside. Hospitals, municipal and voluntary, passed into the hands of the Minister but were to be run by regional boards and committees. The sum of £66 million was provided for what was in effect the purchase by the state of all private practices.

9 *P. J. Madgwick et al:* Britain Since 1945 *(1982)*
The Labour government enacted the principles of the Beveridge scheme for social insurance (National Insurance Act 1946). This ended four centuries of the Poor Law. Under the new legislation, it was intended that the citizen would be adequately safeguarded against old age, sickness and unemployment, by an insurance-based system without the much resented means tests of the 1930s. Poverty was not abolished, but there is no doubt that the number of people seriously lacking in food, clothing, shelter and warmth was very substantially reduced compared with the 1930s (or indeed any previous period).

10 *C. Cook and J. Stevenson:* The Longman Handbook of Modern British History 1714–1980 *(1983)*

1946 New Towns Act set up a number of development corporations entrusted with the building of new towns in various parts of the country.

1947 Town and Country Planning Act. County councils compelled to prepare plans for the development of their areas and given powers of compulsory purchase. Planning permission required for major alterations to buildings or changes in land use by owners.

11 *D. Coates:* The Labour Party and the Struggle for Socialism *(1975)*
Behind this structure of public ownership and State planning of the private sector the Labour Government created its system of welfare provision. True to its promise of alleviating the individual insecurities and destitution endemic to untrammelled private capitalism, it created a system of universally available social insurance, which provided guaranteed minimum incomes and provisions to those subject to unemployment, ill-health, industrial accidents, disablement, infirmity and old age. It continued the new family allowances as a form of supplementary benefit to those with children of school age or under. It raised the school leaving age to fifteen, and continued the guarantee of secondary education for all embodied in the 1944 Education Act. It created a national health service. It committed itself to a house-building programme which, though subject to economic retrenchment and resource-starvation later, still built 806,000 permanent houses and carried out 333,000 conversions in the first five years of office. Its taxation initiatives, especially in the early years, placed an even heavier burden on higher incomes than had the Coalition Government. Combined rates of surtax and income tax reached 19s. 6d. in the pound on incomes in excess of £20,000 a year, and taxation on inheritances, and on luxury and semi-luxury goods, was greatly increased. Distributed business profits were taxed at 50% by 1951, and the remaining 10s. in the pound was then subject to income tax at the standard rate.

THE ECONOMY

12 *K.O. Morgan: 'The Twentieth Century 1914–1984' in* The Oxford Illustrated History of Britain *ed. K.O. Morgan (1984)*
Later legend made this era one of austerity and general gloom. So in some ways it was. From the outset, Britain faced a huge post-war debt. There were continuous shortages of raw materials and of basic food supplies, made worse by the lack of dollars which led to a severe imbalance of trade with North America. There were moments of near-panic like the run on sterling, following convertibility of the exchanges, in July 1947; the decision to impose devaluation of the pound against the dollar in September 1949; the balance of payments difficulties during the Korean War in July–August 1951. Rationing for food, clothing, petrol, and many domestic commodities survived until 1954. Planning and controls, administered by faceless bureaucrats in Whitehall (and circumvented by 'spivs' and the 'black market'), became part of the conventional stereotypes of the time. For all that, most working-class people, the vast majority of the population, viewed the years since 1945 as much as the best that had been generally known since the late-Victorian heyday. Wages rose to 30 per cent above their 1938 level. There were higher living standards, guaranteed employment, more satisfying environmental and educational facilities. In a world, too, where popular sport such

as football and cricket, and also the cinema and the dance-hall, were readily accessible, the leisure aspects of the good life were catered for as well. Foodball stadiums such as Highbury, Villa Park, or Old Trafford attracted each week over 60,000 enthusiastic (and entirely peaceable) spectators. In 1951, in its last few months in office, the Labour government launched a Festival of Britain, to commemorate the centenary of the Great Exhibition of 1851.

13 *Some relevant economic statistics*

	Index of Industrial Production (1963=100)	Net balance of payments on current account £m.	Un-employment in thousands	Income Tax Rate in £
1931	38	−104	2,630	4/6
1938	53	−70	1,865	5/–
1946	55	−230	374	10/–
1947	58	−381	480	9/–
1948	62	26	310	9/–
1949	66	−1	308	9/–
1950	70	307	314	9/–
1951	72	−369	253	9/–
1952	71	163	424	9/6

Adapted from D. Butler and A. Sloman: British Political Facts 1900–1979 *(1980)*

14 *A. Gamble:* Britain in Decline *(1981)*
The economic policy of the Labour govenment was naturally dominated by the problems of reconstruction. The loss of exports and of overseas investment income during the war meant a huge structural deficit on the balance of payments. Essential imports could not be financed. The difficulty of quickly switching the economy back to peacetime production, the backlog of demand built up during the war, and the continuance of public spending at a high level, mainly because of the new welfare plans, all added to the pressure of demand and the risk of a very rapid inflation. These difficulties, however, were overcome with assistance from the United States, exports were expanded enormously and the export gap closed. Manufacturing output recovered. Strikes remained illegal under wartime regulations, rationing and many physical controls stayed in force to restrain consumption and direct investment, interest rates were

kept at 2 per cent, the trade unions accepted wage restraint and the electorate accepted austerity. Inflation was not entirely avoided but fairly successfully suppressed, until the decision to rearm in 1951.

A measure of the success of reconstruction was the fact that Britain still accounted for 25 per cent of exports of world manufacturers in 1951. At the beginning of that decade the British economy looked strong.

FOREIGN POLICY

15 *K.O. Morgan: 'The Twentieth Century 1914–1984' in* The Oxford Illustrated History of Britain *ed. K.O. Morgan (1984)*
However, Britain's international position was qualified by the gradual, but necessary, retreat from empire that the post-war period witnessed. It was a relentless process, even during the regime of such a veteran imperialist as Sir Winston Churchill. The granting of self-government to India, Pakistan, Burma, and Ceylon (Sri Lanka) by the Attlee government in 1947–9 was the key moment in the transfer of power. It was an unambiguous statement of Britain's military and financial inability, and above all lack of will, to retain possession of distant lands by force.

16 *P. Calvocaressi:* The British Experience 1945–1975 *(1979)*
There was no question about the development of nuclear power for domestic purposes and the Atomic Energy Act 1946 gave the government authority to do this, but bombs were another matter and it was not until 1947 that the decision to manufacture bombs was taken. This decision was taken by a sub-committee of the cabinet and was kept virtually secret until the Conservatives returned to office in 1951.

17 *H. Pelling:* A Short History of the Labour Party *(1982)*
By far the most contentious areas of policy within the Labour Party itself were foreign affairs and defence. Bevin, as Foreign Secretary, soon found that he was faced by an unexpectedly intransigent attitude on the part of the Russian Government. Realising the economic weakness not only of Bri-

tiain but also of the rest of Europe, Bevin therefore worked for effective collaboration with the United States. He did much to bring the 'Marshall Plan' into existence, which had a powerfully invigorating effect in stimulating recovery throughout Western Europe; and he was a prime mover in creating the North Atlantic Treaty Organisation. This policy of association with the United States and of rearma-ment to resist Russian pressure did not commend itself very warmly to the rank and file of the Labour Party. The concept of a 'Socialist' foreign policy, it was felt, had been abandoned: at the very least, an attempt should have been made to retain a position of independence between the capitalist and the Communist world – if possible, to form a bridge between them.

H ISTORIANS' VIEWS & OPINIONS

CONSENSUS AND COLLECTIVISM 1940–51: THE LABOUR ACHIEVEMENT

Historians can sometimes agree on what the important 'facts' are in a particular historical topic, but they can hardly ever agree on a common interpretation of those 'facts'. History, therefore, is almost always controversial. This particular theme, centring on the Labour governments 1945–51, is no exception and has generated a particularly vehement range of arguments. This section includes a cross-section of typical view-points for you to analyse and use as the basis for reaching your own verdict on the Labour achievement. Some of you may still be rather baffled by the terms 'consensus' and 'collectivism' and what they mean when applied to British society and government since 1940. Hopefully, the activities below will help you improve your understanding.

Activity I

a Of the ten historians' views in this section, two criticise the Attlee governments (and the coming of the post-war consensus) from a left-wing point of view, three criticise these governments from a right-wing point of view, another passage provides a short summary of the left and right-wing critiques and two of the extracts provide a defence of the record of the Attlee governments. The remaining two passages do not fall into any of these categories. Try and identify which extract is which. Make sure you have reasons for your choices.

b Working with a partner, compare each other's selections to find out if you have reached similar conclusions about the different points of view taken by the historians.

Activity II

Working individually or in pairs, carry out the following tasks based on the sources you have been investigating.

a Summarise in your own words what historians mean by the term 'consensus' in relation to the politics of the 1940s and afterwards. In your summary try to incorporate the terms 'collectivism' or 'social democracy' (this of course means discovering what these terms mean as well).

b Re-read extract 2. Think about the work you have already down on the period 1940–5. What point is Addison making about the Churchill Coalition government, especially in relation to the post-war consensus – what he calls 'peacetime collectivism'? What implications does Addison's view have as regards an assessment of the achievements of the Labour administrations 1945–51?

c Make lists of the distinct arguments used by left-wing critics, right-wing critics and defenders of the Labour record 1945–51.

Discussion

Discuss in groups and/or as a class the work you have carried out above. Given all the work you have done on the theme, which particular view of the Labour governments do you support? What are your reasons and your evidence?

Class Debate

The motion is: 'The record of Labour governments 1945–1951 was one of unsurpassed achievement'.

1 *P. Addison, quoted in P. Hennessey: 'The Attlee Governments 1945–1951' in* Ruling Performance *eds P. Hennessey and A. Seldon (1987)*
When the Marxist Left and the radical Right emerged in the 1970s there was one point on which they were agreed: that many of the seeds of decline were planted in the immediate post-war years. According to the Marxist Left, this was because socialism and the class struggle were betrayed. According to the radical Right, it was because free market forces had been stultified by the Welfare State and the managed economy. Both rejected the social democratic legacy inherited by the Conservatives from Labour in 1951.

I do not believe that either of these theories is plausible as a reading of post-war history or workable as a means of governing Britain.

2 *P. Addison: 'The Road From 1945' in* Ruling Performance *eds P. Hennessey and A. Seldon*
The coalition government of Winston Churchill, which took office on 10 May 1940, was formed for the sake of national unity and an all-out effort in the struggle against Nazi Germany. To this end it pressed ahead with the task of mobilizing resources for total war. By the end of 1941 a command economy had been established on the basis of state control of industry without state ownership: socialism without tears. In his determination to mobilize every resource and fling it into the battle, Churchill reflected the general will. But he could not have anticipated that wartime collectivism would metamorphose, at a later stage of the conflict, into peacetime collectivism. Between 1942 and 1945 the coalition government committed its

successors, in a series of White Papers, to major initiatives in the fields of education, health, housing, employment, social security, industry and environmental planning. But this is to say nothing of the preparations made for the liberalization of world trade, the reform of the colonial empire, the setting up of the United Nations, the manufacture of the atom bomb, the occupation of Germany, the settlement with the Soviet Union and, most importantly of all, the maintenance of the 'special relationship' with the United States. The Churchill coalition was truly seminal.

3 *D.N. Pritt:* The Labour Government 1945–51 (1963)
What went wrong from the start? The Government, overwhelmingly right-wing in composition and outlook, far more conscious of the supposed "enemy on the left" than of her real enemy that the electorate had sent them to power to conquer, accepted the capitalist *status quo*, political and economical, as if it were a law of nature, and never really sought to alter the class-structure of the nation, to attack the seats and sources of power, or even to weaken the ruling class. It was in reality, as Emile Burns puts it at p. 12 of *Right-wing Labour*, "no instrument of social change, but a valuable instrument of the monopoly capitalists in damping down the post-war unease and in helping the monopoly capitalists to solve the contradictions that faced them". It is not surprising that the ruling class soon recovered from its panic and managed to hold a very large measure of its old power.

4 *Tory election broadcast, 1983*
To understand why today we are fighting a war against rising prices we need to go back to the end of the Second World War, to 1945. The people of Britain had a new vision of how they wanted life to be. An end to poverty and squalor, decent homes for families and plenty of jobs for everyone. To pursue this vision, the Attlee Government committed itself to spending virtually half of what this country earned. The intentions were good but such massive spending soon made the people feel poorer, not richer, and it created even more problems than it seemed to be tackling.

5 *A. Sked and C. Cook:* Post-War Britain *(1979)*
The advent of the Labour government in 1945 gave rise to many hopes and fears: hopes of a new and better age in which values would be transformed; fears that a bureaucratic socialism would slow the beat of the nation's pulse. In fact, life continued much as before for the society which had experienced the war: the nation's leaders were familiar and its social and political structures remained essentially, if not entirely, unaltered. Both optimists and pessimists were proved right in their predictions, although the former more profoundly so than the latter. For despite the rationing and the controls, society's values were transmuted for the better. The Labour governments refused to put the clock back and pursued a programme designed to consolidate and strengthen the social cohesion engendered by the war. And so successful were they in their aims that they even converted the Conservative Party. By 1951 there could simply be no return to the society of the 1930s: the Welfare State had been accepted; full employment had become a common objective; and the social morality of the means test had given way to the doctrine of universality. The Labour Party itself had changed by becoming a respectable and natural party of government. The Conservatives in this respect could claim it as a convert and did so by pointing to its tough and realistic policy on foreign affairs. The idea that 'Left could speak unto Left' had little basis in fact by 1951. The foreign policy of the Labour Party now resembled very closely that of the Conservative Party. The truth was that the parties had come together in their vision of the post-war world. If there were still important differences between them, their similarities outweighed these differences.

6 *K.O. Morgan:* Labour in Power *(1984)*
It is easy to go too far in criticizing or debunking the Attlee government. Arguments from hindsight often neglect the realities actually confronting the administration in the very different world of 1945. Critiques of that government in particular tend to underestimate the overwhelming financial and economic pressures resulting from the loss of overseas assets, the imbalance of trade, the loss of markets, the shortage of raw materials, and the vast dollar deficit which was the government's *damnosa hereditas* from the war years and from the pre-war heritage of industrial decay. In large areas of policy, the Attlee government had a clear record of achievement and of competence, which acted as a platform for successive governments, Conservative and Labour, throughout the next quarter of a century. The advent of a monetarist Conservative government under Mrs Thatcher in 1979 signalled the first real attempt to wrench Britain out of the Age of Attlee. It received a huge endorsement at the polls in 1983. Yet until late 1983 at least, the economic record of well over three million unemployed, a severe contraction of manufacturing industry, eroding public and social services, and some threat of social and racial disorder, did not suggest that this alternative ideological approach had so far provided more coherent or acceptable answers to Britain's acknowledged problems. . . .

The Attlee government was thus unique in its structural cohesiveness and in its legislative vitality. Its legacy lived on in a broad influence over the Labour and progressive left, over political and economic thought and, indeed, over much of British intellectual and cultural life for a full quarter of a century after 1951. It was without doubt the most effective of all Labour governments, perhaps amongst the most effective of any British government since the passage of the 1832 Reform Act.

7 *D. Coates:* The Labour Party and the Struggle For Socialism *(1975)*
For the impact of the Labour Government of 1945–51, for all its promise and its vast body of legislation, was 'profoundly ambiguous'. When the rhetoric of partisan debate had died, this became quickly apparent, and was almost taken for granted by academics and commentators of the mid 1960s. There had undoubtedly been important social reforms. But power had not shifted between classes. Qualitative social transformation had not come. Nor was it any nearer for the six years of office. In essence the Labour Government of 1945–51 had not created a socialist commonwealth, nor even taken a step in that direction. It had simply created a mixed economy in which the bulk of industry still lay in private hands, and the six years of its rule had only marginally altered the distribution of

social power, privilege, wealth, income, opportunity and security.

8 *D. Kavanagh:* Thatcherism and British Politics *(1987)*

By the early 1950s it was already possible to refer to a post-war consensus about many, though not all, policies. In foreign affairs there developed a general agreement about such issues as Britain's role as a nuclear power, membership of NATO, and decolonization.

The package of policies on the domestic front is familiar: full employment budgets; the greater acceptance – even conciliation – of the trade unions, whose bargaining position was strengthened by an increased membership and full employment; public ownership of the basic or monopoly services and industries; state provision of social welfare, requiring in turn high public expenditure and taxation; and economic management of a sort, via a large public sector and a reduced role for the market. This is the vocabulary, as it were, of modern capitalism and social democracy.

9 *Marilyn Daljord in an essay in* The New Right Enlightenment *(1985)*

People would learn to swim, would learn to build rafts, if government did not destroy initiative through welfare and taxation. No one is done a favour by being made dependent on others permanently; only cripples can be produced by that method. Many abdicate responsibility for their own lives because the state ruins their ability to take care of themselves. On either end of the spectrum, people are damaged – the producers in society through heavy taxation, the non-producers by being kept that way through the expectation that someone will *have* to take care of them. When people feel they have no control over their lives, some will sink into passivity, their outlook and existence increasingly dull and narrow. Others feel that, if they have no control over their lives, they cannot be held responsible for their actions. Whatever they may do, it isn't their fault, it is society's. This view provides a justification for violence against others. Whether the response to womb-to-tomb subsidy is passive or violent, neither can produce a healthy society; in concert, they are deadly.

10 *C. Barnett:* The Audit of War *(1986)*

... by the time they took the bunting down from the streets after VE-Day and turned from the war to the future, the British in their dreams and illusions and in their flinching from reality had already written the broad scenario for Britain's postwar descent to the place of fifth in the free world as an industrial power, with manufacturing output only two-fifths of West Germany's, and the place of fourteenth in the whole non-Communist world in terms of annual GNP per head.

As that descent took its course the illusions and the dreams of 1945 would fade one by one – the imperial and Commonwealth role, the world-power role, British industrial genius, and, at the last, New Jerusalem itself, a dream turned to a dank reality of a segregated, subliterate, unskilled, unhealthy and institutionalised proletariat hanging on the nipple of state maternalism.

B ACK TO THE PRESENT

It should be clear from the range of views in the 'Historians Views and Opinions' section that the debates about the performance and legacy of the Attlee governments and the Churchill Coalition government before it are rooted in the continuing differences in political beliefs of the historians themselves. Indeed, similar kinds of arguments about the merits of individualism in relation to collectivism or socialism – the role of the market in relation to the state – have continued unceasingly since the nineteenth century right up to the present time. The character and quality of our own society, now and in the future, will be determined by how these arguments are resolved.

It is not surprising then that historians, caught up in ideological struggles in the 1980s and 1990s similar to those in the 1940s that they may be writing about, should be influenced in their historical judgements by their present beliefs. In fact, the so-called break up of the post-war consensus in the 1970s has intensified ideological debate about how our society is best organised, and this in turn has given renewed urgency to the way historians interpret and re-interpret modern British history in contradictory ways. The striving for objectivity is an ideal which historians will hopefully always try to pursue in their research and analysis but ultimately they cannot rise above the controversies which shape the society in which they live in and are a part of. Here are some questions to provoke further thought and discussion which link up the history of the governments and society of 1940 to 1951 with similar concerns and problems today.

1 What are the arguments for and against the privatisation or nationalisation of (a) industries such as coal, electricity and water, (b) welfare provision such as health, education and housing? Which arguments do you support and why?
2 What do existing political parties say in general about the role of the market *vis à vis* the state in terms of providing prosperity, freedom and equality?
3 To what extent is the social democratic consensus (which some historians believe was established by 1951) now at an end?
4 Is socialism any longer a viable doctrine, especially given the changes taking place in the formerly Communist states of the eastern bloc countries?

ACKNOWLEDGEMENTS

The author and publishers thank the following for their permission to reproduce copyright material:

Edward Arnold Ltd for extracts from J.R. Hay, *The Development of the British Welfare State 1880–1975* (1978); S. Pollard, *The Development of the British Economy 1914–50* (1962); H.A.L. Fisher, *History of Europe* (1936). Barrie and Jenkins for the extract from Peter Rowland, *Lloyd George*. B.T. Batsford Ltd for extracts from A.E. Musson, *The Growth of British History* (1978); R. Eatwell, *The 1945–1951 Labour Government* (1979). A & C Black (Publishers) Ltd for extracts from P. Hayes, *Modern British Foreign Policy – The Twentieth Century 1880–1939* (1978). Basil Blackwell Ltd for extracts from M. Pugh, *The Making of Modern British Politics 1867–1939* (1982); Asa Briggs, *They saw it Happen 1897–1940* (1960); K. Robbins, *Appeasement* (1988); P. Hennessey & A. Seldon, *Ruling Performance* (1987). Blandford Press, a division of Cassell Publishers plc for extracts from M.St.J. Parker and D.J. Reid, *The British Revolution 1750–1970 – A Social and Economic History* (1972). Cambridge University Press for extracts from W.H.B. Court, *British Economic History 1870–1914 Commentary and Documents* (1965); D. Coates, *The Labour Party and the Struggle for Socialism* (1975); K.M. Wilson, *The Policy of the Entente* (1985). Century Hutchinson for the extract from J. Barnes and D. Nicholson (eds), *The Leo Amery Diaries*. Curtis Brown on behalf of the Estate of Sir Winston Churchill for extracts from Winston Churchill, *Liberalism and the Social Problem* (1909). Evening Standard for the extract from *The Evening Standard* March 27th 1936. Express Newspapers plc for the extract from *The Daily Express* July 6th 1945. Victor Gollancz Ltd for the extract from E. Shinwell, *I've Lived Through It All* (1973). Grafton Books for the extract from G.M. Young, *Stanley Baldwin*. Hamish Hamilton for extracts from S. Koss, *They saw it Happen 1897–1940* (1960); J. Grigg, *Lloyd George, Twelve Essays* (1971). Harper Collins Publishers for extracts from K.W.W. Aikin, *The Last Years of Liberal England 1900–1914* (1972); J.A.S. Grenville, *A World History of the Twentieth Century* (1980); Trevor Wilson, *The Political Diaries of P. Scott 1911–1928* (1970); T. Wilson *The Downfall of the Liberal Party 1914–35* (1966); R. Jenkins, *Baldwin* (1987). William Heinemann Ltd for the extract from Clement Attlee, *As it Happened.* H.M.S.O. for the extract from Arthur Ponsonby speech in the House of Commons August 3rd 1914. Hodder and Stoughton Publishers for extracts from R. Moore, *The Emergence of the Labour Party 1880–1924* (1978); S. Baldwin, *This Torch of Freedom* (1935). The Labour Party for extracts from Frank Bealey, *The Social and Political Thought of the British Labour Party* (1970); *Labour Party Annual Report 1929.* Lawrance and Wishart Ltd for *The General Strike, 1926* ed. J. Skelley (1976); Paul Adelman, *The Labour Government 1945–51.* Longman Group UK for the extracts from P. Thane, *Foundations of the Welfare State* (1982); R.D. Cornwell, *World History in the Twentieth Century* (1980); K. Robbins, *The Eclipse of a Great Power* (1983); J. Joll, *Origins of the First World War* (1984); P. Adelman, *The Rise of The Labour Party* (1952); C. Cook & J. Stevenson, *The Longman Handbook of Modern British History 1714–1980* (1983). The MacDonald Group for extracts from E. Shinwell, *The Labour Story* (1963); J.P. Kenyon, *Dictionary of British History* (1988). Macmillan for extracts from Harold Macmillan, *The Middle Way*; D. Fraser, *The Evolution of the British Welfare State* (1973); *The Relief of Poverty 1834–1914* (1972); J.R. Hay, *The Origins of the Liberal Welfare Reforms* (1975); M.E. Rose, *The Relief of Poverty 1834–1914* (1972); D. Butler & A. Sloman, *British Political Facts 1900–1979* (1980); J. Wroughton & Denys Cook, *Documents on World History 1870–1918* (1976). Manchester University Press for the extracts from A. Morgan, *J.R. MacDonald*. Methuen and Co for extracts from L.C.B. Seaman, *Post-Victorian Britain 1902–1951* (1966); R. Rhodes James, *The British Revolution – British Politics 1880–1939* (1978); L.C.B. Seaman, *Post-Victorian Britain 1902–1951* (1966); G.D.H. Cole & R. Postgate, *The Common People 1746–1946* (1949); C.L. Mowat. *Britain between the Wars* (1955). John Murray Publishers for the extract from Edward David,

ACKNOWLEDGEMENTS

Inside Asquith's Cabinet – From Diaries of Charles Hobhouse (1971). Thomas Nelson for extracts from D. Read, *Documents from Edwardian England 1901–1915* (1973). Oxford University Press for extracts from K.O. Morgan, *Labour People*; K.O. Morgan, *Labour in Power*; S. Steiner, *Britain and the Origins of the First World War* (1977); E. Brock, *H.H. Asquith letters to Venetia Stanley* (1982); R. McKibbon, *The Evolution of the Labour Party 1910–24* (1974); K.O. Morgan, *The Oxford Illustrated History of Britain* (1984). Penguin Books Ltd for extracts from D. Thomson, *England in the Twentieth Century* (1965); J. Stevenson, *British Society 1914–45* (1984); A. Skeed & C. Cook, *Post-War Britain* (1979). Bernard Barker, (ed) *Ramsay Mac-Donalds Political Writings* (Allen Lane The Penguin Press, 1972) copyright © Bernard Barker, 1972. Peter, Fraser & Dunlop for extracts from A. Calder & D. Sheridan, *Speak for Yourself* (1984). Prentice Hall for the extract from M. Gilbert, *Lloyd George* (1968). Random Century Group for the extract from D. Marquand, *Ramsey MacDonald*. Routledge for extracts from E.J. Evans, *Social Policy* (1978); C.J. Lowe & M. Dockrill, *The Mirage of Power* (1972); P. Thompson, *Socialists, Liberals and Labour – The Struggle for London 1895–1914* (1967); J.H. Bettey, *English Historical Documents 1906–1939* (1967); G.D.H. Cole, *History of the Labour Party from 1914*. Sidgwick and Jackson for the extract from R. Douglas, *The History of the Liberal Party 1895–1970* (1971). Sphere Books Ltd for the extract from J.P. Kenyon, *Dictionary of British History* (1981). Thames and Hudson for the extract from A. Marwick, *The Illustrated Dictionary of British History* (1980). Times Newspapers Ltd for the extract from *The Times*, 1st August 1914. Stanley Thornes for the extract from W.O. Simpson, *Changing Horizons – Britain 1914–80* (1986). Unwin Hyman for the extracts from K.O. Morgan, *The Age of Lloyd George* (1971); G. Williams, *The Coming of the Welfare State* (1967); R.K. Webb, *Modern England* (1980); *The Autobiography of Bertrand Russell vol II, 1914–1944*; A.P. Adamwaite, *The Making of the Second World War* (1977); J.H. Bettey, *English Historical*; H. Morrison, *The Peaceful Revolution* (1949). Weidenfeld and Nicolson for extracts from K.O. Morgan, *Lloyd George* (1974); K. Young, *Stanley Baldwin* (1976); K. Middlemas and J. Barnes, *Baldwin* (1969); J.P. Mackintosh, *British Prime Ministers in the Twentieth Century* (1977).

The publishers would also like to thank the following for permssion to reproduce copyright illustrations:

Associated Press (p. 111); *Express Newspapers* (pp. 92 and 98); Hulton-Deutsch (cover, pp. 10, 17, 77, 78, 104 and 131); Illustrated London News Picture Library (p. 46); Imperial War Museum (p. 44); David Low/*Star*/Centre for the Study of Cartoons and Caricature, University of Kent at Canterbury/Solo Syndication (p. 13); David Low/*Evening Standard*/Centre for the Study of Cartoons and Caricature, University of Kent at Canterbury/Solo Syndication (pp. 68 and 119); National Portrait Gallery, London (p. 31); Popperfoto (p. 88); *Punch* (pp. 11, 57, 82, 119 and 135); Philip Zec/*Daily Mirror Newspapers*/Centre for the Study of Cartoons and Caricature, University of Kent at Canterbury.

Every effort has been made to trace and acknowledge ownership of copyright. The publishers will be glad to make suitable arrangements with any copyright holders whom it has not been possible to contact.